THE MORAL LIFE: EIGHT LECTURES

The Moral Life: Eight Lectures

Martin D'Arcy, SJ, Memorial Lectures

These books are based on lectures given at the Jesuit Campion Hall of the University of Oxford. The author of each book is a distinguished member of the Society of Jesus, and the goal of the series is to present the very best of Jesuit scholarship. The series honors Fr. Martin D'Arcy, SJ, the celebrated Master of Campion Hall from 1933 to 1945.

Human Dignity and Liberal Politics: Catholic Possibilities for the Common Good
Patrick Riordan, SJ

The Moral Life: Eight Lectures
James F. Keenan, SJ

THE MORAL LIFE

EIGHT LECTURES

JAMES F. KEENAN, SJ

GEORGETOWN UNIVERSITY PRESS / WASHINGTON, DC

© 2023 Georgetown University Press. All rights reserved. No part of this book may be reproduced or utilized in any form or by any means, electronic or mechanical, including photocopying and recording, or by any information storage and retrieval system, without permission in writing from the publisher.

The publisher is not responsible for third-party websites or their content. URL links were active at time of publication.

Library of Congress Cataloging-in-Publication Data

Names: Keenan, James F., author.
Title: The moral life : eight lectures / James F. Keenan.
Identifiers: LCCN 2023011218 (print) | LCCN 2023011219 (ebook) |
   ISBN 9781647123994 (hardcover) | ISBN 9781647124007 (paperback) |
   ISBN 9781647124014 (ebook)
Subjects: LCSH: Christian ethics—Catholic authors.
Classification: LCC BJ1249 .K37698 2024 (print) | LCC BJ1249 (ebook) |
   DDC 241/.042—dc23/eng/20230822
LC record available at https://lccn.loc.gov/2023011218
LC ebook record available at https://lccn.loc.gov/2023011219

24 23   9 8 7 6 5 4 3 2   First printing

Cover design by Brad Noor. Cover image *Noli me tangere* by Anton Raphael Mengs, reproduced by permission of the Warden and Fellows of All Souls College, Oxford. The painting is on loan and hangs in the chapel of Campion College, where the D'Arcy Memorial Lectures are given.
Interior design by BookComp, Inc.

To my teachers and mentors who helped me prepare for the moral life and encouraged me to cultivate the vision, the ideas, and the passion that run through these pages

John O'Malley, SJ; Josef Fuchs, SJ; Klaus Demmer, MSC;
John Langan, SJ; Jack Mahoney, SJ; Sr. Mary Emil Penet, IHM;
Lisa Sowle Cahill; David Hollenbach, SJ; Edward Vacek, SJ; Charles Curran

CONTENTS

Preface ix

Acknowledgments xiii

1 Grief 1

2 Vulnerability 19

3 Recognition 38

4 Conscience 55

5 Discipleship 75

6 Grace and Sin 93

7 The Virtues 112

8 The Communion of Saints, the Works of Mercy, and the Beatitudes 131

Bibliography 151

Index 169

About the Author 177

PREFACE

In 1982 I was ordained a priest, and shortly afterward I went to the Gregorian University to pursue a licentiate and a doctorate, studying with both Josef Fuchs and Klaus Demmer. In 1987, at the end of my studies, Jack Mahoney published his magisterial work, *The Making of Moral Theology*.[1] Reading that book, I learned about the Martin D'Arcy Memorial Lectures, and from that time I sincerely hoped that one day I too would be invited to give those lectures.

Now thirty-five years later, I confess that I am honored to be delivering them. Thank you, Nicholas Austin, SJ, Master of Campion Hall, for this invitation.

Over the past ten years I have been developing my own account of the history of theological ethics, which builds on and develops from Mahoney's groundbreaking account. Happily, that work, *A History of Catholic Theological Ethics*, was published by Paulist Press in early June 2022.[2]

These D'Arcy lectures derive from another inquiry that I began about five years ago by asking, What prompts human beings to act morally? The first of those investigations were provoked by an invitation I received from David DeCosse, who invited me into a project entitled *Conscience and Catholic Education*.[3] These lectures are the fruit of that first and subsequent inquiries. I have entitled these lectures: The Moral Life. They are an attempt to investigate what we need to know not only to be and live morally but also to teach and share with others what they need to know as well.

They are in eight stages: Grief, Vulnerability, Recognition, Conscience, Discipleship, Grace and Sin, the Virtues, and the Communion of Saints, the Works of Mercy, and the Beatitudes. The first four chapters are the foundations for contemporary ethics. Even though I use biblical texts, I think the questions and insights in the first four chapters could resonate with many people regardless of their ethical or religious traditions. The final four chapters, however, are a distinctive pathway for realizing a contemporary vulnerability ethics in the context of Christianity and, more specifically, Catholicism.

While I believe the lectures are rooted in the research of contemporary philosophers and theologians, they were delivered to be more broadly engaging.

Furthermore, in consultation with the editor of Georgetown University Press, Al Bertrand, I have decided to make this publication the actual collection of the eight lectures themselves. I found that the lectures generated considerable questions and discourse, and at fifty minutes for a read of each, they helped me to encapsulate my ideas and positions into a fairly strict but evocative framework.

I hope therefore in this collection you hear my voice. Lectures, unlike book chapters, tend to be more engaging and more open ended; matters are less settled and more subject to further investigation. They are meant to elicit a response from the listener or, in this case, the reader. There's also an immediacy, less of a formal setting, and more of an openness between the speaker and the audience. The lectures themselves tell you not only about the lecturer's ideas but also about the lecturer.

This format is very helpful for me because I am seeking to develop an ontologically social anthropology. I am interested in the Ubuntu insight that "I am because we are." For this reason, I begin these lectures on grief because I believe that the experience of grief highlights just how deeply connected one human being is with another. Still, grief is an experience rarely reflected on by ethicists in either philosophy or theology. Instead, in the Christian tradition, we developed the tradition of the art of dying, or the *ars moriendi*, by which the Christian is asked to anticipate her or his deathbed experiences so as to prepare for the art of living, the *ars vivendi*. I have always thought of these exercises as somewhat narcissistic, and so I invite us, instead, to reflect on our own experiences of grief where we are overwhelmed by how much another human being means to us.

That experience of deep connectedness I want to investigate with you as foundational for understanding the moral life. It leads, I think, to vulnerability, recognition, and conscience.

Finally, each lecture builds on the prior. This means that I presume that ideas in an earlier lecture that were explained do not need to be repeated later. But they also capture my own struggles with generating these lectures, for, indeed, though they were written and planned ahead of delivery, as any lecturer knows, in the lecture itself the claims are finally verbalized for the first time. Hopefully as you read these lectures, you hear my delivery.

They were delivered in the library at Campion Hall, the Jesuit Hall at Oxford University, on Tuesday evenings from April 26 to June 14, 2022. There was an in-person and live-streamed audience, and they were subsequently posted on YouTube for greater access.[4] They were in honor of Fr. Martin D'Arcy, SJ, the celebrated Master of the Hall from 1933 to 1945, having been established in 1976, shortly after D'Arcy's death.

NOTES

1. Mahoney, *Moral Theology*; Keenan, "John Mahoney's *The Making of Moral Theology*," 503–19.
2. Keenan, *A History of Catholic Theological Ethics*.
3. Keenan, "Building Blocks for Moral Education." DeCosse had engaged many of us on conscience earlier; see my "To Follow and to Form," 1–15.
4. The recordings may be found here: https://www.campion.ox.ac.uk/news/darcy-lectures-2022.

NOTES

ACKNOWLEDGMENTS

I am very grateful to Nicholas Austin for the invitation to Campion Hall to deliver the Martin D'Arcy SJ Memorial Lectures of 2022. Nick was an inspiration as Master of Campion Hall, a perfect host, but even better, a fellow pilgrim and a dear friend. Then, Trudi Preston, by her style and support, made every day a delight to be at Campion Hall. I especially enjoyed my breakfast crew—Frank Turner (our Jesuit Superior), Patrick Riordan (my D'Arcy predecessor) and Rob Marsh (the kind commentator)—who helped me start each day for those glorious ten weeks. I am indebted to the dedicated talent of Sarah Gray and Yingying Jiang, who made sure each lecture was advertised, each guest was welcomed, and each session was posted, and to Tom Lucas and his team, who livestreamed and edited each transmission.

I want to also thank in a particular way Jack Mahoney, who inspired me by his 1981 D'Arcy lecture, "The Making of Moral Theology: A Study of the Roman Catholic Tradition" and encouraged me through the years.

Several friends came to Campion Hall to visit me and, often, to hear one of the lectures: Linda Hogan, Antonio Autiero, Alice Goodman, Liam Hayes, Anna Abram, Ladislav Šulik, and Gina and Steve Wolfe. Each friend made my stay particularly memorable.

To the faculty, fellows, students, and friends of Campion Hall who moderated and attended my lectures, engaged me in discourse, and hospitably made my stay a wonderful experience, thank you Alec Thorp, Andrew Hochstedler, Anna Chewter, Artur Suski, Austen Ivereigh, Bethany Sollereder, Carl Scerri, Celia Deane-Drummond, Chase Hasenoehrl, Christopher Fleming, Cory Rodgers, Daniel De Haan, David Braithwaite, Diarmaid MacCulloch, Emilio Chuvieco, Gavin Flood, Gilbert Kilroy, Gilbrian Stoy, Graham Ward, Hiba Salem, Isidoros Katsos, James Hanvey, Jane Stevenson, Jennifer Cooper, Jijimon Joseph, Joel Gutteridge, Joel Rasmussen, John Barton, John Berkman, Joseph Simmons, Juan Iglesias, Juan Iglesias Martinez, Lucinda Armstrong, Maikki Aakko, Maria Roginska, Marten Bjork, Matthew Dunch, Matthew Whelan, Olivier Delouis, Pamela Armstrong, Paolo Monzani, Peter Davidson, Philip Kennedy, Philip Moller, Rachael Chan, Rebecca Artinian-Kaiser, Sarah

Ogilvie, Stephen Withnell, Timothy Howles, Vincent Gillespie, Wilin Buitrago Arias, William Lamb, and Wilma Minty.

I close thanking Al Bertrand and his team at Georgetown University Press for the publication of these lectures and in a very special way, my indefatigable undergraduate research fellows Samuel Peterson and Steven Roche, as well as Jacob Ottiger, who joined them in the home stretch, for catching infelicitous expressions and outright errors, converting multitudinous footnotes to one bibliography, and, for many other ways that they accompanied me in getting this work into your hands, THANK YOU.

1

GRIEF

I begin this lecture series with grief, and I begin this lecture on the grief of the followers of Jesus gathered in the Upper Room. Let me offer you first three governing insights to help you follow my argument.

First, the disciples were gathered in the Upper Room from the death of Jesus to the Pentecost, moving initially from grieving to evangelizing Jesus as risen Lord. There, in the Upper Room, their experiences of grief led them to become even more vulnerable to Jesus, and they were subsequently incited to recognize him as risen Lord through the Holy Spirit.

Those in that Upper Room experienced grief, vulnerability, and recognition. While I have argued in my writings over the past four years that vulnerability and recognition are the preconditions for the moral life,[1] I propose to begin now with grief and then turn to the two "preconditions" so as to offer you the first three lectures. Thus, just as all three experiences were, as I will argue, constitutive for the birth of the church, they are also constitutive for the birth of the moral life.

Second, remembering that the *ars moriendi*, or the "art of dying" tradition, was often invoked to exhort others to pursue the *ars vivendi*, or "the art of living," I similarly want to begin at the end of the moral life, that is, with death. But rather than propose that we look forward imaginatively to what one's exemplary deathbed experience ought to be, I want instead to look back to the actual experience about how we grieve and, as Judith Butler recommends, tarry there.

Third, I hope that by giving grief its due we might raise up in these lectures a theological anthropology for the moral life that is far more affective, relational, connected, vibrant, and life giving than we normally encounter. Though starting with grief might be unsettling, I hope you find that in preparing for the moral life, grief conveys how much we matter to one another such that the moral life should never forget this.

GRIEVING AT PENTECOST

On Tuesday May 19, 2015, I received word that my best friend, the Hong Kong Jesuit Yiu Sing Lúcás Chan, had just died of a heart attack, having collapsed on a bench in the corridor of the theology department of Marquette University. Trying to get to his office as he was returning from his daily early morning workout at the university gym, Lúcás gave up his last at 6:45 a.m. before any of his colleagues arrived. He was forty-six years old, the epitome of healthy living, and his death was overwhelming for all of us, his family, friends, and colleagues.

His funeral at Marquette would not be for at least a week, but on May 24 I was scheduled to preside at the Sunday liturgy at St. Peter's Parish in Cambridge, Massachusetts, where I have now worked for nearly twenty years. That Sunday would be Pentecost Sunday. Facing Pentecost, the so-called birthday of the church, the celebration of the Spirit descending into the midst of the gathering in the Upper Room and sending them out, inspired by and with tongues of fire, I asked how could I bring my grief to that celebratory liturgy.

I had known sudden death before. My brother Bob died during an early morning seizure of epilepsy when he was twenty-six years old. That day, June 2, 1980, changed the lives of all of us. From Bob's death I learned the importance of grieving with others and that grief alone is a dreadful, painful practice. Grief is meant to be shared, whether at a wake, sitting Shiva, or at a Janazah.

In preparation for the Sunday liturgy, I began asking myself, What were the disciples of Jesus doing in the Upper Room on the eve of what we now call Pentecost? Certainly, they were there in fear as is often noted, though in time they also began to wait for the Holy Spirit, as Luke tells us. But they were also there in the Upper Room to grieve. In fact, I began to see that their grieving was constitutive to the process of the coming of the Spirit and of their recognizing Jesus as risen Lord. Moreover, their ability to subsequently witness to Jesus, the very message of Pentecost, was prompted by their grieving. The Scriptures, I believe, bear this out.

GRIEVING IN THE UPPER ROOM

In the later, so-called long canonical ending of Mark's Gospel, we learn that Jesus rose early and appeared "first" to Mary Magdalen (Mk 16:9). The eleven were gathered in the Upper Room, where they were, we are told, "mourning and weeping" (Mk 16:10). Mary Magdalen knows they are there and reports to them that Jesus is alive, but they do not believe her (Mk 16:11). Again, two more come to report to them in the Upper Room that they met Jesus on a road, but again they do not believe (Mk 16:12–13). Later—we do not know how much later—Jesus himself comes to the Upper Room. Now that they recognize him, he rebukes them for not believing the reports but then commissions them to preach and ascends to his Father (Mk 16:14–20).[2]

In Matthew 28, Mary Magdalene and the other Mary arrive at the tomb and see the angel who tells them to not be afraid, that Jesus has risen, and to hurry to tell his disciples (Mt 28:5–7). But as they begin to depart, afraid but filled with joy, Jesus appears to them, and they "clasped his feet" and "worshipped him." Jesus instructs them to "[g]o and tell my brothers to go to Galilee; there they will see me" (Mt 28:8–10).[3]

In Luke, everything happens in one day.[4] We hear that on Sunday, three days after the death of Jesus, the women—Mary Magdalene; Joanna; Mary, the mother of James; and the other women—discover the empty tomb and encounter the two men "in dazzling clothes" who tell them that he has been raised; they run to the disciples in the Upper Room, and the grieving disciples do not believe them, though Peter runs to the tomb and is amazed by the tomb being empty (Lk 24:12). Then the encounter at Emmaus occurs where two disciples are described as "looking downcast" (Lk 24:17). These two have already left the Upper Room, where they heard the reports of the women and of those who went to check the tomb and found it as the women had reported. Jesus calls these two "foolish" and "slow of heart to believe" (Lk 24:25). In their shared grief, they still do not recognize him as he tries to open their eyes by recounting from the Scriptures. Finally, in the breaking of the bread, they recognize him (Lk 24:31); the Lord vanishes, and the two rush back again to the Upper Room to tell the eleven; as they enter the room, the eleven tell the two from Emmaus that the Lord has risen and appeared to Peter, and then the two make their report (Lk 24:33–35). Unlike Mark, Luke reports that the eleven believe that Jesus has been raised before Jesus appears. When he does, he extends to them his peace, eats fish, and tells them to stay in Jerusalem because he is "sending upon you what my Father promised." He walks to Bethany and then ascends.

In the Acts of the Apostles, after the ascension of Jesus, the disciples return to Jerusalem and immediately go to the Upper Room, where we are told the eleven were staying (Acts 1:13) "together with certain women, including Mary the mother of Jesus, as well as his brothers" (Acts 1:14). Luke makes a point that they are there for days (Acts 1:15). When the Pentecost occurs, again it seems as though they are in the Upper Room (Acts 2:1–2).

In John, everything, including the Pentecost, happens in one day. Mary Magdalene discovers the empty tomb, rushes to report the missing body of Jesus to Peter and the disciple whom Jesus loved, and they rush to the tomb, and then return to their houses. Mary returns to the tomb and is grieving outside the tomb, distressed that not only has Jesus been put to death but now even his body has been taken as well. The Gospel refers to her weeping four times, with both the angels and Jesus asking, "Woman, why are you weeping?" (Jn 20:13,15). Jesus approaches her in her grief and confusion; like the two in Emmaus, she does not recognize him, but then he calls her by name (Jn 20:18). She clings to him, he tells her to stop holding on to him as he is ascending to his Father, and then commissions her to tell the disciples. Jesus later that day goes to the disciples who are gathered in the Upper Room and breathes on them, which Bruce Vawter holds as the culmination in one day of the resurrection, ascension, and Pentecost.[5] Jesus returns a week later again to the Upper Room to reveal himself to Thomas (Jn 20:19–31).

Their grief was not an obstacle to their capacity to recognize Jesus but rather the passageway itself to the recognition. Through their grieving they became more vulnerable to their love for Jesus so that they could recognize his risen presence. These words—grief, vulnerability, and recognition—are here inextricably linked to the Pentecost story and, in particular, to the role the Spirit plays in our lives and in the church.

The phenomenon of grief is, I think, the willing openness to recognize and experience the loss of a loved one.

During that Pentecost, I discovered that my grief was a form of love. In fact, whenever I touch that grief, I encounter the love that connected me to my friend Lúcás. Entrance into grief is not solely an encounter with absence but with presence as well. The more one feels the presence of the love, the deeper one feels the loss, and yet the gulf of love remains; like the Upper Room itself, it is a place of vulnerability.

When I think of the disciples, Mary, and the others in the Upper Room, I think it was there that they gathered to grieve. There, after all, was where they celebrated the Last Supper, a meal that Jesus initiated on the night before he was to die, though also as a meal to be repeated after his departure. It is good to remember that right after that meal, they fell into sorrow in the Mount of Olives; Mark tells us (14:33) that Jesus was greatly distressed and filled with sorrow, as does Matthew. Luke helps explain the tiredness of the disciples when he says they fell asleep due to their sorrow (22:45). Clearly the Synoptic Gospels register the sorrow of the disciples leaving the Upper Room.

There they returned after the death of Jesus. When the twelve are gathered in the Upper Room with Mary, they are grieving with one another.

Clearly, they went there out of fear, having witnessed the terrorizing arrest, humiliating and violent passion, and the barbaric crucifixion of the one whom they called Master and Lord. But they also went there precisely to grieve.

Still, their grief was not probably like a contemporary therapeutic check-in where they were asking one another: "Are you OK?" "Mary, how are you coping?" "Peter, are you handling your grief well?" I think instead that they were just sharing stories of the love that they experienced from Jesus. In their grieving, they wanted to hear from Peter, Mary (the Mother of Jesus), the Magdalene, John, and the others, stories of how Jesus loved each of them. In hearing these narratives, I think they were consoled. In their shared grief they gave one another to experience their love for and from Jesus. And into the loving grief of the Upper Room, in that vulnerable space, first Jesus and then the Spirit found the place to enter.

In a similar way every Christian funeral is a replay of the Upper Room. When I preside at a funeral, I enter, not primarily the presence but rather the felt absence of the person loved, the raw, emotional, gut-wrenching experience of love exposed because the loved one has died. Those who believe the promise of the resurrection encounter it, not by negating grief nor by "transcending" it but by entering it. The promise is not a quick fix imposed but rather something believers recognize as they grieve. Through grief we experience and eventually recognize the promise of the resurrection. The felt love with the now deceased remains as the bridge through grief.

MINDING THE GAP OF GRIEF

Several weeks after my brother Bobby died, I received from a Jesuit, Stanley Marrow, a beautiful letter of condolence with these words from Dietrich Bonhoeffer:

> Nothing can fill the gap left by someone we love, and we should not attempt to find anything. We must simply endure and hold out. That may sound very harsh at first, but at the same time it is a great comfort, because as the hole that he has left remains unfilled, so the connection with him remains. It is wrong to say: "'God, fills the gap.'" God doesn't fill it at all. Rather he leaves it unfilled, and in this way,

he helps us to maintain our true communion with our loved one, even though it is painful.⁶

Bonhoeffer wrote these words on Christmas Eve 1943 to his closest friends, Renate and Eberhard Bethge, as he lay in prison in Tegel, Germany, later to be executed on April 9, 1945.

These words of Bonhoeffer were an enormous consolation to my family; we experienced precisely in the gap of grief the way "to maintain our true communion with our loved one."

I have come to believe that grief reveals human vulnerability, which is, I will posit later, not our weakened nature but rather our capacious ability to be connected and responsive to one another. Grief that arises from the separation of being connected is the exposition of our underlying vulnerability. Thus, in the Christian funeral, we do not deny the pain of death but rather touch precisely the loss through grief.

I think that is how the disciples recognized Christ, not in spite of the grief but through it. They dared to feel the loss of Jesus, to share the love he had for them and they for him. They grieved. Their grief made them more aware of their own personal and collective vulnerability to Jesus, to the love of God, and to the working of the Spirit. Their grief was/is integral to their recognition of the resurrected Jesus.

Let me add: They grieved his death even after the resurrection appearances. Mary Magdalene grieved that she had to let go of the risen Jesus and could not hold him again. Jesus's command to her to stop clinging, the so-called *Noli me tangere*, captures her grieving that remains and endures. In fact, the iconography of the Magdalene after the resurrection of Jesus shows her almost always alone, minding if you will, the gap. She waits her whole life long for when she will finally be reunited with him.

The disciples of Emmaus grieved also after Jesus vanished. They returned to the breaking of the bread again and again to encounter their grief, the gap, and the love until they too would be reunited with him.

Peter and John assuredly looked for Jesus time and again on that beach. It was that grief that gave them the conviction to preach Jesus raised, but they, like Paul in Philippians (1:21–23), longed for death so as to be reunited with the one they lost on earth. Peter grieved until he was crucified and Paul too until he was executed.

Let us not think that the appearances eradicated the grief but rather gave grief a new energy, a new reason to hope though grief. They minded the gap.

Let us turn to the Scriptures and see this more clearly.

GRIEVING ELSEWHERE IN THE SCRIPTURES

We all know the shortest verse in the Bible is "Jesus wept" (Jn 11.35). In that pericope, Jesus does not begin to weep when encountered by Martha or Mary but rather when he literally is brought to the tomb and confronts the reality of Lazarus as dead. Grief exposed Jesus's vulnerability to Lazarus. And that is revealed to us in the very next verse. "Then the Jews said, 'See how he loved him!'" (Jn 11.36). Though some say that grief is the price of love, I say instead that grief is a form of love. It is not an effect of love; it is an act of love. Jesus grieving for Lazarus is Jesus entering into his love for Lazarus, experiencing painfully, vulnerably, the love they had. Though grief overcomes us, still we, like Jesus, choose to grieve, choose to encounter the love we have for the one who has died.

As we know, through grief the Spirit leads us as vulnerable in the face of death through love to the discovery of hope.

Another significant biblical text is the second of the eight Matthean beatitudes, "Blessed are they who mourn." In his book *The Ten Commandments and the Beatitudes: Biblical Studies and Ethics for Real Life*, Lúcás Chan opens up the beatitudes by appropriating John Climacus's notion of a ladder of ascent.[7] In this way Chan recommends we see that each beatitude makes possible the next one. As he tells us, we can only ascend the ladder, one step at a time.

Chan notes, therefore, the overarching importance of the first beatitude, where we start by turning our gaze on the poor in spirit who are the most poor of the poor, economically deprived, *and* socially alienated. Turning to the second beatitude, "Blessed are they who mourn," Chan notes that we are to turn our gaze on those who mourn.[8] Reading the beatitudes along with the exegetical claims of Hans Dieter Betz, William Davies, and Dale Allison Jr., as well as of the theologian Gerald Vann, Chan notes that the second beatitude is not about mourners grieving their own condition or loss. The second beatitude is not a self-help instruction in which those who have experienced loss are being encouraged to grieve.

He writes: "The object of mourning is not so much one's own suffering or sins, but rather the concrete human experience of poverty and suffering encountered by community members"; that is, the gaze of our consideration turns to those in the first beatitude, "the poor in spirit." Chan continues: "Mourning points to an other-oriented moral value. . . . It is about a certain disposition that genuine disciples have with one another, such that if one suffers, the other mourns as well."[9] He adds, "Mourning is then the ready subordination of one's own comfort and wellbeing to the suffering of others."[10] Blessed are those who mourn is therefore about those community members who mourn the condition of the poor in spirit. (We will see later how Butler suggests an invitation to grieve for the other, which is not far from, I think, the second beatitude.)

Similarly, it is important to note in the Scriptures that mourning always encounters a responsive God. Mourning is always a sign of the human's hope to be visited by God. Just as Jeremiah consoles the mourners of Zion (Sir 48:23–25), so God turns mourning into joy (Jer 31:13), like a mother who comforts her child (Isa 66:13). Thus, "The Lord (who) is close to the brokenhearted" responds to "those who are crushed in spirit," as the Psalmist says (Ps 38:14).[11]

Grieving for the other's loss, their alienation, suffering, or death, is the beginning of the beatitudinal response of the call to genuine discipleship, that is, of responding to the poor in spirit. By grieving for the poor in spirit, our empathy, the virtue of our vulnerability, connects us to the poor and those who grieve for them. It is that shared grief that the Spirit recognized in the Upper Room, and it is what precedes all else in the ladder of ascent. For the Christian it is not the denial of suffering and death but the encounter with loss and suffering of another; entering into their loss, we are led by the Spirit as the disciples were led to not only recognize the Risen Christ but to unabashedly preach him.

THE SICK SELF

Between the deaths of Bobby and Lúcás, I also experienced an advanced cancer and learned a little bit about the notion of the sick self by the American philosopher and pragmatist William James. Additionally, during that time, I was invited by Bryan Massingale, the president of the Catholic Theological Society of America, to give a plenary address on the theme of "impasse."[12] Though I was tempted to speak about impasse in the church, I spoke instead about the fact that I was living then with an advanced melanoma that gave me a 50 percent chance of survival over the next five years.

After extensive surgery, I went through a fairly brutal regime of twelve months on interferon. Despite the sustained and compelling depression and fatigue as well as the nightly sweats and the low-grade, and sometimes spiked, fevers that I got from interferon, I was experiencing a new and reconciled peace in my life that I never knew before I became ill. I saw how I found myself experiencing something akin to William James's twice-born person.

In my recovery I was discovering a newfound ability to appreciate the present, to attend to those whose lives were far more in jeopardy than my own, to appreciate more deeply the humanity of the people I met, to sense the abiding presence of the Lord, to be far less trapped by my own fears, and to stand in hope, not despite, but because of the ambiguity with which I live. Though these sentiments were still in their early stages, all of this was very reconciling, and I found that the more I identified with others' suffering, the more able I was to bear mine, though with others.

James distinguished between the healthy soul and the sick soul. The healthy soul is a person who is able to pursue her or his own desires; the sick soul has conflict, struggle, and frustration throughout life and knows a great deal about evil and sin. Because of this striving, only the sick soul can become a twice-born person. This rebirth resonates with my own experience. James writes: "The process is one of redemption, not of mere reversion to natural health, and the sufferer, when saved, is saved by what seems to him a second birth, a deeper kind of conscious being than he could enjoy before."[13] You can hear in the background echoes of "O Happy Fault!"

I know that many, many of you have had similar experiences of the sick soul: whether from disease, alcoholism, drug addiction, betrayal, censure, job loss, a divorce or abandonment, or the death of a spouse, child, or loved one. I am deliberately trying to tap here into another precarious experience like grief, that is, your experiences of the sick soul as well.[14] I think the key to life is an ability to live cognitively, emotionally, and spiritually with one's own precarity while being in union with others in theirs.

I do not think that Peter, the Magdalene, Mary, the Mother of Jesus, Thomas, or John ever really left their grief behind. In fact, Paul himself so resonated with the death of Jesus that he therein found his freedom and the promise of life. I think for them, as for Bonhoeffer, the gap that death causes was never really closed.

I think this is why Paul in Romans 8 assures us that we are led by the Spirit precisely in our sufferings. We groan through our sufferings into becoming the children of God, and this groaning occurs through, as Paul notes, "the present time" (Rom 8:22). He adds, "The Spirit helps us in our weakness. We do not know what we ought to pray for, but the Spirit himself intercedes for us through wordless groans" (Rom 8:26). Whether in grief, in suffering, or in the sick self, we experience the Spirit leading us, accompanying us, expressing for us and from us what we yearn and hope for. In the rawest moments of human vulnerability, the Spirit gives us hope by her own actions.

I need to acknowledge here that in the summer of 1977, on an eight-day retreat that I made under the direction of Fr. Thomas F. Walsh, my former master of novices, he gave me some texts, including Romans 8, to start my retreat. On the second day I reported to him that I found some consolation in that text. He told me to follow the consolation and simply stay only with that text. I returned on the third day and reported the same. He responded the same. And so it went, for eight days. The experience of the retreat became instructive after Bobby's and Lúcás's deaths.

Where we are precarious and vulnerable, the Spirit finds her home.

A MORE EXISTENTIAL AND RELATIONAL ENCOUNTER WITH DEATH

In the sixteenth century, a period when Christian piety greatly developed, ascetical manuals on the preparation for dying proliferated across Europe. It is hard to underestimate the extent to which this form of meditation became a constitutive part of the Christian spiritual life. Its thesis was simple, by preparing for death one could learn how to live. The tradition of the ars moriendi ("art of dying") was the first lesson to the ars vivendi ("art of living").

In a way, this explains, in part, my reason for beginning this project with a reflection on grief, for just as earlier traditions on the art of moral living began with an anticipation of or a memento of death, so too do I. It may be jarring, but it has been long the necessary first step.

In his significant work *Patience, Compassion, Hope and the Christian Art of Dying Well*, Christopher P. Vogt begins by noting how in contemporary times, we avoid talk of death and have so medicalized death so as to take it from view, from being seen or witnessed.[15]

Vogt takes us through four major texts to consider how rich the ars moriendi tradition was: Erasmus's *Preparing for Death* (1533), William Perkins's *Salve for a Sicke Man* (1595), Robert Bellarmine's *The Art of Dying Well* (1619), and Jeremy Taylor's *Rule and Exercises of Holy Dying* (1651). Each of the texts is an invitation to consider not only what right dying looks like but also at the same time to anticipate or imagine oneself on that very deathbed. In a way the texts proffer an exemplar, and for that reason Vogt provides in another chapter Luke's account of the death of Jesus as such a worthy model.

For me, what Vogt describes is an antidote to what Ernest Becker captured in his award-winning work *The Denial of Death*, that is, the contemporary flight from engaging with our human mortality. In his foreword to that work, Sam Keen prepares us for Becker's claims by noting "that the terror of death is so overwhelming we conspire to keep it unconscious."[16] Keen adds, "The basic motivation for human behavior is our biological need to control our basic anxiety, to deny the terror of death. Human beings are naturally anxious because we are ultimately helpless and abandoned in a world where we are fated to die."[17] Becker says it even more uncomfortably: "What does it mean to be a *self-conscious animal*? The idea is ludicrous, if it is not monstrous. It means to know that one is food for worms. This is the terror: to have emerged from nothing, to have a name, consciousness of self, deep inner feelings, an excruciating inner yearning for life and self-expression—and with all this yet to die."[18]

Of course, as your memory turns back to Becker's work, you probably are also thinking of the famed Elizabeth Kubler-Ross, who domesticated death and offered our trajectory toward accepting it through six separate steps. As Keen notes: "Elizabeth Kubler-Ross and Ernest Becker were strange allies in fomenting the cultural revolution that brought death and dying out of the closet. At the same time that Kubler-Ross gave us permission to practice the art of dying gracefully, Becker taught us that awe, fear, and ontological anxiety were natural accompaniments to our contemplation of the fact of death."[19] As Becker, Kubler-Ross, and Keen remind us, unless we face death we will never live.

When Christians hold up the ars moriendi tradition, they anticipate it in the confidence of faith and hope. But this can be as misleading as the cultures we live in that counsel us to avoid thoughts of death. Allen Verhey reflects on this in his *The Christian Art of Dying: Learning from Jesus* and warns against the tendency to commend death so as to subdue it. Rightly, Verhey argues this is not a healthy nor an honest move. The threat of death is, as he and I think, terrifying.[20] Like Christian grief at a funeral, we face and feel the impact of death; but we enter the experience as believers, sometimes coming out of it looking as haggard as Piero della Francesca's *Risen Christ*.

Hopefully, you can see then, that I am trying something different than what we find in the anticipatory ars moriendi exercises. That tradition is not far from the memento mori tradition, in which mementos of death, like someone's skull, is kept at hand, whether in Hamlet considering poor Yorick, or Saint Jerome or the Magdalen, who often, like Hamlet, is seen holding a skull as a memorial of death. Invariably the practice reminds us that we are food for worms. Ars moriendi, like the memento mori, are, however, imaginary exercises. In fact, they are often solitary ones, imagining my own death.

Grief is not an act of imagination. It is existential. Grief is also not a onetime affair but an ongoing one; following Bonhoeffer, it's a lifelong one. And, in this sense it is an awakening or, as I like to say, an epiphany of the gap. Grief is not an imaginary encounter with death; it is death interrupting life. It is love exposed, raw. It is a space that we enter and feel transformed by the loss of, and yet the presence of, love.

As Becker seeks to challenge our culture's easy efforts to obscure death, I too want to reject the so-called psychological advice that advises those who grieve to get back on track and put grief "behind" them. I have learned to tarry with grief, and I cannot tell you how many friends respond to my comments on grief as liberating. They find helpful my talking of grief, as a form of love, as a life-giving pathway to enter without shame and without losing themselves in despair. And, yet they find the invitation an honest one. They stand boldly on the brink of the gap and embrace Bonhoeffer's admonition to not fill it but to trust in God as the witness to it.

In a recent essay on lessons learned about grief in light of COVID entitled "We Must Learn to Look at Grief, Even When We Want to Run Away," Sunita Puri, the palliative care physician, writes: "I don't believe in 'moving on' and 'finding closure.' This language distills the messy complexity of grief into tidy sound bites and asks people to leave something behind, bury it or lock it away. The challenge for my patients and their families is the challenge for all of us: Can we instead move *forward* with grief? Can we find a way to integrate loss into life, to carry it with us?"[21]

Moving forward with grief is what those gathered in the Upper Room did.

I also turn to grief because it exposes the theological anthropology that I want to pursue in these lectures. I think grief reveals the breadth and the depth of the human capacity for relationality, and it is for that reason I suggest that we tarry with it. It is for this reason that C. S. Lewis's *A Grief Observed* is so remarkably disquieting. It conveys how he grieved the dying and death of his wife, Joy.[22] Without apology Lewis conveys his grieving, and we are left speechless.

But can we not move beyond that speechlessness? Like those who try to help the grieving find "closure," there are those who believe that grief is too messy for philosophical reflection. The philosopher Michael Cholbi disagrees. In the first philosophical examination of the topic, *Grief: A Philosophical Guide*, he argues that the importance of grief deserves better attention: "The centrality of grief to the human experience makes it ripe for philosophical investigation, so the paucity of philosophical attention it has received is lamentable."[23]

Though Melissa Kelley reminds us in her classic work on grief in pastoral ministry that there are many matters over which we grieve,[24] Cholbi focuses, as I am doing here, exclusively on the death of persons and investigates the question, For whom do we grieve? He asks: Do we grieve for the one who has died, for ourselves, or for the relationship itself? He answers: "We grieve for those in whom we have invested our practical identities, that is, we grieve those who come to play crucial roles in our aspirations and commitments—indeed, in how we understand ourselves and in what we find valuable or worthwhile in our lives."[25]

Furthermore, he outlines three descriptions about the way grief functions. First, grief is "a series of affective states." While recognizing Kubler-Ross's contribution, Cholbi adds that his series is not reducible to five stages, nor limited to any particular order, nor exclusive of the emotions he proffers. His thoughts resonate with Sunder John Boopalan, who insists on grief as "a profound multidimensional experience," in his illuminating work *Memory, Grief and Agency*.[26]

Cholbi names the second descriptive as a "kind of emotionally driven *attention*." He explains: "Grief responds to the death of others, not by immediately disclosing their importance but by motivating us to take notice of their deaths and interrogate how those deaths matter to us."[27] That attention leads us to the gap where we find not only the death of the other but the relationship. In grief, we attend to the loss, trying to comprehend it in its fullness, just as those did collectively in the Upper Room and we do today at shiva or at funerals. It is not simply something that just happens to us; it is something that we do. I want to add here that, mindful of Bonhoeffer's admonition, when we Christians grieve, we do so mindful of the presence of God who witnesses to our own belief that our relationship with the other is not lost because the other is not lost. For this reason, our attentiveness in grief is a matter of faith and hope precisely in the tangible, emotional, and spiritual experience of the death of a loved one.

Finally, Cholbi provides the third description: "Although grieving is not a process we can dictate, it is nevertheless an *activity* that responds to our choices and actions and that has a discernible aim."[28] Grief is then a process, a kind of attention, and a purposeful activity. In sum, he writes: "Grief's object—what grief is ultimately about—is the bereaved individual's relationship with the deceased, a relationship that invariably has been transformed by the latter's death."[29] Cholbi's griever has agency, through the emotions, through the attention, and through activities.

Nonetheless, grief is disruptive. Cholbi writes: "Grief can be seen as corresponding to a *narrative disruption* in our lives."[30] And, he adds, it can be a "pivotal juncture" in the story one makes out of life. He proposes, therefore, that grief can lead to "narrative building," that "grieving has both backward- and forward-looking dimensions." He adds that "it can be seen as an activity of revising one's existing life narrative in light of the death of one of that narrative's principal characters": Cholbi concludes that grief leads us to ask the larger question "Who shall I be in light of who I have been?"[31]

TURNING TO GRIEF AS A RESOURCE FOR THE MORAL LIFE

Obviously, I am not the first to turn to grief as a resource for ethics, though before doing research on the topic, I thought I was. Indeed in 1992, like Keen, Jerome Miller critically noted that much of contemporary therapy brought grief out into the open so as to subdue it, so that we could "undergo it without being ultimately upset by it."[32] Later, in 2003, Bruce Rogers-Vaughan wrote an essay to recover grief as a resource for theological reflection. He rightly noted: "What we direly need today is not 'grief recovery,' but the recovery of grief.[33]

In 2004 the philosopher Judith Butler wrote *Precarious Life: The Powers of Mourning and Violence*,[34] as a response to the United States' response to the attack of September 11, which she believed was "missing an opportunity to redefine itself as part of the global community."[35] While noting that President Bush announced on September 21 that after ten days as a nation it was time to replace grief with resolute action,[36] she posed instead: "If we are interested in arresting cycles of violence to produce less violent outcomes, it is no doubt important to ask what, politically, might be made of grief besides a cry for war."[37] She argued instead that we should "tarry with grief," to remain "exposed to its unbearability," so as to make grief "into a resource for politics" "not to be resigned to inaction" but as a slow process to "develop a point of identification with suffering itself."[38]

Butler sees grieving as not in itself negative but rather as productive of new social relationships. Grieving opens our eyes to a new appreciation of our relatedness; it challenges our self-understanding, our autonomy, and our understanding of our independence. Butler wants us to appreciate the experience of being decentered by precarity and loss, to understand how we are understood when we experience loss and grief. The evocation of supreme sovereignty or even self-sufficiency is delusional, though a disturbing default. Grief teaches us that we are not sovereign but relational, more than we actually know.

She writes: "If my fate is not originally or finally separable from yours, then the 'we' is traversed by a relationality that we cannot easily argue against; or, rather, we can argue against it, but we would be denying something fundamental about the social conditions of our very foundation."[39] Warning us against unreasoned flight, she writes, "Our political and ethical responsibility are rooted in the recognition that radical forms of self-sufficiency and unbridled sovereignty are, by definition, disrupted by the larger global processes of which they are a part, that no final control can be secured, and that final control is not, cannot be, an ultimate value."[40]

I like to think that grief provides as it did for the disciples at Emmaus, as it did for the Magdalene in the Garden, an epiphany, disclosing at once who Jesus is and who we are, and how we learned love through the one we lost and yet continue to love as we stand at the gap.

That image of epiphany helps us, I think, appreciate all the more what Butler is suggesting, as grief provides a foundation for our political lives. Grief displays, she writes, "the thrall in which our relations with others hold us, in ways we cannot always recount or explain, in ways that often interrupt the self-conscious account of ourselves that we might try to provide, in ways that challenge the very notion of ourselves as autonomous and in control."[41] Grief allows us to see the fragility of the narrative we are trying to build. She writes: "I tell a story about the relations I choose, only to expose, somewhere along the way, the way I am gripped and undone by these relations. My narrative falters, as it must." She adds, "Let's face it. We're undone by each other. And if we're not, we're missing something." She concludes, "One does not always stay intact. One may want to, or manage to for a while, but despite one's best efforts, one is undone . . . by the memory of the feel."[42]

As the disciples who sought one another in the Upper Room knew, grief is not "privatizing," nor does it return us to the solitary self. Luke might not have said this, though Butler did: grief "furnishes a sense of a political community of a complex order" and brings "to the fore the relational ties that have implications for theorizing fundamental dependency and ethical responsibility."[43]

Besides grief revealing to us how embodied, interdependent, and relational we are, and how fundamentally problematic an ethics invariably is that tries to imagine the self as singular; grief also reveals, as Butler sadly suggests, those who do not matter. She writes, "I am as much constituted by those I do grieve for as by those whose deaths I disavow, whose nameless and faceless deaths form the melancholic background for my social world."[44]

In 2008 she investigated the issue of lives as grievable or not in *Frames of War: When Is Life Grievable?*[45]

In 2015 she returned to them again, asking which lives are disposable and ungrievable.[46] By looking at the ungrievable she sees that we can find "whose lives matter? Whose lives do not matter as lives." She recognizes that the ungrievable "have ways of grieving one another." That "the ungrievable gather sometimes in public insurgencies of grief," but to say that one is ungrievable is to say that there is no present structure of support that will sustain that life, which implies that it is devalued, not worth supporting."[47]

When we consider that there are the ungrievable, then we must ask, What will it take for us to recognize their lives as worthy of our grief? But in order to get to that recognition, we need to discover our own vulnerability first and therein see how it so deeply depends on recognizing human dignity. And those two themes, vulnerability and recognition, are the topics for our next two lectures.

Still, I want to close by saying that when it comes to grief, Christians have a lot more to say than being undone by it. For myself, the love I encounter in my grief for Lúcás is not simply mine for him or even the Spirit for me. I encounter his love as well.

Fittingly, I conclude with the words of my friend Yiu Sing Lúcás Chan. Three days before he died, on May 12, 2015, he presided for the first time at the Jesuit community liturgy at the close of the academic year at Marquette University, having just finished his first year of university teaching. He had had a very successful year of teaching, and he had already published two books and about a dozen peer-reviewed articles, but now he preached these prescient words on John 16:5–11.

> In the Gospel, Jesus was saying farewell to his beloved ones. Likewise, it is supposed to be a very sad moment, yet he turned the situation into one of great hope for his disciples. "For if I do not go, the Advocate will not come to you." Of course, from a human earthly point of view, it may be better still to have Jesus around instead of letting him go. Why are we afraid of separation!
>
> I think it is very true when we see our beloved ones leaving us (or we leaving them). Whenever I preach in a Funeral mass, I always remind myself that, if without faith, death would only mean eternal separation. Yet with faith in the Lord, the deceased, the beloved one is actually closer to us than before as he or she is now next to the Lord who is always around to teach, stand by, and walk with us.[48]

Thank you.

NOTES

1. Keenan, "Vulnerability and Hierarchicalism," 129–42; Keenan, "The World at Risk," 132–49; Keenan, "Rethinking Humanity's Progress," 713–35; Keenan, "Linking Human Dignity," 56–73; Keenan, "Building Blocks for Moral Education." On bringing both into the University, see Keenan, "Vulnerable to Contingency," 221–36; Keenan, "The Community Colleges," 143–64.
2. Malley, "The Gospel according to Mark," 20–61.
3. McKenzie, "The Gospel according to Matthew," 62–114.
4. Stuhlmueller, "The Gospel according to Luke," 115–64, at 162.

5. Vawter, "The Gospel according to John," 414–66, at 464.
6. Bonhoeffer, *Letters and Papers from Prison*, letter no. 89, 238.
7. Chan, *The Ten Commandments*, 153, 164. See Climacus, *Ladder of Ascent*; Forrest, *Ladder of the Beatitudes*.
8. Chan, *The Ten Commandments*, 171.
9. Chan, *The Ten Commandments*, 171. See Betz, *Sermon on the Mount*; Davies and Allison Jr., *According to Saint Matthew*; Vann, *The Divine Pity*.
10. Chan, *The Ten Commandments*, 172.
11. Chan, *The Ten Commandments*, 170.
12. Keenan, "Impasse and Solidarity," 47–60.
13. James, *The Varieties of Religious Experience*, 157. In a similar, but more confessional, vein, Alison tells his painful story of having been "caught and held through the depths in which the utterly terrifying and yet completely gentle, unambiguous 'yes' of God to suggest into being the consciousness of a son, to bring forth the terrifying novelty of an unbound conscience." He learns of a new faith beyond resentment. Alison, *Faith Beyond Resentment*, 95.
14. Kaag, *Sick Souls, Healthy Minds*.
15. Vogt, *Patience, Compassion, Hope and the Christian Art of Dying Well*, 1–13.
16. Keen, "Foreword," xii.
17. Keen, xii.
18. Becker, *Denial of Death*, 87.
19. Keen, "Foreword," xii.
20. Verhey, *The Christian Art of Dying*, 89–109.
21. Sunita Puri, "We Must Learn to Look at Grief, Even When We Want to Run Away," *New York Times*, February 23, 2022, https://www.nytimes.com/2022/02/23/opinion/death-grief-covid.html. In a similar way, Kaveny argues that "the book of Lamentations teaches us that the practice of lament calls us to look at the devastation, not to look away from it, even in the name of fixing it." In "Anger, Lamentation, and Common Ground," 663–85.
22. Lewis, *A Grief Observed*.
23. Cholbi, *Grief*, 16.
24. Kelley, *Grief: Contemporary Theory*.
25. Cholbi, *Grief*, 16.
26. Boopalan, *Memory, Grief, and Agency*, 156.
27. Cholbi, *Grief*, 17.
28. Cholbi, 17.
29. Cholbi, 17.
30. Cholbi, 81.
31. Cholbi, 82.
32. Miller, "The Way of Suffering," 21–33, at 27.
33. Rogers-Vaughn, "Recovering Grief," 36–45, at 37–38.
34. Butler, *Precarious Life*.
35. Butler, *Precarious Life*, xi.
36. Bush, "A Nation Challenged."
37. Butler, *Precarious Life*, xii.
38. Butler, *Precarious Life*, 30.
39. Butler, *Precarious Life*, 22.
40. Butler, *Precarious Life*, xii.
41. Butler, *Precarious Life*, 53.

42. Butler, *Precarious Life*, 23–24.
43. Butler, *Precarious Life*, 22.
44. Butler, *Precarious Life*, 46.
45. Butler, *Frames of War*.
46. Butler, *Notes*, 152.
47. Butler, *Notes*, 197.
48. Griener and Keenan, *A Lúcás Chan Reader*, 255. Some of his essays are in this collection. See also, Chan, *Biblical Ethics in the 21st Century*; Chan, Keenan, and Kochuthara, *Doing Catholic Theological Ethics*; Chan, Keenan, and Zacharias, *The Bible and Catholic Theological Ethics*.

2

VULNERABILITY

I began the last lecture proposing that grief provides an epiphany of human connectedness and invited us to consider two very different sites, the biblical gathering of the disciples in the Upper Room from the death of Jesus to the birth of the church at Pentecost and the fairly common gathering of Christians as they accompany their loved ones to the place of rest at a Christian funeral. Both are very vulnerable places where the reality of death intersects with Christian hope, and neither is compromised while they remain together painfully true and present.

I want to begin this lecture with another site.

VULNERABILITY AT THE FOOT OF THE CROSS

I propose we focus on Mary Magdalen. She appears at the Deposition, or later in the Garden, or even later in life, as a contemplative, for instance, in the *Penitent Magdalene* by Caravaggio. In each of these, she grieves. Many of us can think especially of the frescoes and paintings of the grieving Magdalen attempting to clutch the Risen Jesus in the *Noli me tangere*, an icon that captures I think Christian grief and hope together, suspended.[1]

Her visible grief helps us understand Christian hope in all its truthfulness. The poet Richard Crenshaw (1612–49) dedicated a poem to her and called it "St. Mary Magdalene or The Weeper." There he describes her eyes as "two faithfull fountaines, / Two walking Baths, two weeping motions; / Portable and compendious Oceans."[2] Taking her cue from Crenshaw, the writer Susan Haskins similarly dedicates her longest chapter to "The Weeper" in her work *Mary Magdalen: Myth and Metaphor*.[3]

I would like to stay with the Magdalen but look on her specifically at the foot of the cross, standing with Mary, the mother of Jesus, and John, as Jesus is dying. At Golgotha, we get an epiphany of true human vulnerability as we gaze on the three grieving, present to Jesus and present to us as they witness the death of the Savior. I think there, in that icon, we see that Christian hope is born on Golgotha, precisely in their vigilance, in the face of death. As if at the brink of Bonhoeffer's gap, they are at once in their grief, their presence, and their vulnerability, the icon of what we understand to be Christian hope. By standing and witnessing to his passion and death, by accompanying Jesus, Christian hope is born.

Please note, Christ crucified is a sufficient icon of our salvation; Christ crucified captures the faith of Christians. Still, Christ crucified with Mary, John, and the Magdalene in accompaniment not only captures our desires to be present with Jesus as he dies for us but also models for us how we too can stand and witness to the actual kenosis of Christ. As they hear the lament of Christ, "My God, my God, why have you forsaken me" (Psalm 22) they know as we know that this is a lament of abandonment transfigured into one of deliverance.[4] As we contemplate that they hear those words as we gaze on the entire composition, we too enter into that mystery where kenosis is irrevocably witnessed, where we move from the brink of despair to the brink of hope.

In that self-emptying we stand in grief recognizing that our hope is in that body on that cross, and we contemplatively enter into the moment in salvation history in which death continues to have its say, but Christian hope is born as the three witnesses are, in their exhaustion, inevitably transfigured into Christian history by their accompaniment.

That particular composition captures, I think, Christian vulnerability. I focus here on the Magdalen because it is she that keeps the composition from falling into a Stoicism where grief is hard to see, hidden, or even suppressed. The Magdalen invariably keeps the grief apparent, and therein we witness their vulnerability to the scene. The vulnerability that I see there is not so much in the wounds of Jesus as in the connectedness of the four actors.

In this lecture it will be that connectedness that we have with one another that conveys our vulnerability to one another. I want to say that the connectedness of the four on Golgotha mirrors, in a way, other scenes that we have in Christian anthropology where the Throne of Grace or the Mourning Trinity reflects how the Trinity was bound up in Golgotha as well. Each, by focusing on the Body of Christ of Golgotha, highlight how all of humanity and all of divinity are intimately connected, vulnerably inseparable.

Here, hopefully you now see that through the honest embrace of grief, whether at Golgotha or at that the death of a loved one, we encounter love and, in that love, find Christian hope. Attending to grief allows us to encounter the gap, sense the impact of death on human vulnerability, but, in that honest presence, by standing there, by being present, we experience Christian hope. We are called to join in that vulnerability, not only because it is in our nature, not only because we are made in the image of the vulnerable one but also because it is the key to our destiny. We are meant to be connected. That is, after all, what Golgotha seals.

As we now move to consider human vulnerability, this introduction serves, I hope, as a bridge between what we have already considered and what now, in the eyes of faith, we see as the source of our hope, the human as fully, kenotically vulnerable.

INVESTIGATING THE STAGES OF MORAL FORMATION

My thesis in this talk is that in preparation for the moral life, *vulnerability* and *recognition* are necessary preconditions even before conscience comes into play. This thesis develops, however, from an ongoing concern of mine.

Years ago, I became worried about teaching and conscience formation. It seemed to me that we were designing ethics courses as if the students just needed a number of instructions to form their consciences. I began to see that we were thinking of conscience as a disposition, as something the students had, that we wanted to form. Now I am beginning to think that conscience is not a disposition but actually follows from some other disposition. Interestingly, Thomas Aquinas held the same position. As we will see, for him conscience was not a disposition or even a habit, but rather an act, that is, something we needed to do.

While I teach courses in ethics about HIV/AIDS and public health, my students learn a lot about the matter, but not all are responsive to it. In fact, in general across my campus, I see some students who are responsive to the need for moral assistance and others who are not. If they all take courses on conscience formation, why is it that afterward some respond to the need for moral assistance and others do not?

Of course, failing to respond *in the first place* is pretty significant. It emerges as the predominant form of moral failure in the Bible. In fact, in the moral life, people do not often fail by responding; rather, they fail beforehand: they fail to bother to respond and therein fail morally. The priest and Levite pass by the man on the road in the parable of the Good Samaritan in Luke 10:30–37; the goats do not see the hungry and the naked in the last judgment in Matthew 25:31–46; and the rich man steps over Lazarus in Luke 16:19–31. None of them respond. It is not that they do something wrong; rather, they do nothing. They do not seem to even notice the people in absolute need.

Is there something about preparing for the moral life that precedes the act of conscience? If we are forming the conscience intellectually, is there something we are not forming that eventually gets one to stop and recognize the need to respond in conscience in the first place? This is the question that has guided me to these lectures.

I think the problem is that we think of the beginning of the moral life as the conscience, but I now believe that the beginning of the moral life is first being vulnerably disposed to the other, and then subsequently recognizing the other, and then acting in conscience. In other words, I think there are two steps before acting in conscience: being vulnerably disposed and then actually recognizing. These are the preconditions to the conscience act. What the nonresponsive students lack is not knowledge but vulnerability, a call to responsiveness, a call to be answerable.

Let us return to the Good Samaritan parable. Neither the priest nor the Levite were vulnerably disposed to the injured man, and therefore neither recognized him as injured and in need. On the other hand, the Good Samaritan's recognition of the man gives evidence of his vulnerability to the injured man. Then, after the Samaritan recognized the man as being in need, he in conscience went about considering the details of what he needed to do. Acting in conscience, he needed to address a wide array of matters that his conscience had to consider: assess the man's condition, clean the wounds, get him to a safe place, make inquiries about the appropriate place in which to leave him, negotiate and secure from the newly found innkeeper his oversight of the injured man, dispense with his funds, redesign his return to this particular inn and innkeeper so as to take the man with him, etc. The Good Samaritan's conscience got a workout, but the work of his conscience only began after his vulnerable disposition *recognized* the man; the vulnerable recognition led then to the conscience question: Now what do I do?

One reason why we do not see what precedes the conscience is because, disregarding Thomas Aquinas, we think of conscience as essentially both a disposition and an act. We think of conscience as something one has *and* as something one does. I know I did. But I do not anymore. I think something else precedes the act of conscience.

In the *Summa*, Thomas wrote that conscience was not a faculty or a habit, but simply an act (*Summa Theologiae* [*ST*] I.79.13).[5] According to him, when we act in conscience, we try to descend into the particulars to consider what we should do.

In the *Summa* article prior to the one on conscience, Thomas asked about a closely related aspect of the moral life called *synderesis*. There he argued that synderesis is a habit that inclines us to the good and murmurs at evil; this initial habit is for Thomas what eventually launches the act of conscience (*ST* I.79.12). Here, Thomas first notes that the human's "act of reasoning . . . is a kind of movement." Then, about this idea of movement, he writes: There is "a special natural habit, which we call *synderesis*. Whence *synderesis* is said to incite to good, and to murmur at evil, inasmuch as through first principles we proceed to discover, and judge of what we have discovered." This prompting to discover is, I think, akin to recognition. I think this notion of synderesis that "incites to good, and to murmur at evil" resonates very much with what we will see shortly about vulnerability and also recognition.

Still, when Thomas moves to the question on conscience, he acknowledges that we confuse conscience with synderesis but insists that conscience is an act, an effect of synderesis. This is not far from my suggestion that the act of conscience—that is, answering the question, "Now what do I do?"—is the effect of recognizing out of vulnerability the presence of another in need. Thomas explains his terms:

> Now, it is clear that all these things follow the actual application of knowledge to what we do. Wherefore, properly speaking, conscience denominates an act. But since habit is a principle of act, sometimes the name conscience is given to the first natural habit—namely, *synderesis*: thus Jerome calls *synderesis* conscience (Gloss. Ezech. 1:6); Basil, the *natural power of judgment*, and Damascene says that it is the *law of our intellect*. For it is customary for causes and effects to be called after one another. (*ST* I.79.13)

Like Thomas, I want to argue that something precedes conscience that inclines us toward recognizing the neighbor. Thomas called this inclination synderesis. I want to explore what that something is in different, more contemporary terminology like "vulnerability," so that we can better educate our students to be responsive, that is, to vulnerably recognize and act in conscience.

Returning to this first movement, then, what the goats, the rich man, the priest, and the Levite have in common is that they were not vulnerable to, and therefore did not recognize, the other, that is, the homeless and the naked, poor Lazarus, and the wounded stranger. If they had been responsive and recognized these persons as such, then they would have needed in conscience to figure out what the other exactly needed from them. I believe that these instances of "overlooking" others happen precisely because these agents were not incited or prompted to see or imagine the others as like them. In that same moment, they (and their cultures) gave them permission not to be bothered by the others or by their situation. Lacking the vulnerable disposition and the habit of recognizing these people, they passed them by.

Before moving on, let us acknowledge that assuredly, like my smart but nonresponsive students, they knew ethics. Certainly, the priest and the Levite did. But they only knew ethical conduct for those whose dignity they recognized: the priest and Levite for their colleagues, the rich man for his business partners. But they are not interested in ethics for those whom they do not recognize, for those who are, in a word, as Butler says, "ungrievable." They practice ethics with selective bias. If they had recognized them as worthy, then they would think in conscience about what they needed to do.

What we have to address is their particular indifference arising from their lack of vulnerability and recognition. We need to tap their vulnerability and then train them to recognize others beyond family, friends, and caste. In this lecture I want to focus on vulnerability; in the next lecture, I turn to recognition.

VULNERABILITY AS FOUNDATIONAL

Like many others, when I first thought of vulnerability, I considered it singularly as being wounded, weak, at sea, as primarily a condition that raises in others alarm and concern. From the writings of the philosopher Judith Butler, among others, however, I began to see vulnerability as less about being wounded and more about being responsive.

Then I recognized that the word "vulnerable" does not mean "having been wounded" but rather "being able to be wounded." I began to see how it means being exposed, open, or responsive to the other; in this sense vulnerability is the human condition that allows me to hear, encounter, receive, or recognize the other even to the point of being injured.

Thus, at Golgotha, the vulnerability I see from Mary, John, and the Magdalene is in their openness to bear with Jesus his pain, his sorrow, his death; their vulnerability is a capacious accompaniment, a faithful courageous presence, and an unquestionable witness to the ultimate rejection of the Savior.

Being human is being vulnerable, and as such being vulnerable should not be reduced to being precarious, that is, being in an unstable or a risky situation where the possibility or the continuation of harm occurs. Judith Butler realizes that too many people think of vulnerability as primarily being in an unstable context. She, rather, wants us to understand that all of us as human beings are vulnerable to one another; when one is at risk, however, she describes them as in "precarity." She notes: "Precarity exposes our sociality, the fragile and necessary dimensions of our interdependency."[6]

Butler's move is very important. This is developed in a very fine book, *The Ethics of Vulnerability: A Feminist Analysis of Social Life and Practice*, where Erinn C. Gilson considers the implications of a reductively negative view of vulnerability as being in need, being precarious, or even being wounded. She argues rightly that if vulnerability is only the object of concern and *not* the very condition for responsiveness, then when we are in precarity, we would be inevitably looking for moral responsiveness from someone who is anything but vulnerable, that is, those who "occupy the role of the invulnerable" one.[7] In fact, she advertises her book as a corrective to the discourse:

> The meaning of vulnerability is commonly taken for granted and it is assumed that vulnerability is almost exclusively negative, equated with weakness, dependency, powerlessness, deficiency and passivity. This reductively negative view leads to problematic implications, imperiling ethical responsiveness to vulnerability, and so prevents the concept from possessing the normative value many theorists wish it to have. When vulnerability is regarded as weakness and, concomitantly, invulnerability is prized, attentiveness to one's own vulnerability and ethical response to vulnerable others remain out of reach goals.[8]

Retrieving vulnerability as capacious and responsive allows us to see that it is precisely in the Good Samaritan parable that the Samaritan is the one who is vulnerable to the wounded man lying on the road.

Certainly, in being vulnerable, we have the capacity to encounter and respond to another whose life is precarious, as also in the Prodigal Son parable (Lk 15:11–32), where the younger son's own precarity is evident. But, while the beginning of that parable focuses on the younger brother, the center of that parable emerges as we recognize the vulnerability of the Father who recognizes his son in the distance, embraces him, reincorporates him, and works to restore all that was unstable, threatened, exposed, and jeopardized. Like the vulnerable Good Samaritan, the vulnerable father recognizes his son as the precarious one, having a humanity not recognized by those who left him to eat with the pigs.

Butler insists on how fundamentally foundational vulnerability is. She writes: "Ethical obligation not only depends upon our vulnerability to the claims of others but establishes us as creatures who are fundamentally defined by that ethical relation."[9] Vulnerability is what defines and establishes us as capable of being moral among one another. As such, our vulnerability precedes everything else that we can say about ourselves.

Again, emphasizing the priority of vulnerability, she contends: "This ethical relation is not a virtue that I have or exercise; it is prior to any individual sense of self. It is not as discrete individuals that we honor this ethical relation. I am already bound to you, and this is what it means to be the self I am, receptive to you in ways that I cannot fully predict or control."[10] She acknowledges that our vulnerability is woundable and adds: "This is also, clearly, the condition of my injurability as well, and in this way my answerability and my injurability are bound up with one another. In other words, you may frighten me and threaten me, but my obligation to you must remain firm."[11] I am answerable to you and therein I am injurable or woundable, as I prefer to say. But it is our answerability that vulnerability first signifies, or as Charles Mathewes writes: "Vulnerability seems better understood as a description of our openness than our woundable-ness; the way we are porous to what is not self."[12]

Vulnerability essentially is what most qualifies ourselves as being bound to and among others, and this, we shall see, is what prompts our recognition of the other. In fact, the act of recognition reciprocates and affirms our vulnerability.

Butler returns to the priority of vulnerability, this notion that "I am *already* bound to you" that is prior even to the moan from another in need. She writes: "You call upon me, and I answer. But if I answer, it was only because I was already answerable; that is, this susceptibility and vulnerability constitutes me at the most fundamental level and is there, we might say, prior to any deliberate decision to answer the call. In other words, one has to be already capable of receiving the call before actually answering it. In this sense, ethical responsibility presupposes ethical responsiveness."[13] Our vulnerability is our answerability; like synderesis it incites and prompts us to recognize, to respond, to communicate, in short, to love.

The theological ethicist Jennifer Lamson-Scribner dedicated half of a chapter in her recently defended dissertation on "Disorder and Distortion: Theological Approach to Addiction" to how the ontology of relationality in Butler sets the trajectory for moral responsibility. She writes: "For Butler, vulnerability is constitutive of the ontological precondition that allows for the emergence of responsibility. Butler revises the meaning of responsibility by seizing on our limitations. In her estimation, '... to take responsibility for oneself is to avow the limits of any self-understanding and to establish these limits not only as a condition for the subject but as the predicament of the human community.'"[14] Instead of conceiving of responsibility as concomitant with our freedom, "Butler tethers responsibility to vulnerability."[15] By tethering responsibility to vulnerability, we will together in the third and fourth lectures examine both recognition and conscience from that foundational, primal point of departure of moral agency which as prior to the self is constitutively relational and connected.

DIVINE VULNERABILITY

One of the first places that vulnerability appears as foundational in theology is in 2005, in the Irish moral theologian Enda McDonagh's book *Vulnerable to the Holy: In Faith, Morality and Art*.[16] McDonagh began his treatment on vulnerability not with the human but with God. God reveals to us God's self as vulnerable by the very act of creation in which God lets the light be, life be, nature be, animal life and human life be. McDonagh adds, this is a God who lets go and takes risks.[17] Noteworthy, McDonagh sees in Mary's reply to the annunciation, "Be it done unto me according to thy Word," another moment of risk, of letting go, that at once engages the divine initiative. The riskiness of the Creation extends into the Incarnation.

Implicit in this then is the assumption that if God is vulnerable, then we in God's image are made vulnerable. In all this vulnerability, there is great risk. God takes risks in all that God does because God is vulnerable and God's vulnerability informs our own.

Similarities to McDonagh's claims can be found in a variety of other works of theology. Before the discourse on vulnerability developed, in fact, before it was even articulated, Abraham Heschel wrote about a divine "sympathy" in his work on prophets and divine pathos; this sympathy captures in these divine sensibilities a vulnerability that the prophets tangibly breathe when they echo the voice of God. Heschel writes: "An analysis of prophetic utterances shows that the fundamental experience of the prophet is a fellowship with the feelings of God, a *sympathy with the divine pathos*, a communion with the divine consciousness which comes about through the prophet's reflection of, or participation in, the divine pathos. The typical prophetic state of mind is one of being taken up into the heart of the divine pathos. Sympathy is the prophet's answer to inspiration, the correlative to revelation." He adds: "Prophetic sympathy is a response to transcendent sensibility.... The emotional experience of the prophet becomes the focal point for the prophet's understanding of God. He lives not only his personal life but also the life of God. The prophet hears God's voice and feels His heart. He tries to impart the pathos of the message together with its logos. As an imparter his soul overflows, speaking as he does out of the fullness of his sympathy."[18]

Vulnerable to the voice of God, the prophet receives the sensibility of that voice and in the very reception encounters and discovers the capacity to express the sympathy of God. Like the prophets we too can be like those at Golgotha who breathed with Jesus up until his last. When we are vulnerable to the holy, we tap into that divine self-expression of sympathetic responsiveness. And then spirit-filled, we may speak with tongues of fire.

Though not theology, T. H. White's wonderful *The Once and Future King* provides another account of creation that captures vulnerability beautifully.[19] The narrative goes like this: On the sixth day of creation, God gathers all the embryos of each and every species of animal life that God has created; these embryos are rolling around all over the place with each looking exactly like the others. But God offers each species' embryo the opportunity to ask for an addition that will distinguish its own species. One after another species' embryo takes God up on the offer. The giraffe embryo gets a long neck for tree food, the porcupine asks for quills for protection, and so it goes for the entire animal kingdom. The last embryo is the human, Adam, who when asked by God what Adam wants, responds, "I think that You made me in the shape which I now have for reasons best known to Yourselves, and that it would be rude to change.... I will stay a defenceless embryo all my life." God is delighted and lets the human embryo have no particular protection, to be the most vulnerable of all newborns and says: "As for you, Adam.... You will look like an embryo till they bury you."

Behind White's imaginative portrayal of creation is his remarkable vision of the human embryo as the bearer of human vulnerability. By positing the human as willing to remain vulnerable, White is able to disclose further God's delight in that the human now is capable of being in God's image, precisely because of the decision to "stay as a defenceless embryo all my life." White concludes his account with God revealing to the human: "Adam ... eternally undeveloped, you will always remain potential in Our image, able to see some of Our sorrows and to feel some of Our joys. We are partly sorry for you, Adam, but partly hopeful."[20]

Creation narratives help us to see the vulnerability of humanity from the nakedness of Adam in Genesis to the creation of Adam on the Sistine Chapel ceiling. But I have always been struck by a passage in the tenth book of *Paradise Lost*, where John Milton describes how the Son of God encounters the nakedness of our first parents. Milton, by putting the Son of God in the Garden, becomes the one who clothes our first parents in the garden. Milton emphasizes that the one who clothes them is the one who will disrobe himself at the Last Supper to wash our feet and therein begins the process of our salvation, which ends with him hanging naked from the cross. In becoming vulnerably responsive to and for us, he teaches us how we are connected.

Milton writes:

then pittying how they stood
Before him naked to the aire, that now
Must suffer change, disdain'd not to begin
Thenceforth the form of servant to assume,
As when he wash'd his servants feet so now
As Father of his Familie he clad
Thir nakedness with Skins of Beasts. (bk. 10, lines 211–17)[21]

But then Milton adds that he dresses not only their outward nakedness but their inward nakedness as well with the robe of righteousness:

Nor hee thir outward onely with Skins
Of Beasts, but inward nakedness, much more
Opprobrious, with his Robe of righteousness,
Arraying cover'd from his Fathers sight. (bk. 10, lines 220–23)

In their precarity they are restored by his vulnerability.

So as to conclude on vulnerability as foundational, I would like to return to the Good Samaritan parable again. In the parable there is an inversion that we encounter once the parable gets underway, an inversion that we forget until the parable is told again and then we recall it. Remember, the parable is told in answer to the Scribe's question, "Who is my neighbor?" a question from the Scribe who already asked the question regarding inheriting eternal life. The Scribe's second question was not "Who is my neighbor to be loved?" but simply "Who is the neighbor?" In a way, Jesus takes advantage of the Scribe's tendency to ask quickly not-yet fully developed questions. Naturally, knowing what the Scribe wanted to ask, we think that the wounded man is the neighbor, but the neighborliness of the Samaritan is so overwhelming that by the end, we have to answer with the Scribe that the neighbor, in the truncated question, has to be the towering figure of mercy. Therein, Jesus teaches us a new lesson on neighbor: the neighbor has gone from being an object of concern to being a responsive agent or subject.

In a similar inversion the concept of vulnerability in contemporary literature has moved from the wounded one to the responsive one.[22] The inversion about vulnerability mirrors the inversion of our understanding of neighbor. It redeems the notion of vulnerability from being something to avoid to being something to express.

VULNERABILITY GOING FORWARD PHILOSOPHICALLY

Much of the contemporary discourse on vulnerability is indebted to Emmanuel Levinas for his appreciation of the human condition needing to recognize the other. McDonagh acknowledges it,[23] as does the renowned Belgian ethicist who brought Levinas into Catholic moral theology, Roger Burggraeve.[24] In a new work by the Australian ethicist Daniel J. Fleming, we find an excellent summary of Levinas's contribution. There Fleming rightly underlines how for Levinas vulnerability precedes all else in the framing of the moral life:

> Levinas' foundational understanding is not, as is commonly suggested, something that proceeds from our understanding of what it means to be human but rather it is the very structure out of which the possibility for this process arises. Levinas's challenge is that our encounter with the other person *precedes* consciousness: because of this it also *precedes* the meaning we make of the encounter, the meaning we make of ourselves and the rational activity of making decisions regarding the nature of our response to this other person.[25]

The American philosopher Judith Butler gives an extraordinary rendition of Levinas's contributions in her *Giving an Account of Oneself*.[26] It is Butler, as Gilson acknowledges, who has truly developed an ethics of vulnerability.[27] In her own work, she recognizes how fundamentally "prior" vulnerability is, a point similar to the "precedence" that Levinas gave to it. Vulnerability precedes everything about being human. In theological language, the priority of vulnerability is precisely that ground on which the *imago* rests and from which it emanates. The divine enters the human through our shared vulnerability, just as for Heschel the divine sensibilities are what makes us in God's image. Or another way, the covenant, which binds us to God, is as vulnerable as the bonds that bind us to one another. Our vulnerability is what allows us to be connected and therefore to love.

VULNERABILITY UNDER CRITIQUE

Still, I want to acknowledge that on a variety of instances in speaking on vulnerability I have been challenged by the question: Is everyone as able to be vulnerable to the other, *and* should everyone be as vulnerable to the other? Invariably the critique comes from feminist voices. So, in Vienna when I presented a paper on vulnerability and human dignity, I was faced with the critique of Lisa Tessman on *Burdened Virtues*,[28] and asked did I not appreciate that many persons were more burdened than others, while some were also less capable as well. I responded that "I was very sympathetic" with those "with less power due to gender, class, race, or caste to respond to those in need" and invoked Valerie Saiving Goldstein's foundational essay.[29] I added, though, that I shared the feminist presuppositions of Butler, Gilson, and others of learning "to be vulnerable, to give due recognition, and to conscientiously respond to those who are so burdened."[30]

In October 2021, at Duquesne University, I delivered the annual Holy Spirit lecture on grief and vulnerability, where some of the insights for the first lecture were earlier developed.[31] The Latina theologian Neomi De Anda responded and helpfully introduced the difference between chosen and *forced* vulnerability. The distinction was wonderfully complex, as she noted how she hated binaries while offering Mary's yes at the Annunciation as a chosen vulnerable response but adding that Mary was a young woman in occupied lands who by that yes would find "herself in further places of forced vulnerability."[32]

It was here in Campion Hall, however, in 2019, when I gave the Campion lecture,[33] that someone recommended to me afterward Hille Haker's significant essay from 2004 "The Fragility of the Moral Self." Reading that essay, I began to see the need to incorporate her work into my argument. No contemporary Catholic theologian follows the work of Butler, Levinas, Ricœur, and Taylor the way that Haker does, and she critically incorporates them into her own complex and important theological arguments. In her earlier essay, Haker explores both Levinas and Butler and notes: "What becomes important for the concept of the moral self, however, is that from the ethical perspective of 'giving an account of oneself,' both the narrative and the failure of the narrative are addressed toward the other."[34] Haker's concern is what do we make of it when all is being determined by the claims of the other?

As a corrective she earlier introduced the significance of narrative in order to fill out the exchange. "The role of narrative goes far beyond being a constitutive part of self-identity. The self—who is indeed, as Butler and Ricœur claimed, dependent on the narratives of others, as well as on self-narratives, to develop or uphold an identity over time—is likewise dependent on narrative as a moral self, questioning moral convictions and visions of the 'other' from the point of view of the self as sameness."[35]

These narratives require an account not only of the self to others but of the self to oneself, and those self-reflexive narratives do not, as Haker wisely remarks, always get resolved. On the contrary, the "deeply reflexive narratives" highlight that invariably there is no final resolution. She writes: "Thus, what is expressed through the medium of narrative is the impossibility of overcoming the tension between speaking and keeping silent, between agency and non-agency (by way of passivity or suffering), between being oneself and another, between fragility and sovereignty, between forgetting and memory, and finally between life and death."[36] In short, these narratives reveal more a dilemma than a solution. I recognize the other is in need; should I be the one to respond, again?

More recently in her major book *Towards a Critical Political Ethics: Catholic Ethics and Social Challenges*, she develops an argument for what she calls "vulnerable agency" in which she further develops both Levinas and Butler and incorporates a moral self, now not only in a self-reflexive narrative but as having moral agency within it. She writes, implicitly presupposing that shaped by vulnerability we are first answerable but that our agency *subsequently* shapes that answerability: "Vulnerability encompasses the radical ambiguity of human relations. We do not 'naturally' develop into agents; rather, we are addressed and shaped by others *as* (potential, actual, or former) *agents*, in order to *see* ourselves *as* agents, beings who are able to act on one's own account. Vulnerability refers as much to the social constitution of the self as to the general affectability of human beings."[37] In short, she writes: "In any action we take the risk to affect the other and be affected by them, and morally speaking, we aim to affect others (and be affected) in a positive way."[38]

To remedy the overlooking of the self as agent, she integrates a notion of autonomy into this vulnerable context. First, she notes that Levinas "increased the power of the other so far that the response of the self to the other was completely determined by the other." She calls this, with uncanny reserve, "a stretch." She adds, instead, a form of autonomous ethics so as to determine "ultimately which claims the other can make or makes are *justified*." She concludes, "The ethics of vulnerable agency embraces autonomy, but it understands it and reinterprets it, in part, as the capacity to open up to the other, in part as the capability to respond to the other, including in the right to say no to the other's demands or desires."[39]

This agency in a vulnerable context then takes account of one's freedom and one's burdens but is still shaped and constituted as moral because it is first vulnerable, before being agential or autonomous. Haker's proposals take us further than anyone into making vulnerability more attainable and expressible for ordinary life. Vulnerability is still prior to all, but we need agency to decide whether and how we should recognize and respond.

VULNERABILITY GOING SOCIAL

Linda Hogan, of Trinity College Dublin, highlights vulnerability's social significance. In 2018 in Sarajevo, at the close of the third international conference of Catholic Theological Ethics in the World Church (CTEWC), Hogan, the co-chair of CTEWC, gave the final plenary, proposing an ethics of vulnerability for a divided world, describing "vulnerability as a way of being, as the ground of our relationality, and as a mode of social engagement."[40]

She asks, "Can this existential experience of vulnerability be deployed in the service of a politics that unites rather than divides? This depends on whether this recognition of vulnerability can generate a new kind of conversation: about how we act in the world; about our ethical obligations towards each other; about how to oppose the conditions under which some lives are more vulnerable than others."[41]

She concludes:

> Mutual dependence, shared vulnerability, these are elements of human experience that have rarely featured in the ways in which politics is constructed or ethical theories are framed. Indeed, much of our politics and ethics seems to be intent on foreclosing this recognition. And yet shared vulnerability and mutual dependence may be precisely the qualities that have a resonance with the individuals and communities world-wide who are struggling to find the grounds for the hope of a shared future in a world divided.[42]

Along with others,[43] Hogan amply shows how vulnerability could well animate the discourse regarding how we encounter human dignity across the world. Indeed, Hogan herself is one who has offered a significant and hope-filled apology for a human rights discourse, animated by the language of human dignity. Insisting that our expectations ought to be more modest and realistic, she suggests in her work *Keeping Faith with Human Rights* that human rights discourse can amply support our work to achieve greater equity universally. For her, vulnerability, human dignity, and human rights are mutually engaging and illuminating.[44]

Finally, as I was leaving Boston to come to Oxford to deliver these lectures, I received Carolina Montero's *Vulnerabiliad: Hacia una ética más humana*, a foundational investigation of its philosophical foundations from Hegel to Levinas to Ricœur.[45]

THE VIRTUE OF VULNERABILITY

I often write on the virtues, and it is here that I would like to begin incorporating them along the way. So, I ask you, what is the virtue of vulnerability?[46] I suggest humility, a redemptive humility, a humility burdened not with self-deprecation but rather with an unabashed self-understanding of being called to moral responsiveness.

A humble vulnerability helps us to see our interrelatedness, that incites us to mutual recognition, where we see ourselves constituted as connected, interdependent, and responsive in the further realization of human dignity. Throughout the Scriptures, we discover a humble vulnerability that, like Mary as she sings the *Magnificat*, recognizes her place in God's world.

Humility keeps us grounded. Inasmuch as the word "humility" derives from *humus*, meaning soil or dirt, humility keeps us close to the moral terrain in which we find ourselves. A humble vulnerability keeps us alert to our environment, our neighbor in need, our own responsibilities, and the need to take account of ourselves, the future, and its challenges.

Finally, humility affects not only how we understand our place in God's world but also how we think, learn, and understand. This insight into a humble way of thinking that rejects the imperial ego is complemented by what other theologians call the "grace of self-doubt."[47] In humility we discover that there can be a real grace in doubting ourselves and our opinions. This grace animates and informs our humility and helps us to see that the work of realizing ourselves as disciples of Christ is a formidable lifelong task fraught with misperceptions and yet possible, precisely because of that humility. We will see more on this "epistemic humility" in the seventh lecture, on the virtues.

The foundational stance of humility as the virtue for all Christians is found in Augustine. He writes in *Letter 118* that the way to seek abiding truth "consists, first, of humility, second, of humility, and third, of humility. . . . It is not that there are no other precepts to be mentioned. But, unless humility precedes, accompanies, and follows whatever we do, unless it is a goal on which we keep our eye, a companion at our side, and a yoke upon our neck, we will find that we have done little good to rejoice in; pride will have bereft us of everything."[48]

For Augustine, humility is the way of the vulnerable Christ and therefore the way of the disciple. He writes: "Christ Humbled is the Way; Christ the Truth and the Life, Christ Highly Exalted and God. If thou walk in the Humbled, thou shalt attain to the Exalted. If infirm as thou art, thou despise not the Humbled, thou shalt abide exceeding strong in the Exalted. For what cause was there of Christ's Humiliation, save thine infirmity?"[49]

Humility is rightly the virtue of vulnerability as the virtue prior to all; it reminds us of God's world and our place in it.

A FINAL WORD

In the next lecture we will still talk about vulnerability as we talk about recognition, but, here, I want to get you into the practice of recognizing vulnerability not as being needy but rather as being capaciously responsive. In looking for the vulnerable one, I want you to change your gaze.

So let us return to the Prodigal Son parable. Earlier I suggested the father's vulnerability and the younger son's own precarity; now, I hope you see how central the father's vulnerability and the son's precarity are to the story. Together they present a good way of appreciating both concepts. In the beginning of that parable, we encounter the younger brother's rapid decline into precarity, but the center of the parable turns to and focuses on the vulnerable father, who has originally given his son his inheritance but who welcomes his son's return. The same father remains vulnerable to his older son as well, who does not suffer from precarity but from resentment. Let us not think, however, that the father is surprised by the older son's resentment. When he sees his younger son in the distance, he knows that his movement toward the younger son will trigger the older son's own insecurities. The father's vulnerability frees him to anchor both sons in his household and in their relationships. The stability in the story is the vulnerable father, as the precarious son returns and the resentful one tries to leave; the centrality of the story is the enduringly vigilant, attentive, responsive, indeed humble father, who is so because he is vulnerable and therein capable of responding to them in their own respective needs for one another.

Thank you.

NOTES

1. Katsanis, "Meeting in the Garden," 402–16; Baert, "The Gaze in the Garden," 187–221.
2. Crenshaw, "St. Mary Magdalene or The Weeper."
3. Haskins, *Mary Magdalen*, 224–90.
4. Carey, *Jesus' Cry from the Cross*.
5. Throughout I cite the Summa from the universally standard *Summa Theologiae of St. Thomas Aquinas* Second and Revised Edition, literally translated by Fathers of the English Dominican Province (London: Burns Oates and Washbourne, 1920–22).
6. Butler, "Precarious Life, Vulnerability," 134–51, at 148; See also her *Precarious Life*.
7. Gilson, *The Ethics of Vulnerability*, 35.
8. Gilson, i.
9. Butler, *Notes*, 110; See also her *Giving an Account*.
10. Butler, *Notes*, 110.
11. Butler, *Notes*, 110.
12. Mathewes, "Vulnerability and Political Theology," 165–84, at 168.
13. Butler, *Notes*, 110. See also Butler, Gambetti, and Sabsay, *Vulnerability in Resistance*.
14. Butler, *Giving an Account*, 83.
15. Lamson-Scribner, *Disorder and Distortion*, 231.
16. McDonagh, *Vulnerable to the Holy*.
17. McDonagh, 12–20.
18. Heschel, *The Prophets*, 25–26.
19. White, *Future King*, chap. 21.
20. White, chap. 21.
21. John Milton, *Paradise Lost*, 2nd ed. (London: Samuel Simmons, 1674).
22. A noteworthy philosophical engagement with vulnerability that remains in ancient Greek literature and philosophy is McCoy, *Wounded Heroes*. For a breathtaking, comprehensive Spanish theological foundational work on vulnerability, see Orphanopoulos, *Vulnerabilidad*.
23. McDonagh, *Vulnerable to the Holy*, 7–8.
24. Burggraeve, *The Wisdom of Love in the Service of Love*; Burggraeve, *The Awakening to the Other*.
25. Fleming, *Attentiveness to Vulnerability*, 23.
26. Butler, *Giving an Account*, 84–101.
27. Gilson, *The Ethics of Vulnerability*, 40–71.
28. Tessman, *Burdened Virtues*.
29. Goldstein, "Human Situation," 100–112.
30. Keenan, "Linking Human Dignity," 56–73, at 73. Among such accounts, see the essays in Mackenzie, Rogers, and Dodds, *Vulnerability: New Essays*.
31. Keenan, "Grieving in the Upper Room."

32. De Anda, "Spirit of Community: Forced Vulnerability, the Little Details as Realized Hope and Lament as Prophetic Protest."
33. Keenan, "Exploring Vulnerability."
34. Haker, "The Fragility," 359–81, at 366.
35. Haker, "The Fragility," 377.
36. Haker, "The Fragility," 380.
37. Haker, *Towards a Critical Political Ethics*, 138–39.
38. Haker, *Towards a Critical Political Ethics*, 143.
39. Haker, *Towards a Critical Political Ethics*, 157.
40. Hogan, "Vulnerability," 216.
41. Hogan, "Vulnerability," 219.
42. Hogan, "Vulnerability," 219–20.
43. Leclerq, *Blessed Are the Vulnerable*.
44. Hogan, *Keeping Faith*.
45. Orphanopoulos, *Vulnerabiliad*.
46. Brown, *Daring Greatly*.
47. Farley, "Ethics, Ecclesiology," 55–77.
48. Elsewhere he writes: "Wherefore did it behove Christ to be born? Wherefore did it behove Christ to be crucified? For if He had come to point out the way of humility, and to make Himself the way of humility; in all things had humility to be fulfilled by Him. He deigned from this to give authority to His own baptism, that His servants might know with what alacrity they ought to run to the baptism of the Lord, when He Himself did not refuse to receive the baptism of a servant. This favor was bestowed upon John that it should be called his baptism" [Tractate 5 (Jn 1:33)]; "We have learned, brethren, humility from the Highest; let us, as humble, do to one another what He, the Highest, did in His humility. Great is the commendation we have here of humility: and brethren do this to one another in turn, even in the visible act itself, when they treat one another with hospitality; for the practice of such humility is generally prevalent, and finds expression in the very deed that makes it discernible" [Tractate 58.4 (Jn 13:10–15)].
49. Sermon 92: Jn 14.6.

3

RECOGNITION

Like Levinas, Butler, and Haker, I think of vulnerability as pre-personal, constituting us as human and in God's image. When thinking of God's image, it is helpful to remember that early images of God were more Trinitarian than Christological. The Trinity as three persons in one God accentuates the "person" not as autonomous but as constituted by others. Like the Triune God, we are humans by our being connected to other persons. Our personhood derives from our vulnerable humanity. I will return to this Trinitarian source of ourselves later in the seventh lecture.

Thus, in this project of "Preparing for the Moral Life," I am interested in a theological anthropology that takes seriously not that we are social before we are personal, or personal before we are social, but that we are in our natures, or as philosophers would say we are, "ontologically" (that is, in our being) connected before we are either and therefore the act of recognition will always somehow refract to this underlying prior state of us as connected.

Having had many African students and colleagues such as Laurenti Magesa, Agbonkhianmeghe Orobator, John Ghansah, Bénézet Bujo, Azétsop Jacquineau, Leocadie Lushombo, Ann Nasimiyu, Veronica Rop, Hilary Nwainya, Lazarus Onuh, and Anne Achieng over the years, I have always been impressed by their insistence that as Ubuntu philosophy teaches us "I am because we are." The interrelatedness of people is not only between being connected among persons and across societies but also through time, by being connected not only to the ancestors but to those forthcoming. Vulnerability helps establish the givenness of our connectibility.

I began these lectures with grief to highlight how profoundly we are connected, such that separation from others is always grievous. On this note, in light of vulnerability, now let us move on to recognition, a recognition that furthers the appreciation of our interconnectedness.

GOOD SAMARITAN AS ALLEGORY

I begin this section on recognition with a meditation that highlights the long history of the allegorical understanding of the Good Samaritan parable so as to see that for Christians the recognition of the other is always first a secondary recognition deeply refracted by our first recognition of Christ, who stopped on the road, recognized humanity, and saved us, and therein liberated us for the work of vulnerable recognition and mercy.

As we saw earlier, the parable of the Good Samaritan is an odd one because in the beginning of the parable we think the neighbor is the one in need, but at the end the neighbor is the one who responds. We recognize too that the scribe's question at the beginning, "Who is the neighbor?" becomes Jesus's question at the end, with the scribe actually answering his own question. The answer is the "Samaritan" because on hearing the story, the Samaritan's enormous responsiveness in mercy to the wounded man eclipses all else: neighbor is no longer an object to be loved but a subject to be emulated.

Though many do not know this, the parable has been preached through allegory, basically from the early third century through to the Reformation. It highlights how significantly the agency of the Samaritan is. Let us turn now to that allegorical retelling of the parable.

Throughout the tradition, many preachers and theologians saw in the story of the Good Samaritan an allegory (in miniature) of our redemption by Christ, a story of what Christ has accomplished for us.[1] Starting with Clement of Alexandria (ca. 150–ca. 215), then Origen (ca. 184–ca. 254), Ambrose (339–97), and, finally, Augustine (354–430), the Good Samaritan parable was explained as how mercy was first given to us. Later from Venerable Bede (673–735) to Martin Luther (1483–1546), preachers and theologians appropriate and modify the narrative.[2]

The basic allegorical expression of the parable was this: The man who lies on the road is Adam, wounded (by sin), suffering outside the gates of Eden. The priest and the Levite (the law and the prophets) do not and cannot save Adam; they pass him by. Along comes the Good Samaritan (Christ), one not from here, who tends to Adam's wounds (our salvation), takes him to the inn (the church), makes a down payment (toward our redemption), and promises to return for him (the second coming), when he will pay in full (our redemption) and take him with him to his home (the kingdom of God).

The parable then is first and foremost *not* a moral story about how we should treat others. Though often forgotten today, this interpretation of the parable shows us that it is *first* a narrative of Jesus's redemptive work for us and *then and only then* a call to go and do likewise. The parable reveals that Jesus was first vulnerable to us when he recognized us on the road. Jesus's recognition of us makes possible our recognition of others. This is a lesson we must never forget, for our capacity to recognize is made possible by his recognition of us first. He recognized first how we were wounded by sin and death. He stopped and saved us. In light of that, we need to go and do likewise.

MUTUAL RECOGNITION

I first came upon the notion of recognition not from a philosopher or a theologian but from the psychoanalyst and feminist theorist Jessica Benjamin, who reflected on infancy and mutual recognition among infants. In fact, even before Benjamin, it was James Hanvey, SJ, the previous Master of Campion Hall, who first urged me in this direction. Mutual recognition is the central experience of infants among infants; after being the object of the attention of people much bigger than themselves, mutual recognition is where an infant finally encounters another infant that seems much like itself and yet, not. They want to touch the face of the other child; they are fascinated that this child in front of them is just like them. They mutually recognize each other: in that moment they recognize their humanity. They cry when the other cries, smile when the other smiles, touch when the other touches.

Benjamin writes, "Mutual recognition is the most vulnerable point in the process of differentiation." She adds, "In mutual recognition, the subject accepts the premise that others are separate but nonetheless share like feelings and intentions."[3] In a more recent work in 2017, she turns again to mutual recognition and among other matters finds the language of vulnerability key for recuperating and restoring the experience of mutual recognition.[4]

As we mature, the experience of mutual recognition can and should happen time and again as part of our growth as moral agents. The mutual recognition in infancy becomes the foundation for subsequent expressions of due recognition whenever we encounter humanity in its greatest precarity or neglect. From that first recognition, where we acknowledge the other's and our own humanity, we learn to develop a sense that the other in need is another human being. Of course, as we saw earlier in the biblical stories, overlooking the humanity of another is what gives us the unfortunate "permission" to withhold due recognition. Thus, the work of education is to help one another to be vulnerable and vigilant enough so that due recognition and appropriate response to the other are actualized as the worthy alternative to the customary but harmful stance of overlooking or neglect.

THE THREE STAGES OF RECOGNITION

The philosopher Paddy McQueen provides a foundation for explaining the way recognition unfolds. He proposes it as an insight and a practice that develops, going from first being an awakening; to second, making a form of identification; and, finally, to acknowledging the other or appreciating the other as such in relation to ourselves. Let me repeat that—recognition is first an awakening; then makes a form of identification; and, finally acknowledges the other as such in relation to ourselves. Do you see the Samaritan here? First, awakening to the wounded man, then identifying the wounded one as a fellow human, and finally, even in silence acknowledging the other's call for help.

McQueen expands these steps:

> The term "recognition" has several distinct meanings: (1) an act of intellectual apprehension, such as when we "recognize" we have made a mistake or we "recognize" the influence of religion on American politics; (2) a form of identification, such as when we "recognize" a friend in the street; and (3) the act of acknowledging or respecting another being, such as when we "recognize" someone's status, achievements or rights.... The philosophical and political notion of recognition predominantly refers to (3), and is often taken to mean that not only is recognition an important means of valuing or respecting another person, it is also fundamental to understanding ourselves.[5]

The move from recognizing someone as familiar to giving recognition to one to whom it is due is, I think, the threshold into the moral life.[6] What we learn in infancy is literally a first lesson: in our vulnerability we recognize that we are related one to the other, that we are not alone and that the other is not alone. We are awakened to being connected. Then, we move from an awakening to a form of identification. We are connected because we are human beings. Later, as children, we realize that that form of identification calls us to a form of responsiveness, especially when the other is neglected, in need, or oppressed. The awakening to and the identification with another's humanity are therefore the first steps toward the moral threshold wherein through recognition we become ethically responsive.

I think we need to highlight this point of moving from awakening and identification to the act of acknowledgment as the threshold of the moral life, for therein in our vulnerability, we, like the Samaritan, recognize the other and begin the process of ethical responsiveness. Three major scholars stay with us as we pause at this threshold of recognition.

AT THE THRESHOLD OF RECOGNITION WITH HILLE HAKER AND AXEL HONNETH

First, Hille Haker reflects not on recognizing but on being recognized. She writes: "It is through recognition—or, more precisely, through the experience of being recognized by others—that the self is enabled to keep the *tension* between sameness and uniqueness or one's otherness in balance."[7] Then she asks the question, "Why does recognition matter so much?"[8] After reflecting on the spectrum of the threefold meanings of recognition as awakening, identification, and acknowledgment, she notes the "close relationship between identity and ethics. Both identity and morality are actualized in acts of mutual recognition—or prevented in acts of domination and subjection, which are forms of failed or refused recognition." She highlights the power of recognition, when it is given and when it is withheld. "Because not only the *failure* of recognition but, actually, the intentional *refusal* of recognition is possible at any point, individuals who interact with others are always and necessarily exposed to the risk of being mistreated by others. Individuals are not only dependent on being identified as the same over time; they are also dependent on being recognized as equal to others in relevant aspects." She concludes: "The evaluations and self evaluations constitute one's standing in the eyes of others and oneself, and it is through acts of misrecognition as well as through systemic forms of misrecognition that foster denigrative gestures and/or acts that persons are morally harmed."[9]

In a more recent article, entitled "Recognition and Responsibility," Haker seeks to remedy her finding that "while the concept of responsibility is a cornerstone of Christian ethics, recognition theory still lacks a thorough theological-ethical analysis."[10] Among other matters, she proposes a consideration of the murder of Abel by Cain in Genesis 4:1–16,[11] which she calls "the paradigmatic story of morality told as part of the narrative of the origins of humans and the history of their faith."

She describes the famous narrative in this way: "Cain misunderstands God from the beginning, mistaking his own sacrifices as a conditional gift to God for which he expects something in return. God refuses to act accordingly, although God does receive the sacrifice of Abel."[12] Though she does not do it, I think it might be worth our while to linger a moment on the text itself to see how much the text centers on recognition. We are told that, "The LORD looked with favor on Abel and his offering, but on Cain and his offering he did not look with favor" (Gen 4:4–5). Still, recognizing Cain's anger, YHWH warns Cain, "Sin is crouching at your door; it desires to have you, but you must rule over it" (Gen 4:7). Nonetheless, Cain does not heed the counsel but lures his brother out to the fields, where he kills him. The text continues: "Then the LORD said to Cain, 'Where is your brother Abel?' 'I don't know,' he replied. 'Am I my brother's keeper?'" (Gen 4:9). I do not think it is without relevance that the Lord does not simply ask where is Abel, but where is your brother? Cain has destroyed the one human who is without doubt the one closest to and most identified with him.

When Cain is punished to be a "restless wanderer," Cain responds in terror: "My punishment is more than I can bear. Today you are driving me from the land, and I will be hidden from your presence; I will be a restless wanderer on the earth, and whoever finds me will kill me" (Gen 4:13–14). The text continues, "But the Lord responds: 'Not so; anyone who kills Cain will suffer vengeance seven times over.' Then the LORD put a mark on Cain so that no one who found him would kill him" (Gen 4:15). The Lord not only assures Cain that he will not be hidden from the Lord but also that he will be recognized by the Lord and by all others.

Haker comments on the passage: "The story depicts Cain's desire to be recognized by God, spelling out the tragic consequences of misunderstanding God's love and demands. Cain becomes as much the symbol of the desire for recognition as for the failure of responsibility. Being marked *and* put under God's protection in one symbol, Cain survives his moral failure, just as the people of God survive all following failures and mistakes despite all the catastrophes that pile up over the course of history."[13]

I will return shortly to the question about recognizing one's brother, but before I move to the second scholar on recognition, let me acknowledge how it is through contrast, through what Haker calls misrecognition, that we see the true power of recognition. Invariably the failure to appreciate the significance of identification leads to the failure to acknowledge, and the failure to cross that threshold leads to moral failure.

The second scholar is the German philosopher Axel Honneth, whose 1995 work *The Struggle for Recognition: The Moral Grammar of Social Conflicts* is a foundational exposition on the urgency of recognition for the moral life.[14] Honneth posits a social philosophy that undergirds the personal understanding of the good life, which he describes as the "process of realizing, without coercion, one's self-chosen life-goals."[15] Honneth argues that recognition plays a constitutive role in the attainment of these goals. Positively, recognition supports the agent's pursuit of agency that requires self-trust and the ability to name, set, and realize one's goals. As Bart van Leeuwen notes, "What characterizes the intersubjective character of Honneth's theory is that this positive self-relation becomes possible only through patterns of recognition; hence, these represent the intersubjective conditions that we must presuppose in order to describe the general structures of the good life."[16]

Just as we saw the ontological priority of vulnerability as a condition for our moral responsiveness, Honneth sees these intersubjective conditions as foundational for the pursuit of the moral life. Negatively then, the social failure to recognize, the social refusal to recognize, or the actual stance of social disrespect compromises the other's "potential to exercise his own freedom in order to realize those values that he deems to be constitutive of his own personality."[17]

The human needs recognition to flourish.

Famously, Honneth argues, "The reproduction of social life is governed by the imperative of mutual recognition, because one can develop a practical relation-to-self only when one has learned to view oneself, from the normative perspective of one's partners in interaction, as their social addressee."[18] So as to further the realization of "the imperative of mutual recognition," Honneth invokes the "common good," the very topic of last year's D'Arcy lectures by Campion Hall's own Patrick Riordan.[19] Honneth notes, "That puts everyone in the same position to understand his or her value for the community without restricting the autonomous realization of his or her self. In this kind of society, subjects with equal rights could mutually recognize their individual particularity by contributing in their own ways to the reproduction of the community's identity."[20]

As we can see, for Honneth, mutual recognition provides the constitutive foundation of the personal and social realization of the good life, the moral life. More recently, Honneth engaged with the American philosopher Nancy Fraser in a debate concerning the common good with each investigating the terms of distributive justice and mutual recognition and with each asking with what priority and with what strategy a more just social life is attainable by emphasizing one over the other.[21] The debate highlights how interconnected recognition is to the actual realization of the more just redistribution of goods through moral responsiveness. It also highlights the power of social disrespect and its impact on very particular cultures as a real institutional obstacle.

JUDITH BUTLER ON GRIEVABILITY

Following then on this theme of contrasts in both Haker and Honneth, we turn now to Butler and return to her concept of grievability, which we saw at the conclusion of the first lecture. In a way that reflects Honneth's own concerns, Butler frames her concept in this way: "The most individual question of morality—how do I live this life that is mine?—is bound up with biopolitical questions distilled in forms such as these: Whose lives matter? Whose lives do not matter as lives, are not recognizable as living, or count only ambiguously as alive?"[22]

Butler directs us then to her question, "Whose lives are grievable and whose are not?" And, in order to help you to appreciate the question, I want to share with you how the question affected and continues to affect my reading now of the morning newspapers.

I remember well now with shame and guilt that before learning this concept of grievability, and before the emergence of Black Lives Matter (BLM) through the deaths of George Floyd, Breonna Taylor, and Ahmaud Arbery, when I read the newspaper some stories of tragedy caught my eye, my recognition, and prompted me to read their story, see what happened, reflect on it, and consider their loss. I attended to their tragedy. But there were others that I did not pause to read, that I thought to myself, oh yet again, another person shot by police, or another homeless person found dead. I exercised an economy with my time and realized I was stopping at those who were grievable in my estimation, and simply considered the others as not. Invariably, in many instances, the stories I did not read were stories of Black men being killed. I was wrong to do that. In order to correct my ways, the notion of grievability now serves as a new examination of conscience for me, or what the Jesuits refer to as the "examen."[23] I stop and read now and take in accounts that I formerly, wrongfully overlooked. It prompts me to an awareness of how white supremacy operates within and without me and why I need to expose and dismantle it. And, as embarrassing and as shameful as it is to say it, I do not think my own interior disposition to "pass by" such news is over, though I try and pray that it be so. For it is really not about my shame but rather about the recognition long overdue.

Butler talks about how we individually and collectively live out the matter of grievability in powerful and prophetic terms. She writes: "The biopolitical management of the ungrievable proves crucial to approaching the question, how do I lead this life?" Terrifyingly, Butler reflects on the person who understands themselves as not grievable. She notes: "This question becomes most acute for someone, anyone, who already understands him or herself to be a dispensable sort of being, one who registers at an affective and corporeal level that his or her life is *not* worth safeguarding, protecting, and valuing."[24] She adds, "If it turns out that I have no certainty that I will have food or shelter, or that no social network or institution would catch me if I fall, then I could come to belong to the ungrievable."[25]

Powerfully, Butler sums up her argument about how social structures effectively make the determination of the ungrievable:

> The reason that someone will not be grieved for, or have already been established as one who is not to be grieved for, is that there is no present structure of support that will sustain that life, which implies that it is devalued, not worth supporting and protecting as a life by dominant schemes of value. The very future of my life depends upon that condition of support, so if I am not supported, then my life is established as tenuous, precarious, and in that sense not worthy to be protected from injury or loss, and so not grievable. If only a grievable life can be valued, and valued through time, then only a grievable life will be eligible for social and economic support, housing, health care, employment, rights of political expression, forms of social recognition, and the conditions for political agency (*Handlungsfähigkeit*). One must, as it were, be grievable before one is lost, before any question of being neglected or abandoned, and one must be able to live a life knowing that the loss of this life that I am living would be mourned and so every measure will be taken to forestall this loss.[26]

I think Butler's concept of the social demarcation of those whose lives are grievable and those whose lives are not helps us to realize the impact of mutual recognition. Before we move on to the question of social structures that make, in part, these determinations, I wish to offer three brief meditations on the misrecognized or the ungrievable.

The first is the actual public murder of George Floyd on May 25, 2020, on the streets of Minneapolis by a police officer. The fact that Mr. Floyd was publicly murdered by a police officer, with other officers assisting over the period of 9 minutes and 29 seconds of having a knee pressed down on his throat as he died uttering "I can't breathe,"[27] provided the social instruction to kneel in grief for the same 9 minutes and 29 seconds as a counterpractice to the festivities that celebrated in years past in my country the lynching of Black men, women, and children.

That history of lynching was finally recognized when in 2015 the Equal Justice Initiative (EJI) released a study that "detailed over 4,400 documented racial terror lynchings of Black people in America between 1877 and 1950." To make those deaths memorable, EJI opened in 2018 the National Memorial for Peace and Justice. Later, in June 2020, EJI reported, "During the 12-year period of Reconstruction (1865–1877) at least 2,000 Black women, men, and children were victims of racial terror lynchings."[28] Not only were these deaths not grieved; their murders were horrendously celebrated with white men, white women, and white children participating. Against that social culture, the Black Lives Matter movement insisted that white culture be taught how to grieve the death of George Floyd, by kneeling for 9 minutes and 29 seconds, by uttering "I can't breathe," and by remembering the name of George Floyd and all those others murdered in the United States.

Black Lives Matter is a way of forcing American white people to acknowledge that George Floyd mattered, that he was and is grievable. As were Ahmaud Arbery and Breonna Taylor and those killed before and after them as well. It calls us to remember their names, their lives, and their deaths as grievable. Black Lives Matter prompts us to recognize how these people died and how until this moment, we could simply overlook these killings and not take note. BLM is a social movement summoning white America to a mutual recognition of Black America. That due recognition is theirs and always was theirs.[29]

A second meditation goes to a film called *Elephant Man*. This David Lynch film came out in 1980 while I was a student at Weston Jesuit School of Theology, learning moral theology for the first time. The climax of this social drama on the life of the severely deformed Joseph Merrick, whose own head he normally hooded, comes when Merrick, unhooded, is hunted down by a crowd that pursues him into a men's public bathroom, where in the midst of urinals this man who is so ungrievable cries out in protest, gasping, "I am not an elephant! I am not an animal! I am a human being! I . . . am . . . a . . . man!" as he collapses amidst the row of urinals. I cannot remember a better, more compelling declaration of the summons to mutual recognition.

The third meditation leads me to return to the prodigal son parable to uncover recognition's rich relationship with both the vulnerable and the familiar. In the parable, as the vulnerable father attends to the prodigal, he remains vulnerable to his older son as well. As we saw in the previous lecture, the father knows that his movement toward the Prodigal will surely trigger the older son's own insecurities. The stability in the story is the vulnerable father, as the precarious son returns and the resentful one tries to leave.[30] Indeed, the father's response to the older brother is extraordinary. As biblical theologian

Greg Forbes notes, "The father again acts contrary to all expectations." Noting that if a son talked to his father as the elder son does in the parable, he "observes that in this situation a Middle Eastern father would lock the son up, finish the banquet, then have him beaten."[31] Instead, the father's patience with the angry older son is not unlike Yahweh warning the resentful Cain. In both instances, the older son needs to recognize his brother. So, when the older son refers to his prodigal brother as "that son of yours," the father urges him to *recognize* that "this brother of yours was dead and has come to life." Still, the brother needs to be vulnerable before he can recognize; without it, due recognition just does not happen. In many ways the older brother of the prodigal is a replay of Cain unable to return to the original mutual recognition of himself discovering Abel.

CORRECTING THE SOCIALLY DIRECTED GAZE: THE CALL TO RECOGNITION

Why is it that our cultures, like the biblical ones, let people fail to recognize their neighbor in need or even to socially disrespect them? I would like to take you to three works that attempt to redirect our gaze.

The question of cultures insulating us from the need to recognize our neighbor was raised in the United States nearly ninety years ago by one of the most famous Protestant American ethicists, Reinhold Niebuhr. In 1932 he warned ethicists that they lacked "an understanding of the brutal character of the behavior of all human collectives, and the power of self-interest and collective egoism in all inter-group relations."[32] There, in *Moral Man and Immoral Society: A Study in Ethics and Politics*, he insisted that we do not see "the limitations of the human imagination, the easy subservience of reason to prejudice and passion, and the consequent persistence of irrational egoism, particularly in group behavior."[33] In many ways we go on teaching today, nearly ninety years later, failing to heed the forces that empower "the inequalities of privilege (that) are greater than could possibly be defended rationally."[34] It is in the interests of such forces that we continue to fail to recognize those whose inequities pay the price of our privilege. No wonder that we rarely recognize; no wonder how we each unreflectively distinguish the grievable from the ungrievable by the read of a morning newspaper.

And yet, reason is often invoked precisely to defend such inequalities of privilege and thus to keep us from giving due recognition to others. In her stunning critique of Adam Smith's *The Theory of Moral Sentiments*, Kate Ward describes how Smith aimed to create a social culture that could tolerate and even promote his economic theory. She laid bare Smith's contempt for "'those whining and melancholy moralists' who call attention to the suffering of distant others'" noting how he considered the moralists' sympathy for those with misfortunes "absurd and unreasonable" and irresistibly unnatural.[35] The father of capitalism understood well the importance of keeping our gaze from those who are victims of our privileged structures.

I remember the first time I taught *The Theory of Moral Sentiments*, I was so astonished at how Smith directed the gaze of "sympathy" upward to the so-called self-made man. That upward gaze of Smith's sympathy never caught a glimpse of the homeless person or some other in need. When Ward submitted for publication her essay that dissected *Moral Sentiments* and in particular the device of the "impartial spectator," and revealed the senior scholars who acquiesced in the Smith agenda, she received numerous rejection notices until finally *Heythrop Journal* published it in 2015. In many ways the journals' rejections were an institutional resistance to her insistence that the *Moral Sentiments* were, well, false. The title of Ward's essay, "'Mere Poverty Excites Little Compassion': Adam Smith, Moral Judgment and the Poor," conveys how effectively Smith validates our daily disinterest in compassion. I recommend it for those who especially think otherwise.

Finally, we turn to Isabel Wilkerson and her magnificent *Caste: The Origins of Our Discontent*, which argues that America's racism is a caste system. Throughout, she provokes the reader to see how our society keeps us from seeing the structures that frame American racism. To awaken us from our compliance with these structures, she proposes the image of a "wordless usher," whose flashlight keeps our gaze focused, not letting our eyes avert to any recognition that caste itself is guiding us to look only at what caste wants us to recognize. She writes:

> As we go about our daily lives, caste is the wordless usher in a darkened theater, flashlight cast down in the aisles, guiding us to our assigned seats for a performance. The hierarchy of castes is not about feeling or morality. It is about power—which groups have it and which do not. It is about resources, about which caste is seen as worthy of them and which are not, and about who gets to acquire and control them and who does not. It is about respect, authority and assumptions of competence—who is accorded these and who is not.[36]

Wilkerson defines caste as "the granting or withholding of respect, status, honor, attention, privileges, resources, benefit of the doubt, and human kindness to someone on the basis of their perceived rank or standing in the hierarchy."[37] In short, discerning the grievable from the ungrievable.

Early in her work she explains how caste can help us understand how race is structured in my country, the United States. "Caste is the infrastructure of our divisions. It is the architecture of human hierarchy, the subconscious code of instructions for maintaining, in our case, a four-hundred-year-old social order. Looking at caste is like holding the country's X-ray up to the light."[38] Nicely, she sums up the way they correlate: "Race, in the United States, is the visible agent of the unseen force of caste. Caste is the bones, race the skin."[39]

Before highlighting the affinities with India's caste and Germany's Nazi history, she invites us to consider how early caste was formed. The arrival of the slave ships in 1619 helps us to see that "before there was a United States of America, there was a caste system, born in colonial Virginia."[40] Against the Blackness of the American slave, "the general white population ... was hardening into a single caste."[41] The impact of slavery was not simply "a dark chapter in the country's history."[42] Nor was it "merely an unfortunate thing that happened to black people."[43] Rather, slavery "was an American innovation, an American institution created by and for the elites of the dominant caste and enforced by poorer members of the dominant caste."[44] Its impact was ferocious: "The vast majority of African-Americans who lived in this land in the first 246 years of what is now the United States lived under the terror of people who had absolute power over their bodies and their very breath, subject to people who faced no sanction for any atrocity they could conjure."[45] She added, "Slavery so perverted the balance of power that it made the degradation of the subordinate caste seem normal and righteous."[46]

Whiteness developed for the sake of caste. Europeans, before coming to America, were Italian, German, French, English, Serbs, Swedes, and Russians. When they arrived in America, they became identified as white and "were fused together ... solely ... to strengthen the dominant caste in the hierarchy."[47] As white, they learned that "hostility toward the lowest caste became part of the initiation rite into citizenship."[48] Through caste, immigrants became white supremacists.[49]

Wilkerson notes that caste is, she writes, "not necessarily personal." Rather, caste is constituted by "patterns of a social order that have been in place for so long that it looks like the natural order of things."[50] In a word, in the United States, caste is familiar, "the investment in keeping the hierarchy as it is in order to maintain your own ranking, advantage, privilege, or to keep yourself above others or keep others beneath you."[51]

The power of these arguments by Niebuhr, Ward, and Wilkerson is that they remind us how prevalent the forces are that keep us from reverting our gaze and discovering a mutual recognition in the other, whose conditions we are socially trained to ignore. Recognition is therefore the act that liberates the vulnerability of both the agent and the other in the face of the distorting power of the castes or social systems that structure our lives.

But, recognition, then, is not simply a personal act. As Haker and Honneth noted, by misrecognition or disrespect, we see those who are not recognized, and generally they are not individuals but collectives, organized by race, tribe, ethnicity, class, caste, gender, sexual orientation, etc. Similarly for Butler, too, the ungrievable are not preeminently singular persons but collectives again. Social structures like those created by capitalism or by a slave market helped to manage us and in particular to distinguish those who count as recognizable or grievable and those who do not.

RECOGNITION AND SOCIAL IMPACT

For the most part, while I began the last lecture with very much the personal as vulnerable though leading us always to see the vulnerable as prior to personhood or social identity, now in concluding this lecture we see recognition as very much having social impact.

We must not think, however, that these structures have agency as critical realists remind us. These ethicists—like Daniel Finn, Daniel Daly, Conor Kelly, and others—help us to see that human persons are agents and their own collectives have agency, but social structures do not. Social structures influence us, tremendously, though we remain the moral agents. This governing insight of theirs rescues us from misplacing our moral freedom and responsibility. Critical realists want us to attend to these structures, to see that we can redirect them, correct them, dismantle them, and rebuild them. We need to see how very much they may, like the wordless usher, try to direct us, but whether we follow or not is for us to decide.

Critical realist social theory is a significant platform, then, that helps us today to better appreciate the influence of those forces. The finest explication of the theory is "The Critical Realist Solution to the Structure-Agency Problem," found as a chapter in Daniel J. Daly's *The Structures of Virtue and Vice*. There, Daly notes, "The critical realist approach presents an account of structures and agency that makes space for both realities." He adds:

> Structures enable persons to act in prescribed ways and constrain them from acting otherwise. In short the possibilities of human action occur within a social context. Critical realism maintains that though

agents are free, structures provide pathways to certain kinds of lives and actions. Structures do not determine actions; rather structures enable and constrain action. Because critical realist thought maintains that there is ontological distance between structures and persons, it preserves space for the person to conduct an internal conversation regarding what she should do given the circumstances.[52]

The key, here, undoubtedly is the importance of recognition, not only to acknowledge those who are not grieved or disrespected but to see the structures that persuade us to not think otherwise. When we recognize that George Floyd matters or that Black Lives Matter, we are not only according the due recognition to the too-long wrongly ungrievable; we also need to recognize the social forces that validated the previous stance. Recognition of the ungrievable can be or should be at the same time an awakening to the forces that lulled us into our original, diverted gaze.[53]

We need to cultivate the virtue of vigilance that prompts us to recognize more often, more clearly, and more universally.[54] With humility as the foundation for our vulnerability, we can cultivate the virtue of vigilance so as to generate a readiness to see the world as it actually is, a mindfulness that we not become as preoccupied as the priest and the Levite in the Good Samaritan parable but rather that we are prompt to recognize and respond to the neighbor in need. But first we need to recognize, as Niebuhr and Wilkerson argue, that our gaze is constantly diverted. Thus, this new vigilance invites us to investigate ourselves as to whether we see the world as it really is in the first place.

I suggest that we start by recognizing that we were once redeemed by the one who stopped along the way and recognized us as wounded, then maybe, by starting there, we too might begin to go and do likewise.[55]

Thank you.

NOTES

1. See, for instance, Augustine, *Quaestiones Evangeliorum*, 2.19; Bede, *Lucae Evangelium Expositio*, III, PL 92, 467–70. See also Clark, "Reversing the Ethical Perspective," 300–309; Stein, *An Introduction to the Parables of Jesus*, 42–52; Roukema, "The Good Samaritan in Ancient Christianity," 56–74; Sanchis, "Samaritanus ille. L'exegese augustinienne de la parabole du Bon Samaritain," 406–25; Lapide, "Who Is My Neighbor?," 256–62; David Gowler, "Venerable Bede and the Parables."
2. Regarding the history of interpretation of the parable, see Levine, *Short Stories by Jesus*, 77–115.

3. Benjamin, *The Bonds of Love*, 53.
4. Benjamin, *Beyond Doer and Done to: Recognition Theory, Intersubjectivity and the Third.*
5. Paddy McQueen, "Social and Political Recognition."
6. Charles Taylor, "The Politics of Recognition," 26. See also Pellauer and Ricœur, *The Course of Recognition.*
7. Haker, *Towards a Critical Political Ethics*, 143.
8. Haker, *Towards a Critical Political Ethics*, 143.
9. Haker, *Towards a Critical Political Ethics*, 144.
10. Haker, "Recognition and Responsibility," 467.
11. Writing on Cain and Abel, Haker refers to Levinas, *Difficult Freedom: Essays on Judaism*; LaCocque, *Onslaught against Innocence*; Vermeulen, "Mind the Gap," 29–42.
12. Haker, "Recognition and Responsibility," 467.
13. Haker, "Recognition and Responsibility," 467.
14. Honneth, *The Struggle for Recognition.* For a much more skeptical view of recognition, see Patchen Markell, *Bound by Recognition.*
15. Honneth, *The Struggle for Recognition*, 174.
16. Van Leeuwen, "A Formal Recognition of Social Attachments," 181.
17. Van Leeuwen, 182.
18. Honneth, *The Struggle for Recognition*, 92.
19. Riordan, "Common Good: Theological, Philosophical, Political Aspects." The lectures will be published by Georgetown University Press.
20. Honneth, *The Struggle for Recognition*, 90.
21. Fraser and Honneth, *Redistribution or Recognition?*
22. Butler, *Notes toward a Performative Theory of Assembly*, 196.
23. Jesuits, "The Ignatian Examen."
24. Butler, *Notes*, 196–97.
25. Butler, *Notes*, 197.
26. Butler, *Notes*, 197–98.
27. McLaughlin, "Three Videos Piece Together the Final Moments of George Floyd's Life."
28. Equal Justice Initiative, *Reconstruction in America: Racial Violence after the Civil War.*
29. Keenan, "The Color Line, Race and Caste," 69–94; On other needs for recognition, see Keenan, "The Community Colleges: Giving Them the Ethical Recognition They Deserve," 143–64; Keenan, "Vulnerability and Hierarchicalism"; McCosker, Gioia, and LaCouter, *Clericalism and Sexuality.*
30. Keenan, "Vulnerability and the Father of the Prodigal Son."
31. Forbes, "Repentance and Conflict in the Parable of the Lost Son (Luke 15:11–32)," 222, referring to Bailey, *Finding the Lost*, 172.
32. Niebuhr, *Moral Man and Immoral Society*, xxxiv.
33. Niebuhr, xxxiv.
34. Niebuhr, 117.
35. Ward, "'Mere Poverty Excites Little Compassion.'"
36. Wilkerson, *Caste: The Origins of Our Discontent*, 17–18.
37. Wilkerson, 70.
38. Wilkerson, 17.
39. Wilkerson, 19.
40. Wilkerson, 41.
41. Wilkerson, 42.

42. Wilkerson, 43.
43. Wilkerson, 44.
44. Wilkerson, 44.
45. Wilkerson, 47.
46. Wilkerson, 47.
47. Wilkerson, 49.
48. Wilkerson, 50.
49. Throughout her work, though there is no space here to engage it, Wilkerson discusses the middle caste, e.g., at 52, "slavery built the man-made chasm between blacks and whites that forces the middle castes... and new immigrants of African descent to navigate within what began as a bipolar hierarchy." Helpfully, see Ki Joo Choi, *Disciplined by Race*.
50. Wilkerson, *Caste*, 70.
51. Wilkerson, 70.
52. Daly, *The Structures of Virtue and Vice*, 63–97, 92–93. See also Cloutier, "Cavanaugh and Grimes on Structural Evils of Violence and Race," 59–78; Finn, *Moral Agency within Social Structures and Culture*; Finn, "What Is a Sinful Social Structure?," 136–64; Darr, "Social Sin and Social Wrongs," 21–37; Kelly, "Everyday Solidarity," 414–37.
53. See Esau McCaulley, "What Good Friday and Easter Mean for Black Americans Like Me," *New York Times*, April 15, 2022, https://www.nytimes.com/2022/04/15/opinion/easter-resurrection-good-friday.html.
54. Metz, *Mystik der offenen Augen*.
55. See the new work by Ryan, *Mutual Accompaniment as Faith-Filled Living*.

4

CONSCIENCE

In 2003, I founded Catholic Theological Ethics in the World Church (CTEWC), a network of roughly 1,500 Catholic theological ethicists around the world. In 2006, Linda Hogan of Trinity College Dublin and I, together with Renzo Pegoraro from Padua, co-chaired the first international conference of the network, where 400 ethicists from fifty-two countries gathered in Padua, Italy. In 2010, Hogan and I hosted with Antonio Autiero, from Trent, a conference of 600 ethicists from seventy-two countries in the beautiful city of Trent, Italy, where the council was held.

In 2014, the Planning Committee of Catholic Theological Ethics in the World Church (CTEWC) began thinking of hosting its third international conference in Sarajevo for those working in Catholic theological ethics. Eventually, 500 participants would gather there from eighty countries in July 2018.[1] In order to get us familiar with Sarajevo, two members of the faculty of the University of Sarajevo, Zorica Maros and Darko Tomašević, invited Antonio Autiero, Kristin Heyer, and me in the fall of 2015 and 2016 to conferences designed to respond to the struggles of the region of Bosnia and Herzegovina.[2] These lectures helped me to develop an understanding of the socially responsible conscience that I did by reflecting on the public remembrance of injustices as an ethical necessity.[3] These public remembrances of injustice are at the heart of this lecture on conscience.

THE MOVE TO A SOCIALLY RESPONSIBLE CONSCIENCE

The move to a socially responsible conscience is not an easy one.

The first difficulty is the enormous plethora of understandings that we have whenever we discuss conscience. Richard Gula has written, "Trying to explain conscience is like trying to nail Jello to a wall; just when you think you have it pinned down, part of it begins to slip away."[4]

Precisely because of the broad diversity of meanings, Alberto Giubilini, in the *Stanford Encyclopedia of Philosophy*, notes that there are "different philosophical, religious and common sense approaches to conscience." Though he develops his essay precisely to define these multitudinous and variegated differences, still he writes: "On any of these accounts, conscience is defined by its inward looking and subjective character."[5]

But here arises the second difficulty. The individual, introspective notion of the individual conscience, as Giubilini proposes, is still quite insufficient. Inasmuch as I have been trying to highlight the connectedness of humanity through the ontological givenness of our vulnerability as prior even to our moral selfhood, I want to resist conscience as singularly or preeminently personal or individual in its self-understanding. Also, by following Thomas in insisting that conscience is an act, and by developing the last lecture on recognition, I believe that conscience ought not to be reflecting on the self as much as on the other. Only by being other-directed will conscience ever be faithful to itself.

These insights align with three issues that I have been aiming at through these lectures: first, the underlying socially connected vulnerability that emphasizes a humble social self-understanding that complements a more individually oriented one; second, the summons to vigilant recognition in which the more privilege and power we have, the more summoned we are to see the structures of vice as needing to be converted into structures of virtues; and, third, the conscientious call to collective, constructive action. These three points highlight, I think, not only a robust socially responsive conscience but also one that needs to be more frequently imagined and developed. These are the goals of this lecture.

SEARCHING FOR A MEDITATION ON A COLLECTIVE GUILTY CONSCIENCE

As I was preparing for this, I very much wanted to offer an extended argument on the need to consider the guilty conscience. I still do. But I began searching for a prefatory mediation on a guilty conscience for you.

First, I wanted to share an experience that I have published elsewhere of my own visit to Dachau, where I experienced profound guilt over my own judgmentalism through a grace-filled illumination. In that narrative, I wanted to share the good of acknowledging one's guilt, but it was fairly private and mostly about myself as an individual.[6] But then, I thought, why not go to the great publicly known guilty conscience of King David. After all, it is hard to think of any earlier exposé on the guilty conscience than David's. In light of the prophet Nathan's accusation of David, "You are the man! . . . You struck down Uriah the Hittite with the sword and took his wife to be your own" (2 Sm 12:7, 9), David's own confession of guilt is displayed for all to see. Not only that; we engage his confession of guilt as a community of faith whenever we read and recite Psalm 51, which is David's confession of guilt.[7]

Yet, even in light of Psalm 51, we are still reflecting singularly on personal guilt, and because I have been insisting on the connectedness of humanity as prior to both the personal and the social, I want to propose something arising from that point of departure of connectedness.

Furthermore, in preparation for this lecture, I came upon two essays by relatively new, though recently tenured, scholars that help us to realize that we need to get to the guilty conscience that expresses its own social rebuke as a way to further the recognition of creating a much more equitable and responsible world order.

These two essays propose three steps not unlike the ones I have outlined: the call to act, to recognize the other, and to witness to the interior, shared social connectedness. Let me briefly turn to them before considering a worthy meditation.

RECENT CRITICAL WORKS ON CONSCIENCE

In a very prophetic essay, "A Call to Action: Global Moral Crises and the Inadequacy of Inherited Approaches to Conscience," Elizabeth Sweeny Block argues that the discourse on personal conscience is so focused on itself that its outward-bearing to act for others is often overlooked. As she writes: "It is precisely in twentieth-century scholars' focus on conscience as a medium between the person and the moral law or as the voice of God echoing in the depths of the person that acting with and for others is eclipsed."[8] Block reminds us: "Although it is deeply personal, conscience as action must draw us out of ourselves and away from our own concerns."[9]

She proposes "to reimagine or refocus conscience, emphasizing action and engagement with the other as equal in importance to the self-knowledge and self-reflection typically associated with conscience."[10] She seeks "to modify" "the reflexive conscience" with what she calls an "engaged conscience"—that is, "a conscience that prioritizes the other and action,"[11] and takes responsibility for "changing unjust structures and institutions."[12]

Block turns for assistance to Elisabeth Vasko's work *Beyond Apathy: A Theology for Bystanders*.[13] There, Vasko wants to expose "the social construction of reality and the silent complicity of the larger community."[14] She sees that our privileged status provides us ways that we can hide from social responsibility within social shelters that implicitly protect our own self-image, letting us acquit ourselves for not recognizing the social structures that oppress others and compromise their lives.

As we saw in the last lecture, both Reinhold Niebuhr and Isabel Wilkerson convey the ways that society soothes our troubled consciences, insisting that we are not responsible for the very inequities that privilege and protect us and compromise others. Mindful of them, we can all the more appreciate it when Vasko and Block indict "unethical passivity" and the "vested interests in not knowing."[15] All of these stances are of misrecognition. These authors look to interrupt our sleeping consciences that indulge themselves "to protect one's moral self-image while maintaining the benefits and privileges one accrues."[16] Block concludes: "If we are using conscience only to dissent, to separate, to protect ourselves, and if conscience is most centrally about identity and self-knowledge, then we are not fully engaged in the work of attending to the other. . . . Conscience can and ought to be that which pulls us out of self-concern and into the work of protecting the other. Conscience must call us into action and hold us responsible for the harms that threaten life."[17] I like Elisabeth Sweeny Block's essay very much, as well as her other investigations.[18]

The second contribution is Brian Hamilton's "It's in You: Structural Sin and Personal Responsibility Revisited."[19] Like Block and me, Hamilton exhorts ethicists to redirect present discourse on conscience. His admonition, as I see it, is to recognize that the social forces that inhibit our moral responsibility are not only externally influential in institutional structures, as critical realists assert, but they are internally engaged and constitutively present in the interiority of our connected, collective selves.

He begins his essay reminding us of another lecture.

> In 1983, the infamous feminist critic Andrea Dworkin gave a talk about rape to an auditorium full of self-declared feminist men. Characteristically, she refused to allow them any cover. She spoke first about the pervasiveness, the inescapability, of men's power over women. She reminded them that "the power exercised by men day to day in life is power that is institutionalized"—protected by law, by religion, by universities, by the police. But she refused to let them think that the real problem was confined to those institutions. "The problem is that you think it's out there: and it's not out there. It's in you."[20]

Hamilton argues that structural sin inheres "not just in policies or institutions or social roles but also in the embodied habits of knowing and willing the good that constitute human agency itself."[21] Hamilton is reacting against the critical realists, especially Daniel Finn, who, Hamilton argues, "does not provide language for talking about how structural sin shapes us from within. Structural sin remains 'out there.'"[22] He adds: "But by conceiving of structural sin entirely in these external ways, they never arrive at a rigorous accounting of its internal dimensions, the way the structures we inhabit reshape us from within."[23]

Hamilton contends that we are formed internally by habits that predispose us, as Aristotle would say, to see the world as we are. Seeing the internal side of social influences helps us to better recognize human moral experience and helps us better understand and act "for the shape of my own moral agency and the shape of the moral communities I am part of."[24]

Hamilton turns to Pierre Bourdieu's notion of "habitus" in his *Outline of a Theory of Practice* and argues, "It is wrong to treat the social world as something outside of and opposed to the individuals who constitute it by their action, and it is wrong to treat each individual action as . . . a *sui generis* confrontation with an alien social world. Instead, the inner life of agents is marked by a habitus: 'systems of durable, transposable dispositions, structured structures predisposed to function as structuring structures.'"[25]

Rather than go into Bourdieu's notion of structuring structures,[26] I would prefer to stay with Hamilton's overriding insight that "my habitus is a determinate way of being in the world, a tendency to think or act or position myself this way rather than that."[27]

Hamilton provides a summary of his argument:

> What Bourdieu's theory captures (and the critical realists, in my judgment, do not) is that part of what social structures structure is me, in all my interiority. My body, my perception, my understanding, my desires—my whole self is already structured. It is not nearly enough to say that social structures influence agents only by way of "constraints and enablements" on our action. Nor does it help to appeal to culture as a supplement to these external constraints, which would fail to make the intrinsic unity of these processes of social formation clear. It is not even enough to say that structures, though existing outside us, have a formative influence over us. "The problem is that you think it's out there: and it's not out there. It's in you." Our habitus is integral to the structure.[28]

We need to acknowledge, however, that these are not all-or-nothing claims. Like Finn and the other critical realists, Hamilton is not arguing that we are irrevocably determined by these habits, but he does want us to see that we are influenced from not only without but within. While not relinquishing human freedom or human responsibility, he still attends to the presence of formative influences that predictably prompt or inhibit us both within and without.

Here Kristin Heyer makes an important differentiation. In addition to recognizing the social structures that are non-agential but influential on human agency, she recognizes actual social agency in human collectives by talking about their social sinfulness. Here she emphasizes not nonpersonal institutional structures like education or the market but rather interpersonal, transpersonal, and socially connected groups of persons whose agency is not individual but plural, that is, any collective groupings like one's family, the Jesuits, or the members of Black Lives Matter.[29] I find this turn to social agency as a worthy place that answers Hamilton's issues about agency while still respecting the function of impersonal structures of virtue and vice. I will be incorporating this turn to social agency throughout; that is, while recognizing social structures, I am much more interested in agency, both personal and social, both the individual and the collective.

As we turn to the socially responsible conscience, then, these authors help us to see conscience formation as a connected enterprise that prompts us to undo the oppressive forces of vice both internal and external to us—collectively and personally and structurally—and to aim for the development of structures of virtue especially for those whom we have not yet recognized as anything but expendable or ungrievable for our own sense of welfare. In other words, we need to think of conscience formation as an interconnective activity that examines our agency, collectively and individually, in the light of our social structures.

It is for this reason that I wish now to turn to the beginning of conscience awakening that I contend arises from the acknowledgment of guilt. I will first give biblical accounts of how acknowledgment of guilt gives birth to conscience and then will consider philosophically the matters of guilt and conscience.

THE COLLECTIVE GUILTY CONSCIENCES OF NINEVEH AND THE ROTHERS OF JOSEPH

In light of my quest for the expression of guilt through the lens of human connectedness and the recognition of the harm to others, I find two biblical narratives that guide us toward a socially responsible form of conscience accountability: the guilt of Nineveh and of Joseph's eleven brothers.

I find the acknowledged guilt of Nineveh in Jonah 3 very helpful. The Book of Jonah begins literally with Yahweh's wanting Jonah to preach against Nineveh because of its wickedness (Jon 1:1). That wickedness is named in chapter three as "violence" (Jon 3:8). Notably there is no mention about false Gods; rather, Yahweh's concern is exclusively about how the Ninevites are treating others and one another. Yahweh's concern is about them simply as a people; after all, they are as Yahweh identifies them a "hundred and twenty thousand people who cannot tell their right hand from their left" (Jon 4:11).

As backward and violent as they are, the guilt of Nineveh is acknowledged notably first by the people and then the king; in both moments the guilt is quickly and completely acknowledged. Here both the individual and social accountability for harming others is publicly summoned and publicly expressed. It serves, as I hope to argue later, as a helpful reason for why the public ritual of repentance is so morally relevant.[30] That an entire city, each and every one of its people, and the king himself become repentant actually is unthinkable for modern times. Still, it should be thinkable, even exemplary. In fact, I think this absence of exemplars in part explains why individuals are so reluctant to acknowledge their own guilt as well.

The second case is not a people but a family. I love the "consciences" of the brothers of Joseph, who first want to kill him, then decide to toss him into a well, and after that retrieve him and sell him into slavery. At the outset, we see their self-interested consciences working. While plotting to kill their brother they are convinced by Reuben to "not draw any blood" (Gen 37:22) and so toss him in the cistern. Reuben uses the ploy so as to later hopefully rescue Joseph. All that the others want is to get rid of their brother with a guiltless conscience, that is, with "no blood on their hands."

The text conveys again the self-regarding consciences of the brothers, as Judah suggests in chapter 37 of Genesis: "What will we gain if we kill our brother and cover up his blood? Come, let's sell him to the Ishmaelites and not lay our hands on him; after all, he is our brother, our own flesh and blood" (Gen 37:26–27).

The story is too long to recount here, but it is worth remembering that after Joseph is sold into Egypt, he becomes in time a trusted executive of Pharaoh, overseeing food supplies in times of plenty and not, times that he foresaw in his dreams. When Joseph's brothers later come to Egypt for grain, Joseph recognizes them, but they do not recognize him. Joseph seeks to undo them by accusing them of being thieves. Afraid of how compromised they seem to be, they immediately believe that their precarity is due to God punishing them for what they did, years ago, to their brother. They talk in Hebrew, thinking that the overseer Joseph does not understand the language.

> They said to one another, "Surely we are being punished because of our brother. We saw how distressed he was when he pleaded with us for his life, but we would not listen; that's why this distress has come on us." Reuben replied, "Didn't I tell you not to sin against the boy? But you wouldn't listen! Now we must give an accounting for his blood." They did not realize that Joseph could understand them, since he was using an interpreter. Joseph turned away from them and began to weep, but then came back and spoke to them again. (Gen 42:21–24)

Joseph releases them but holds one brother as ransom as he gets from them a pledge that when they return they will bring with them the youngest brother, Benjamin. Along the way, Joseph makes them even more anxious by having planted his own silver in their sacks. We are told: "As they were emptying their sacks, there in each man's sack was his pouch of silver! When they and their father saw the money pouches, they were frightened" (Gen 42:35).

As their guilt arises, they are convinced again that their perilous relation with the overseer is wrought with trickery and accusation that they can only believe that God is causing. Still, when the impact of the famine strikes them again, they decide to return to Egypt with Benjamin. The visit goes well. All seems resolved and they seem relieved until, while enroute to the homeland, they are stopped by Joseph's servant, who is looking for Joseph's own silver cup that Joseph made sure to place into the sack of Benjamin. Again, the text highlights their terror of God. "And the cup is found in Benjamin's sack. At this, they tore their clothes. Then they all loaded their donkeys and returned to the city" (Gen 44:12–13).

Judah is beside himself. Now Benjamin is at risk, the youngest son of Jacob, is at risk. Here Judah's sense of responsibility for Benjamin and his father emerges as his guilt keeps surfacing and his conscience is trying to emerge. He begs clemency from Joseph. Joseph can no longer bear the alienation from his brothers and reveals himself to his brothers.

> And he wept so loudly that the Egyptians heard him, and Pharaoh's household heard about it. Joseph said to his brothers, "I am Joseph! Is my father still living?" But his brothers were not able to answer him, because they were terrified at his presence. Then Joseph said to his brothers, "Come close to me." When they had done so, he said, "I am your brother Joseph, the one you sold into Egypt! And now, do not be distressed and do not be angry with yourselves for selling me here, because it was to save lives that God sent me ahead of you." (Gen 45:2–5)

Note that at this point, the brothers have still not yet acknowledged their guilt to Joseph, nor apologized. It will not be until years later that this happens. Indeed, the time from the act of the brothers' sale of Joseph to the actual acknowledgment of their guilt is literally decades.

Chapter 50 records the death of Jacob. But with that, a new fear arises among the brothers:

> When Joseph's brothers saw that their father was dead, they said, "What if Joseph holds a grudge against us and pays us back for all the wrongs we did to him?" So they sent word to Joseph, saying, "Your father left these instructions before he died: 'This is what you are to say to Joseph: I ask you to forgive your brothers the sins and the wrongs they committed in treating you so badly.' Now please forgive the sins of the servants of the God of your father." When their message came to him, Joseph wept.

It is here that the brothers finally acknowledge their guilt.

> His brothers then came and threw themselves down before him. "We are your slaves," they said. But Joseph said to them, "Don't be afraid. Am I in the place of God? You intended to harm me, but God intended it for good to accomplish what is now being done, the saving of many lives. So then, don't be afraid. I will provide for you and your children." And he reassured them and spoke kindly to them." (Gen 50:18–21)

THE CONTEMPORARY RELEVANCE OF THE JOSEPH STORY

Solomon Schimmel calls this account of the Joseph story "A Paradigm for Repentance,"[31] noting that the various manipulations by Joseph are there "to subject his brothers to the experiential situation similar to the one they faced when they committed their crime against him." Joseph wants his brothers to experience anew what they did in selling him into slavery, by making Benjamin a precarious part of the negotiations. Joseph provokes them so that their consciences are awakened by their guilt so that in confessing it they will be liberated.

In another essay, entitled "Joseph and the Politics of Memory," Clarke Cochran suggests that though "their reconciliation is fragile and mixed with other motives, it is real nonetheless and all the more realistic for its fragility. This is not a tidy familial (or political) story of reunion in which all live happily ever after; nor are our own political stories." Remarkably, he notes, "recent students of reconciliation on efforts in the Balkans, Africa, and other conflict situations suggest a dynamic similar to Joseph's."[32]

The story of Joseph's brothers captures then the reality of how a collective sense of guilt emerges clumsily until finally it is collectively expressed with an apology. But it also reveals the difficulty we human beings have in recognizing our guilt, in acknowledging the harm we caused, in apologizing, and, finally, in making restitution to the other. It also highlights how much, because we do not want our consciences disturbed, we try to avoid blame for doing harm. Still, what I most love about the wonderfully complex Joseph story is how long it took for the brothers to actually acknowledge their guilt. Indeed, as I shall now argue, the conscience, personally and socially, is not born, until guilt is confessed. The agency of conscience is born, in fact, only when guilt is acknowledged and confessed, whether individually or collectively.

THE GUILTY CONSCIENCE AND THE BIRTH OF CONSCIENCE

In the Hebrew Bible, the term most analogous to conscience is "heart"—*lebab* in Hebrew, *kardia* in Greek. There are literally hundreds of references to heart in the Bible. Often enough, heart is that which God judges. In Sirach 42:18, God "searches out the abyss and the human heart; God understands their innermost secrets." Sometimes God's examination of the heart empowers it to proceed rightly, as in Jeremiah 17:10: "I the LORD search the mind and try the heart, to give to every man according to his ways, according to the fruit of his doings."

Occasionally, through the heart one recognizes one's guilt. We call this a judicial conscience because it judges our past actions. In 1 Samuel 24:5, for instance, we read that "afterward David was stricken to the heart because he had cut off a corner of Saul's cloak." Here the heart is a conscience convicting the self as guilty.

In theological ethics, we distinguish between a judicial conscience that looks back and a legislative conscience that guides future courses of action; there are a few instances of the latter in the Hebrew Bible. There the word is rarely "heart" but rather akin to a "voice." In Isaiah 30:21, we read: "And your ears shall hear a word behind you: 'This is the way; walk in it,' when you would turn to the right or the left."

When we turn to the history of conscience in western thought,[33] we discover that from Democritus on, conscience is there also primarily judicially. Moreover, while most often God judges the heart in the Hebrew Bible, Greek and Roman notions of conscience highlight the agent's conscience as doing the judging. In fact, most often conscience disturbs as it judges; in most of ancient philosophy the function of conscience is to distress us over our wrongdoing.

The ancient notion of conscience awakens the wrongdoer with its guilt because conscience forces us to recognize our own misdeeds. In that rude awakening, many encounter conscience for the first time. To have a conscience is to recognize one's own guilt. The birth of conscience through remorse is a common theme; Cicero, Julius Caesar, and Quintilian, for instance, refer us to the ways conscience prompts us to recognize these misdeeds. In his *Conscience: A Very Short Introduction*, Paul Strom remarks that this idea of conscience was so evident that in the very popular rhetorical work from the first century, *Rhetorica ad Herennium*, prosecutors were advised to look and see whether their adversary's client shows "signs of conscience." If they did, they knew their adversary was guilty. Thus, they were instructed to look for the face of a person of conscience: "blushed, grown pale, stammered, spoken inconsistently, displayed uncertainty, compromised himself."[34] If you looked guilty, you had a conscience.

It is here that the word "remorse" develops. Richard Sorabji notes in his *Moral Conscience through the Ages*, the Romans referred to this experience as the "bites" of conscience, coming from the word *morsus*, the root for remorse.[35]

Just as conscience makes its appearance in history by first being recognized for the way it disturbed the ancients, so too does it first appear that way in the individual lives of most people. Its pangs not only awaken us to our misdeeds; they awaken us to conscience itself. As we enter adult life, through these pangs we begin to realize that we carry within ourselves a moral beacon that troubles us when we are wrong, and, with time, we also learn that it can validate us when we are right. A guilty conscience is precisely one that recognizes a disconnect between what we thought was acceptable or wanted to be acceptable and the guilt we feel afterward.

I invite you here to think of the disquieting introduction to your own conscience, when as a young person you found yourself very uneasy about something you did and no one was there accusing you but you! Most often our first introduction to conscience is when its remorse tries to emerge.

Yet, by recognizing our guilt, we recognize conscience. The reason why we acknowledge that conscience is born through the awareness of guilt is because only if it has the freedom to indict the agent can it have the power to guide the agent. If it is allowed to disturb the agent, and if the agent recognizes that authority, then it has the freedom it needs to discern the truth.[36] Indeed, conscience is that which does not let us try to operate without surrendering to the truth. In our adolescence, we think we can escape the oversight of others and we can get away with mischief, but we have within us another guardian, one that wants us to be accountable to the truth. It appears within us as a disturbing act, reminding us even when no one else is there, to be accountable to the truth.

Significantly, I think that in the Global north, discussions about socially, collective conscience rose first among continental Europeans anxious about the obediential masses of Catholics following and advancing the cause of Fascism and Nazism. Only later did discussions on conscience emerge in the United States, but here, in a way, I call that development an arrested development.[37]

DIFFERENCES BETWEEN CONTINENTAL EUROPE AND THE UNITED STATES ON THE PHENOMENOLOGY OF CONSCIENCE

My interests are not primarily with the personal conscience, nor only with the social conscience. I am interested in both. I believe that through vulnerability and recognition we see how connected the human is. We are, then, not looking for a personal notion of conscience and then a social; rather we need to acknowledge that we are affected personally and socially by the way conscience acts. It is for that reason of collectivity that we examined the conscience of the brothers of Joseph and not solely King David's. Turning to the collective, we better understand the way conscience functions, both individually and socially.

Years ago, I discovered that before, during, and after World War II, continental European theologians, appalled by the widespread participation of Catholics in the works of the Nazis and the Fascists, developed a robust promotion of the call of conscience for all Catholics, a summons that theologians like Dom Odon Lottin and Bernhard Häring sent in the 1950s to all the seminaries and churches of Europe and that would later bear fruit in the celebrated paragraph 16 of *Gaudium et spes*.

> In the depths of his conscience, man detects a law which he does not impose upon himself, but which holds him to obedience. Always summoning him to love good and avoid evil, the voice of conscience when necessary speaks to his heart: do this, shun that. For man has in his heart a law written by God; to obey it is the very dignity of man;

according to it he will be judged. Conscience is the most secret core and sanctuary of a man. There he is alone with God, Whose voice echoes in his depths. In a wonderful manner conscience reveals that law which is fulfilled by love of God and neighbor. In fidelity to conscience, Christians are joined with the rest of men in the search for truth, and for the genuine solution to the numerous problems which arise in the life of individuals from social relationships. Hence the more right conscience holds sway, the more persons and groups turn aside from blind choice and strive to be guided by the objective norms of morality. Conscience frequently errs from invincible ignorance without losing its dignity. The same cannot be said for a man who cares but little for truth and goodness, or for a conscience which by degrees grows practically sightless as a result of habitual sin.[38]

Before that teaching was promulgated in 1965, these theologians and others developed a theology of conscience because they believed that Catholicism had created a collective, obediential, minimalist passivity in the laity that left them unprepared for participating in the atrocious activities of the Nazis and the Fascists.[39] Too many Catholics, instead of challenging these works, participated in and promoted them.

The rebirth of conscience in continental Europe began in part with collectively acknowledging the profound human wretchedness of their recent history. These moralists invoked conscience to judge, not others, but themselves. The moralists' turn to conscience was precisely the urge to awaken in Catholics emerging from the war's rubble a sense that moral agency needed to be collectively accountable. The locus of that competency was the Christian conscience. Turning to conscience in Europe was not, then, a matter of giving individual Christians the freedom to exercise prerogatives, pursue autonomy, or even to dissent against law; rather, the turn was to place before each and all Christians that they were, in varying ways, both personally and socially responsible for what happened in the war. With this new mindfulness, they would ultimately be a people humbly judged and hopefully redeemed by Christ.

After World War II, Europeans began a process of understanding their capacity for evil by examining the history of their own actions. That understanding continues to be visible today when one visits Germany, for instance, and sees public, social reminders of the nation's own atrocities. From the Concentration Camp Memorial in Dachau to the Berlin Memorial for the Murdered Jews of Europe, we can literally see not only the horrendous treatment of human beings but also the pangs of the European conscience evident in its enduring testimonials. Throughout Europe one finds in these memorials a way of awakening personally and collectively Catholics and other Christians to the monstrosity of their actions.

When appeals to conscience appeared much later in the United States, in fact, during the Vietnam War and in response to *Humanae vitae*, they were, indeed, very different. Rather than a social recognition of guilt, they were individual protests by young men drafted into the undeclared war in Vietnam or by married couples not convinced by the claims of the birth control encyclical. In both instances, the appeals to conscience supported individuals opting out of a claim by a civil or ecclesial law. While the European familiarity with the postwar conscience was begun with the collective social acknowledgment of their guilt for profound human violations of the moral law, the American practice was about personal opting out of social claims.[40] In fact, even more recently, when the US bishops protested against the Affordable Care Act ("Obamacare"), they appeared to be doing what Americans normally do when they turn to conscience: they say, "I am sorry but I have to follow my conscience." Their consciences are invoked momentarily to opt out of an existing law, the draft, *Humanae vitae*, or the Affordable Care Act.[41] These singular exercises of opting out suggest that in fact rarely do the agents otherwise consult their consciences.

Unfortunately, the American use of conscience never really settled into, nor emerged from, the place it did in Europe, that is, as the source of responsible personal and social moral agency that could recognize their own capacity for evil.

The American resistance to recognize its own wrongdoing is long-standing and well rooted in the long legacy of American exceptionalism, in which we excuse many of our actions by presuming that our nation's greatness has a manifest destiny that exempts us from the standards that others must follow.[42]

That exceptionalism allows us the opportunity to avoid any social, public expression of guilt. For instance, despite the nation's own history of enslaving millions of people and the benefits it developed and enjoyed from the enslaved lives of these human beings, Americans have never collectively acknowledged the wrongfulness of slavery.[43] As M. Shawn Copeland reminds us, the American conscience does not realize that it is haunted, profoundly damaged by the complex history of slavery in the United States and by its national willfulness to accommodate and profit from racism.[44] Think here of how the brothers of Joseph were haunted by what they did and continued to be haunted until they threw themselves down before Joseph.

The failure to recognize *morally* the history of slavery in the United States from the first slave ship arrival in 1619 to the Emancipation Proclamation in

1865 led similarly to the failure to recognize the long history of the Jim Crow laws and, with it, its own history of lynching so noted by James Cone's (1938–2018) *The Cross and the Lynching Tree*.[45] As I remarked in the last lecture, The National Memorial for Peace and Justice was established by the Equal Justice Initiative (EJI) led by Bryan Stevenson,[46] and opened in 2018 as "the nation's first memorial dedicated to the legacy of enslaved Black people, people terrorized by lynching, African Americans humiliated by racial segregation and Jim Crow, and people of color burdened with contemporary presumptions of guilt and police violence."[47] It was not founded by the guilt-ridden white supremacists but rather by African Americans who, like Joseph, are prompting the act of conscience to awaken and acknowledge the guilt.

The lynching museum is then a recognition both by and to the victims; it is not an acknowledgment of the guilt of the white oppressors. That has not yet happened. Still, more and more we recognize that racism is, as Barack Obama and others have named it, "our nation's original sin."[48] But because we have not confessed it, we, like the brothers of Joseph, do not recognize how significantly it toxifies our culture.

American exceptionalism also led to the attempted extinction of Native American populations throughout the country. The legendary Trail of Tears is but one of the strategies that the United States took to wipe out the native people of our country.[49] Other instances of American "exceptionalism" include the bombings of Dresden, Hiroshima, and Nagasaki. All of these violent and vicious policies, the so-called American conscience has never publicly acknowledged.

The failure to acknowledge our guilt collectively personally affects the lives of American citizens and permits the myth of innocence to continue.[50] Moreover, without any public, collective apologies, American individuals do not have any exemplars of the apology. Until we can recognize the evidence of our own capacity and realization of evil in the personal and national history of our own actions, we cannot claim to have a conscience, let alone to be exercising one. Indeed, in the United States, the so-called conscience remains self-centered, exempting itself from institutional rules.

A FEW LESSONS TO BE LEARNED

The German memorials that we have seen are reminders of guilt and sin. They are reminders too that people could have acted otherwise. They are not memorials to human weakness but to human power. This is worth noting because until we confess sin, we often think we are less powerful than we were. And here is the first lesson for us to appreciate: we think we sin out of weakness, until we confess and then realize we had the capacity to act otherwise.

The German moral theologian Franz Böckle discussed in *Fundamental Moral Theology* the significance of admitting guilt; for him the confession of sin is itself "effective" and illuminative. It is effective inasmuch as we do not know the scope of our sinfulness *until* we actually acknowledge it. When we do, we can see the history of sinful harm. Until we do, we remain behind artificial blinders (like Joseph's brothers) that keep us from recognizing the trajectory of effects from our sinfulness.[51] Böckle reminds us that "sin is not simply a question of human guilt—it is also guilt in the presence of God."[52] In that effective acknowledgment of our culpability, we are gifted with an illumination by which we understand first, what we did, but second, what we could have done: the confession of our sinfulness lets us recognize that we could have acted otherwise. Until we have that insight and publicly acknowledge it, we are trapped by an understanding of ourselves as weak and constrained, a convenient stance that literally keeps us from believing that we need to confess. When we confess, however, we realize not that we sinned out of weakness but out of strength. We had other options.[53] The myth of our weak capabilities deceives us from acknowledging our guilt.

Second, as we saw in the brothers of Joseph, human beings take an enormous amount of time to acknowledge fault and guilt, let alone memorialize them. For instance, in 2016, in the first visit by a sitting American president to Hiroshima, President Obama, sixty-one years after the bombing of Hiroshima, assiduously avoided any apology for the atomic attack, though clearly his visit was an act of solidarity with the suffering that occurred there.[54] This could be, then, one laborious step on the way to finally acknowledging our culpability and responsibility.

Third, without such admissions, the moral complexity of history remains hidden, and the ruse of purported innocence remains; the "others'" experiences are left out so as to not compromise the myth. For instance, the Vietnam Veterans Memorial on the National Mall honors and grieves the 58,000 American servicemen and -women who died there. There is no mention of "the approximately one million (plus or minus 175,000) Vietnamese who died either as military or civilian casualties, on both sides, from 1965 to 1975."[55] None of their grief enters into ours, nor any of our guilt or possible apologies. They remain ungrievable. Yet, our grief as a nation remains incapable of collective, responsible remorse.

Fourth, still most memorials are not erected by the guilty conscience of the former oppressors but by the insistent memory of the victims who appeal to the consciences of the oppressors, often enough in a global context where power "persuades" others to acknowledge their guilt. Absent the strength of the victim, however, often it is difficult to find the acknowledgment of guilt by the oppressor. Indeed, it was, after all, Joseph who perpetually instigated his brothers' confession. Yet they only confessed when they were desperate. As Jürgen Moltmann reminds us, the real revelation of the confession of guilt occurs when the oppressor understands that one's redemption is found by remembering the victim.[56] But that is usually, again, prompted by the victims' agency.

Fifth, the public lack of remembrance and apology is not singularly an American phenomenon. While I think the United States is an easy example of this exceptional lack of recognition of guilt, the public resistance to acknowledging horrendous complicity in oppressing others is worldwide and is far greater than the urge to publicly acknowledge and remember wrongdoing.[57] Hopefully, though, wherever we are citizens, we might begin to realize if our discourse is so ripe with privilege and yet so terrified of blame; we might begin to interrogate whether our national historical atrocities were ever acknowledged as such. I believe that until we confess our original sin, it continues to infect unabated.[58]

Sixth, by the confession of our guilt, we recognize not primarily our failings, but the victims we harmed, the need for restitution and their pardon, and the vulnerable recognition of their dignity that we once so viciously compromised. The pangs of conscience awaken us to be converted toward a more vulnerable and mutual recognition.

Though deeply interior, the conscience is, then, as the culmination of the movements of vulnerability, recognition, and guilt, the key to our relationships with others, our world, ourselves, and our God. With conscience we continue then to begin the process of response, as we saw in the second lecture where we saw that after the Good Samaritan's vulnerable recognition of the wounded man, he now in conscience determines what he should do so as to bring the man back to good health.

Seventh, it is worth noting in conclusion, that conscience, *suneidēsis*, appears in the New Testament thirty-one times, mostly in Paul, and almost always in terms of our relationships with others, for it is about our recognition of them. A key example of this is the question on idol meat (1 Cor 8:1–13; Rom 14), where Paul asks us whether our conscientious decisions in freedom are mindful of the needs of others growing in faith (see also 2 Cor 1:12, 5.11). Paul is training us there to recognize how exemplary our collective actions are. We are called, he suggests, to a humility to recognize our place in God's world.

Eighth, make no mistake about it; conscience is not infallible—quite the contrary, as *Gaudium et spes* reminds us.[59] But there in conscience we understand that we are bound by the truth as it really is: truth stands in judgment of our own misdeeds, a judgment that we recognize in the pangs of conscience. In that confession, we recognize truth not as something that we made up but rather something that compels us. This phenomenon of "obeying our consciences," "heeding the dictates of conscience," and "recognizing the demands of our conscience" captures the sense that conscience allows us to hear the truth as it is.[60] A well-formed conscience teaches us in humility to allow truth to have its say and does it when we vulnerably recognize the other.

Thank you.

NOTES

1. Heyer, Vicini, and Keenan, "Building Bridges in Sarajevo." For other reports on the conference, see Keenan, "Costruire Ponti a Sarajevo," 513–20. On Catholic Theological Ethics in the World Church (CTEWC), see their website: www.catholicethics.com. See also Heyer and Hogan, "Beyond the Northern Paradigm," 21–38; Keenan, "Pursing Ethics by Building Bridges beyond the Northern Paradigm," 490.
2. Keenan, "Vicious Structures of Social Formation: Acquired Vices, Embodied Anthropology, Social Practices, and Human Freedom," 17–28; Keenan and Murphy, "When the Public Remembrance of an Injustice is an Ethical Necessity," 41–54.
3. I was subsequently invited into other projects on conscience like these in Sarajevo: Keenan, "Collective Conscience and Collective Guilt," 78–86.
4. Gula, *Reason Informed by Faith: Foundations of Catholic Moral Theology*, 123.
5. Giubilini, "Conscience."
6. Keenan, "Faith, A Journey to Dachau," 37–41.
7. DiFransico, "Distinguishing Emotions of Guilt and Shame in Psalm 51," 180–87; Human, "God Accepts a Broken Spirit and a Contrite Heart," 114–32; Brooks, "Psalm 51," 62–66.
8. Block, "A Call to Action," 89.
9. Block, "A Call to Action," 89.
10. Block, "A Call to Action," 89.
11. Block, "A Call to Action," 89.
12. Block, "A Call to Action," 91.
13. Vasko, *Beyond Apathy*. She also notes Cox, *Water Shaping Stone*; Patrick, *Conscience and Calling*.
14. Vasko, *Beyond Apathy*, 54.
15. Block, "A Call to Action," 92.
16. Vasko, *Beyond Apathy*, 80.
17. Block, "A Call to Action," 93.
18. Block's work on conscience is salutary: "White Privilege and the Erroneous Conscience," 357–74; "Moral Intuition, Social Sin, and Moral Vision," 292; "Conscience," 71–82; "Embodied Formation, Embodied Cognition: Incorporating Neuroscientific Findings into Conscience Formation," 45–60.

19. Hamilton, "It's in You," 360–80.
20. Hamilton, 360, qtd. in Dworkin, "I Want a Twenty-Four-Hour Truce during Which There Is No Rape," 164–65.
21. Hamilton, "It's in You," 361.
22. Hamilton, 367.
23. Hamilton, 367.
24. Hamilton, 370.
25. Hamilton, 371, quoting Bourdieu, *Outline of a Theory of Practice*, 72.
26. Hamilton comments in "It's in You," 371–72: "My way of being is a 'structured structure', determinate because it has been determined by the social structures I inhabit. My way of being is at the same time, however, a 'structuring structure', the power that determines the structures that encompass all of us. For Bourdieu, the language of social structure thus encompasses both self and society, dialectically related to one another. The medium of exchange is practice, which is simultaneously constitutive of both."
27. Hamilton, 371.
28. Hamilton, 372–73.
29. Heyer, "Walls in the Heart: Social Sin in Fratelli Tutti," *JCST* forthcoming; "Social Sin and Immigration," 410–36.
30. About the violence and the responsibility, see Timmer, "Jonah's Theology of the Nations," 13–23; Lindsay, "Overthrowing Nineveh," 49–61.
31. Schimmel, "Joseph and His Brothers," 62.
32. C. Cochran, "Joseph and the Politics of Memory," 443. To substantiate his claims, he offers: Volf, *Exclusion and Embrace*; Shriver, *An Ethic for Enemies*; Wink, *When the Powers Fall*; Johnston and Sampson, *The Missing Dimension of Statecraft*.
33. Keenan, "Examining Conscience," 15–17.
34. Strom, *Conscience*, 6.
35. Sorabji, *Moral Conscience through the Ages*, 37–46.
36. Cochran too, on page 212 in "Faith, Love, and Stoic Assent," notes the fundamental significance of finding oneself as profoundly limited as the beginning of a conscience infused by faith. "Luther emphasizes the conscience's recognition of our failure to do good apart from Christ as crucial to the exercise of faith. . . . In order to achieve a true recognition of our moral limitations, the conscience must receive from God a proper understanding of humanity's moral limitations and of the grace and forgiveness God offers in Jesus Christ."
37. James Keenan, "The Arrested Development of the American Conscience in Moral Decision Making," *America*, January 2, 2017, https://www.americamagazine.org/arts-culture/2016/12/22/arrested-development-american-conscience.
38. Paul VI, *Gaudium et spes*.
39. Keenan, "Vatican II and Theological Ethics," 162–90. On Lottin and the other reformers, see my *A History of Catholic Moral Theology in the Twentieth Century*.
40. Keenan, "Catholic Conscience Awakening"; Goertz, Hein, and Klöcker, *Fluchtpunkt Fundamentalismus?: Gegenwartsdiagnosen katholischer Moral*, 305–25; Keenan, "To Follow and to Form over Time: A Phenomenology of Conscience"; DeCosse and Heyer, *Conscience and Catholicism*, 1–15. Additionally, see notes 2 and 3 above.
41. Ad Hoc Committee for Religious Liberty, "Our First, Most Treasured Freedom." For an excellent read on this and other "engagements," see Kaveny, *A Culture of Engagement*.
42. See the foundational essay, Eric Foner, "What Is American Exceptionalism?"

43. Aaron Lazare makes the interesting case that Lincoln's *Second Inaugural* was "an apology for slavery," *On Apology*, 78. While it was perhaps Lincoln's apology, I do not think it has been received in fact as memorial to the atrocious history of slavery in the United States.
44. Copeland, *Enfleshing Freedom*, 2–4; see Lazare, *On Apology*, 78; Townes, "'Wading through Many Sorrows,'" 109–29; Copeland, "Revisiting Racism," 21–24.
45. Cone, *The Cross and the Lynching Tree*.
46. Campbell Robertson, "A Lynching Memorial Is Opening: The Country Has Never Seen Anything Like It," *New York Times*, April 25, 2018, https://www.nytimes.com/2018/04/25/us/lynching-memorial-alabama.html.
47. Equal Justice Initiative, "The National Memorial for Peace and Justice."
48. Obama, "Barack Obama's Speech on Race." See also Alexander, *The New Jim Crow*; Mikulich, Cassidy, and Pfeil, *The Scandal of White Complicity in U.S. Hyper-incarceration*.
49. Ehle, *Trail of Tears*; Brown, *Bury My Heart at Wounded Knee*; Jackson, *A Century of Dishonor*.
50. See Keenan, "Collective Conscience and Collective Guilt," 78–86; "When the Public Remembrance of an Injustice is an Ethical Necessity," 41–54; "On Public Expressions of Guilt, of Conscience, and of Confession," 165–77.
51. Böckle, "Theological Reflection about Guilt and Sin," 88.
52. Böckle, 91.
53. Keenan, "Sin," 45–67.
54. Obama, "Remarks by President Obama and Prime Minister Abe." Still, many news outlets tried to claim that this was part of the president's apology tour! See Evon, "Did Obama Apologize for Dropping the Atomic Bomb on Japan?" For more rigorous consideration of the issue, see Himes, "Hiroshima and Nagasaki," 507–24.
55. Hirschman, Preston, and Loi, "Vietnamese Casualties During the American War," 783–812.
56. Moltmann, "The Justification of Life," 123–43.
57. Haruko Okano from Japan raises a problem, similar to that of the United States, about the inability to apologize, where a people insist on letting bygones be bygones without any acknowledgement of guilt. "Theological Ethics in Relation to Japanese Religions Regarding Moral Responsibility," 194–204.
58. Maria Cramer, "Scotland Apologizes for History of Witchcraft Persecution," *New York Times*, March 9, 2022, https://www.nytimes.com/2022/03/09/world/europe/scotland-nicola-sturgeon-apologizes-witches.html.
59. Paul VI, *Gaudium et spes*, sec. 16.
60. As *Veritatis Splendor* section 64 reminds us, "Freedom of conscience is never freedom 'from' the truth but always and only freedom 'in' the truth." Pope John Paul II, *Veritatis Splendor*.

5

DISCIPLESHIP

While the first four lectures were designed to prepare us for the moral life by developing a theological anthropology that is deeply connected and that regards simultaneously both the personal and the social in talking about moral self-understanding and moral agency in light of vulnerability, recognition, and conscience, the remaining four lectures are now pathways for realizing the personal and social Catholic approach to life.

I begin with discipleship and subsequently build on that with grace and sin in the next lecture, virtues in the seventh, and the Communion of Saints, the Works of Mercy, and the Beatitudes in the eighth.

This lecture claims that a discipleship ethics best names the type of vulnerable ethics a Christian should appropriate today. Inasmuch as disciples are always understood as a collective identity with very different personal expressions, it seems a near perfect point of departure for constructing a Christian virtue ethics out of a theological anthropology based on the connectedness of vulnerability and mutual recognition.

This lecture proceeds in three parts. The first is the remarkable work of Fritz Tillmann, a biblical theologian, silenced by Rome in 1912 for editing a volume of essays in which one of his contributors acknowledged the thesis of the then emerging Q source, that is, a second source for the Synoptic Gospels. Tillmann ended up becoming a moral theologian, developing a biblically based moral theology in which discipleship was central to his work. What you might find surprising is that Tillmann's promotion of the idea of discipleship in the beginning of the last century was innovative and successful.

Second, I then turn to Gerhard Lohfink's *Jesus of Nazareth: What He Wanted, Who He Was* to investigate his understanding of discipleship that gives, I think, greater depth to the meaning of the term "discipleship."[1] Along with Lohfink, I investigate two other works: Richard A. Burridge's *Imitating*

Jesus: An Inclusive Approach to New Testament Ethics,[2] and Howard Thurman's *Jesus and the Disinherited*.[3]

Finally, I conclude with a reflection on discipleship by looking at the sixth sign in John's Gospel, the healing of the man born blind.

Throughout, I hope my earlier claims on the significance of vulnerability and recognition as the conditions for moral agency in conscience emerge.

FRITZ TILLMANN (1874–1953)

On May 10, 2003, on the occasion of the 100th anniversary of the Pontifical Biblical Commission, then-Cardinal Joseph Ratzinger decided to focus on a Vatican ruling regarding a biblical commentary that "had to be banned and withdrawn from sale" because one contributor, Friedrich Wilhelm Maier, as the cardinal explained, "sustained the so-called two-source theory, accepted today by almost everyone." That two-source theory held that Matthew, Mark, and Luke each had their own source for their respective Gospels, but Matthew and Luke also seem to have had access to another text that today we call "Q," a source that we have never seen as such but which biblicists posit because often enough each evangelist seems to be working from the same source.

Curiously, not only was Maier held accountable, but the editor, Fritz Tillmann, was as well. The cardinal disclosed: "This also brought Tillmann's and Maier's scientific career to an end. Both, however, were given the option of changing theological disciplines."

Maier did not take the offer and became, instead, a prison chaplain. Tillmann did, and in the cardinal's words "became a top German moral theologian. Together with Theodor Steinbüchel and Theodor Müncker, he edited a manual of avant-garde moral theology, which addressed this important discipline in a new way and presented it according to the basic idea of the imitation of Christ."[4]

In a strange sort of way, the cardinal seemed to be remarking that if the Congregation had not been intolerant and, well, wrong in not acknowledging what today is the rather broadly accepted Q source hypothesis, we might not have had this great moral theologian.

With that as background, let us look at Tillmann's contribution.

Until 1912, Tillmann had been a successful and influential biblical theologian. The English translations of his German works' titles evidence the focus of the research that he did: *The Son of Man: Jesus's Self-Understanding of His Messianic Nature* (1905), *The Future Coming of Christ according to the Pauline*

Epistles (1909), and *The Self-Understanding of the Son of God: The Foundation of the Synoptic Gospels* (1911).[5] In a word, Tillmann wanted to know who did Jesus understand himself to be?

In 1919, he wrote his first moral theological work, which focused on the personal and the social in terms of the reception of Jesus's preaching: *Personality and Community in the Preaching of Jesus*.[6] In 1934, he collaborated with Theodor Steinbüchel and Theodor Müncker on a three-volume work, which he edited, entitled *Die katholische Sittenlehre* (Catholic moral teaching). Steinbüchel wrote the first volume on philosophical foundations; Müncker authored the second, on the epistemological and psychological foundations; and Tillmann wrote the third, *Die Idee der Nachfolge Christi* (The idea of following Christ), on the idea of the disciple of Christ.[7]

Tillmann's volume was a tremendous success. Seventy years after its publication, Karl-Heinz Kleber writes that in the search to express what the foundational principle of moral theology ought to be, Tillmann came forward and named it: discipleship. Kleber notes that others followed Tillmann's lead, such as Gustav Ermecke, Johannes Stelzenberger, Bernhard Häring, Gérard Gilleman, and René Carpentier.[8]

In 1937, Tillmann published a more accessible text for laypeople, *Die Meister ruft* (The Master Calls: A Handbook of Morals for the Layman).[9] Contemporary reviewers recognized the importance of Tillmann's handbook. One remarked that the new work presented a manual of lay morality not as a list of sins but of virtues animated by the idea of discipleship and guided by Scripture.[10] Another astutely observed two significant achievements. First, Tillmann managed to distill all his previous work, especially *Die Idee der Nachfolge Christi*, into an integrated and accessible expression for interested lay readers. More important, he demonstrated that it was possible to create a sound moral theology based directly on Christian revelation.[11] More recently, Johannes Reiter notes that Tillmann's Christological accent in moral theology influenced a series of subsequent German authors, such as Johannes Steinberger and Bernhard Häring.[12] Bernhard Häring's *The Law of Christ* follows Tillmann's manual seventeen years later in Germany, and in 1960 both books were published in English.

Demonstrating in 1937 a biblically and Christologically based moral theology was, in my estimation, nothing short of miraculous. Catholic moral theology could not make the much needed and extraordinarily urgent turn to the Bible if it did not have within its guild a superb Scripture scholar. One can hardly imagine a moral theologian credibly developing a biblically based moral theology. Tillmann's exile from the land of exegesis and his finding safety and sanctuary in the field of moral theology became itself the fundamental occasion for realizing one of the most significant developments in twentieth-century Roman Catholic moral theology.

The English translation of the 1937 *The Master Calls* is divided into five parts: principles, love of God, love of self, love of neighbor, and social relations. The first four parts are roughly eighty pages each; the final is thirty-five pages long. Without a doubt, a work based on the threefold command of love was radically new.

"Principles" begins with "The Fundamental Idea of the Following of Christ," accompanied by the words of Luke 9:23, "And he said to all, 'If anyone wishes to come after me, let him deny himself and take up his cross daily, and follow Me.'" The passage is key: the call of discipleship is addressed not to a few but to all "whom faith would lead to become His disciples."[13] Tillmann's selection of biblical texts underlining the universality of Jesus's summons offered to the whole church a way of imagining and anticipating a theologically educated laity bent on ministry and service.

Highlighting the immensity and grandeur of the call, Tillmann wrote: "The goal of the following of Christ is none other than the attainment of the status of a child of God." Here Tillmann offered three requisites: "realization of the very highest degree of religious demands and conduct," "a willingness to undergo any sacrifices for the sake of the great task enjoined," and an "absolute conformity to the will of God."[14] These conditions were not matters of privacy or isolation. "Christ's over-all teaching concerning the new man, his duties, and his position with regard to God and His kingdom excludes all isolation, whether in general or in particular, and points out directions and duties which tend toward the community."[15] He concludes stating that baptism supplies the essential foundation of discipleship.[16]

Through emphasis on the virtues, Tillmann built a much-needed bridge to biblical theology. Here he focused more on character traits and internal dispositions, rather than on specific external actions or norms as the moral manuals had. After Tillmann, those who work in biblical ethics frequently turn to the virtues as the most appropriate mode of conveying such an ethics. In fact, Tillmann showed theologians that biblical ethics today must be the result of two competencies: an ability to convey, generally through exegesis, the original meaning of the biblical text, and an ability to bridge that text's original understanding to the present world through an ethical hermeneutics, normally considered to be virtue ethics.[17]

This double normative claim for biblical ethics was first developed and articulated in Lúcás Chan's *Biblical Ethics in the 21st Century: Developments, Emerging Consensus, and Future Directions*, where he appropriated the Tillmann model.[18] Later in advancing the argument, Chan further explored how in contemporary biblical ethics, exegetes and ethicists collaborated together, so as to tap into the much-needed double competency.[19] Of course, the one person who did not need to find a collaborator to bridge the two fields was, in fact, the pathfinder who was exegete turned moralist Fritz Tillmann. As Chan notes, following Tillmann's lead, theologians used virtue ethics as the best way to translate the biblical summons to discipleship.

Tillmann's breakthrough is inestimable. First, as a Scripture scholar he derived from the Scriptures an appropriate identity for the Christian agent both personally and communally: discipleship. His proposal of this identity has had a lasting influence on moral theology.

Second, he developed his argument into a vigorous academic text, *Die Idee der Nachfolge Christi*, which allowed him to engage his colleagues on the intellectual foundations of his proposal.

Third, he made this idea universally accessible and concrete by writing a book for the laity. He also made the text extraordinarily comprehensive, never departing from the double insight that the text had to be fundamentally (and exclusively) based on Scripture (there are no other types of citations in the book), and the text had to give an anthropological shape to the ethical vocation of discipleship.

Fourth, he wisely turned to the virtues most appropriately because, as any reader of the New Testament will note, virtue is the language of Paul and the Evangelists. Virtue is the moral and ethical language of the Hebrew Bible as well. Thus, entering into moral theology, he did not abandon Scriptural language but found in virtue the worthy bridge between Scripture and moral theology.

Fifth, coupled with this, the architectonic structure of the work, two parts bookending the threefold love command, placed charity at the very heart of his ethics. Revelation conveys the singular primacy of charity, a point subsequently argued by Gérard Gilleman in his significant work *The Primacy of Charity* and then developed by Ceslaus Spicq.[20]

Sixth, as a new member of the guild of moral theologians, Tillmann gave his colleagues a text that became a paradigm for others: a biblical ethics based on discipleship. It was a pioneering text that summoned all the baptized to pursue the call to discipleship. It offered an identity that could be understood personally and communally, one discovered by the biblical foundations of the call, along with the virtues necessary to realize that call along the way.[21] Above all, it was a pathway for following Jesus Christ, collectively and personally.

As opposed to the previous manuals of moral theology, which explained what was sin and what was not, Tillmann provided a positive collective- and personal-oriented moral theology that expressed human vulnerable responsiveness by recognizing the call of Christ, the claim of the triple-based love command, and the virtues needed to make that response possible.

GERHARD LOHFINK

Starting in 1996, I had the pleasure to team-teach with the biblical exegete Daniel Harrington first the Synoptic Gospels and virtue ethics, then Paul and virtue ethics, and then finally, just before his death in 2014, John and virtue ethics.[22] As the editor of *New Testament Abstracts*, Harrington wrote more than 35,000 reviews of New Testament publications, making him easily the best-read biblical theologian in the world. On the back cover of Gerhard Lohfink's *Jesus of Nazareth: What He Wanted, Who He Was*, Harrington comments unequivocally: "Lohfink's *Jesus of Nazareth* is the best Jesus book I know." With that endorsement, I turn to the text.

In the beginning of his work, Lohfink notes that the definitive proclamation of the reign of God by Jesus makes clear that "rescue, liberation, and salvation" "had all irrevocably begun."[23] Significantly, Lohfink wants "to show the deep connection between the reign of God and the people of God."[24] Lohfink sees the people of God as the best description of all the baptized and, within that context, reflects on those called to be disciples.

In his chapter on "The Call to Discipleship," Lohfink notes that the term for discipleship, "to follow" (*akolouthēsis*), appears eighty times in the gospels but never as a noun, and only as a verb. "It exists only as a concrete, visible, tangible event," basically meaning "to walk behind."[25] Discipleship then is a movement, an identifiable action.

Lohfink thinks that there might be a temptation to say that the following of a disciple is like a student who follows his rabbi. But Lohfink contrasts how those who follow Jesus are not like rabbinical students. First, rabbinical students mark the beginning of their studies by studying the Torah, not by following a particular rabbi. The Christian disciple, however, is emphatically called by Jesus to follow him. Lohfink writes, "There is not a single story in the rabbinical traditions in which a rabbi called a student to follow him. The reason is very simple: a rabbinic student seeks his or her own teacher."[26] For Jesus, the call comes completely from him; for the rabbinical tradition, there is no call per se, but the decision to follow a rabbi is completely the student's.

Second, Lohfink notes that after a student chooses a rabbi as teacher, "serving the teacher is an essential part of studying Torah." But in the Scriptures, it is Jesus who serves: "The Son of Man came not to be served but to serve, and to give his life as a ransom for many" (Mk 10:45). "For who is greater, the one at table or the one who serves? Is it not the one at table? But I am among you as one who serves" (Lk 22:27). Here Lohfink underlines that by serving them, Jesus is teaching a "new way of being together."[27] Obviously, here we should see how the disciples are vulnerable to the one who serves, vulnerable to the others who are called, vulnerable to those on the road.

Third, rabbinical students learned of the Torah from the rabbi in a specific location, a mark of the school's stability. There was, however, no *stabilitas loci* with Jesus; we follow the one "who has no place to lay his head" (Lk 9:58).[28]

These three differences—regarding call, service, and stability—underline the vulnerable distinctiveness of Jesus's disciples. This leads Lohfink to argue that the disciples' role in following Jesus is for "gathering people for the reign of God."[29]

Lohfink then pursues a subsequent chapter, "The Many Faces of Being Called," where he asks whether Jesus's goal "was that everyone in Israel would become a disciple."[30] While noting that in the Acts of the Apostles "the disciples" refer to the whole community, he considers this "a unique usage" "going back to the earliest Jerusalem community."[31] He also acknowledges that Matthew 28:19 has the great commission: "Go therefore and make disciples of all nations." But still, he seems to think of this as exceptional.

Tillmann based the call of discipleship precisely on the response of being baptized. But, Lohfink argues, "Jesus does not call everyone to follow him." The proclamation of the reign of God "culminates in the call, 'repent and believe the Good News!' but not, 'follow me and become my disciple!'" Lohfink concludes: "He nowhere makes being a disciple a requirement for participation in the reign of God."[32]

Moreover, he adds that "life toward the reign of God—in sociological terms, participation in the Jesus movement—allowed for some very different ways of life." Certainly, Lohfink recognizes many men and women in the New Testament, beyond the Twelve, as called to become disciples.[33] But, he insists, "Jesus by no means called everyone who met him openly and in faith to be his disciple."[34] He names those as *other* "participants" in the story: Bartimaeus (Mk 10:46–52), the "resident members of the Jesus Movement, as in those in Lazarus's household," or occasional helpers "like Joseph of Arimathea or those whom Jesus does not stop who are doing things in his name" (Mk 9:39–40).

Lohfink's overriding concern is that one not be identified as "second class" if they are not considered a disciple. He writes: "Not everyone can be a disciple, since discipleship also presupposes a special call from Jesus. It does not depend on the will of the individual. It can be that someone wants to follow Jesus but is not made his disciple."[35]

It should be noted, however, that Lohfink does underline that all "participants in the reign of God" are "called," but he does not identify how they are called. Tillmann, on the other hand, sees baptism itself as the call to discipleship.

Lohfink concludes his observations, noting that attempts to suggest disciples are top tier and others are second tier ignore "the unity of the people of God and the organization of all its members toward the same goal."[36]

In our first book together, *Jesus and Virtue Ethics: Building Bridges between New Testament Studies and Moral Theology*,[37] Harrington noted that, as we see in the difference between Tillmann and Lohfink, "there has been a long-standing debate on this issue. Some contend that the discipleship teachings are incumbent on all Christians. Others make a distinction between a Christian elite and ordinary Christians." He responded to the question, helpfully explaining that "the major problem posed by these Synoptic Gospel texts is the applicability or transfer to Christians beyond the first century. Or to put the same point in another way, can we use Jesus's instructions to his disciples in Christian moral theology today?"

Harrington resolves the debate as I would, by saying:

> One can and should discern some core values in the discipleship passages in the Synoptic Gospels—absolute dedication to God's kingdom, sharing in Jesus' mission, simple lifestyle, willingness to subordinate or forgo human ties and physical comforts, and the assurance of opposition and suffering for the sake of the gospel—that can give shape to Christian discipleship in any age and place. These core values can serve as the starting points for reflecting on the use of Jesus' discipleship teachings in moral theology today.[38]

Moreover, Lohfink prompts us to see that though discipleship might well be a predominant way of discussing what a Christian's self-understanding before God is, we should be careful to not identify discipleship as a privileging self-understanding. Furthermore, I would suggest that in cultivating the role of discipleship that we be exhorted to consider how it is that we do understand ourselves as having been called. I think as discipleship ethics continues to advance beyond the call of baptism, we should hear from persons and communities how they understand themselves hearing that call beyond the invitation to baptism.

Additionally, Lohfink's emphasis on Jesus as the rabbi who uniquely serves and therein teaches us a new form of being together helps us to see how the call of discipleship is beyond being a solitary call. It is a call to become vulnerably incorporated with those other disciples—this is, in a collective—promoting Jesus's summons for the further realization of the Kingdom of God.

Finally, it is good for us to recognize that the first movement in discipleship comes from the call of God who through Christ invites us to follow him along his way by his grace. The tradition of using journey imagery appreciates the dynamism of the call to follow. If we are going to hear him, we are going to have to keep pace with him. To stand still then on the way of the Lord is then to recede.

The Pier Paolo Pasolini film *The Gospel according to St. Matthew* depicts the pace of Jesus as extraordinarily quick and, as the first disciples realized, not easy to follow. Throughout the film, the viewers watch Jesus stride across the screen heading to Jerusalem, with the disciples stumbling behind trying to catch the words of wisdom Jesus is uttering. The effect is compelling.

This insight is long regarded in the tradition. Thus, Gregory the Great wrote: "Certainly, in this world, the human spirit is like a boat foolishly fighting against the river's rush: one is never allowed to stay still, because unless one forges ahead, one will slide back downstream."[39] Bernard of Clairvaux too emphasized how idleness cannot be a disciple's stance, by writing: "To not progress on the way of Life is to regress."[40] Thomas Aquinas conflated their insights into a motto: "To stand on the way of God is to withdraw."[41] Disciples are always called to move forward so as not to lose sight of the one who summons us. Indeed, I had the privilege at a papal audience on May 13, 2022, to hear Pope Francis echo these sentiments as he urged us to move forward, noting the contemporary tendency that "does so much harm to the church," of wanting to "'turn back,' either out of fear or because of a lack of ingenuity or a lack of courage."[42]

RICHARD A. BURRIDGE

As Harrington introduced me to Lohfink, it was Lúcás Chan who introduced me to Richard Burridge's *Imitating Jesus: An Inclusive Approach to New Testament Ethics*. Burridge offers the hypothesis that the genre of the four Gospels is one of ancient Greco-Roman biography.[43] Arguing that the literary genre is crucial to the interpretation of the text, he stresses, as Chan writes, "the need to focus on the subject in the text; the inseparability between the subject's words and deeds as presented in the text; and the turn to the subject's character which invites us to imitate the subject and appropriate the subject's virtues."[44]

Vulnerably responding to his call means being able to recognize in his life what he wants from us. Nowhere is this more the case than in John's Gospel.

Burridge begins his treatment of John asking, Is Jesus a great moral teacher or a friend of sinners?[45] The question is key: the Gospel is told through a series of encounters—the call of Peter and Nathaniel, the marriage at Cana, the woman by the well, the man born blind, the raising of Lazarus, the Last Supper with the twelve. At the end of the Gospel, we have met Jesus in each of his relationships, whether with the Samaritan woman or Peter, with Martha or Thomas, with the man born blind or Nicodemus, with the Magdalene or Mary of Bethany.

While many argue that there are signs in the Gospel of John, I emphasize the robust dialogical encounters, within and beyond each of the signs. In each encounter, Jesus and the other become better known because Jesus reveals to the other what he knows of them: think here of Nathaniel, the Samaritan woman, Thomas, and Peter (at his call, at the Last Supper, and on the beach). In each, Jesus enters into the life of the other in a transformative way. In terms of a discipleship ethics, we become vulnerable not only to him but to ourselves, both personally and collectively.

There is something very prayerful about these encounters; we are almost eavesdropping on contemplative conversations. These intimate encounters are for Christians deeply moral ones: they are based on love, expressed in faith, maintained by fidelity, and usually accompanied by an instruction about an act of hospitality. These four virtues—love, faith, fidelity, and hospitality—are the moral instructions the reader of John learns.

So much of John's Gospel focuses on love. Even the few encounters with unknown persons, for example, the Samaritan woman and the man born blind, become intimate engagements that are generous, tender, and fairly visceral. Even when Jesus gives the love command, the setting is not public as in the Synoptic Gospels, where there is public questioning and answering. In John, the love command, which is more a gift than a command, is given after Jesus has washed the disciples' feet at the supper (Jn 13:34–35). In fact, the command is incredibly horizontal: love one another as I have loved you. In this instance, as Burridge notes, there is no vertical movement to or from God in the Johannine love commandment.[46] It echoes Lohfink's new way of vulnerably being together.

These loving encounters prompt deeper and more explicit faith. For John, faith is a moral action: we believe in response to the gift given; to not believe is to reject the gift, the person of Jesus. The testimonies of faith from Martha to the man born blind are all deeply relational commitments to Jesus. Indeed, for John, faith is an abiding with Jesus. Jesus's great injunction on the love commandment is not primarily about doing but about abiding with Jesus as he heads toward Jerusalem. So, that faith is always vulnerably relational and therefore the failure to believe is also a failure to be faithful to Jesus.

Sin then is precisely walking away from faith, of being unfaithful or lacking fidelity. Jesus's resurrection admonitions are remarkably moral, as he reprimands the disciples at Emmaus, Thomas in the Upper Room, or Peter on the beach. Fidelity is the trademark of the disciple of Jesus. Believe and remain in my love, believe and abide in my love—these are Jesus's fundamental injunctions. For John sin is the failure to stay in love and to believe in Jesus.

Finally, if anything concrete ever happens in John's Gospel, it is usually an act of hospitality. There is the wedding feast of Cana, but consider other gestures, like Jesus cooking fish, the Samaritan woman offering water, or the disciples on Emmaus inviting Jesus to stay. The key hospitable gesture is the washing of the feet, which is an expression of the love command, to love as Jesus loves. Moreover, that lesson is to be imitated: "Now that I, your Lord and Teacher, have washed your feet, you also should wash one another's feet" (Jn 13:14).

HOWARD THURMAN

In 1935, from the chapel of the famous historically Black research university, Howard University, the Dean of its Rankin Chapel, Howard Thurman (1899–1981), published an essay "Good News for the Underprivileged" that recognized those long overlooked.[47] In 1949, that argument developed into *Jesus and the Disinherited*, a groundbreaking text that precedes any work in liberation or Black theology. In many ways, Thurman asks a series of questions that writers like James H. Cone, Willie James Jennings, M. Shawn Copeland, and Bryan N. Massingale would later pursue in Black theology,[48] and that Gustavo Gutiérrez and others pursued in liberation theology.

He opened his Jesus book with this recognition: "Many and varied are the interpretations dealing with the teachings and the life of Jesus of Nazareth. But few of these interpretations deal with what the teachings and the life of Jesus have to say to those who stand, at a moment in human history, with their backs against the wall."[49]

He added:

> It is urgent that my meaning be crystal clear. The masses of men live with their backs constantly against the wall. They are the poor, the disinherited, the dispossessed. What does our religion say to them? The issue is not what it counsels them to do for others whose need may be greater, but what religion offers to meet their own needs. The search for an answer to this question is perhaps the most important religious quest of modern life.[50]

He reiterates repeatedly, not that the Gospel provides no hope for the "masses with their backs against the wall" but that religion offers them no hope. He writes: "I belong to a generation that finds very little that is meaningful or intelligent in the teachings of the Church concerning Jesus Christ."[51] He adds: "It cannot be denied that too often the weight of the Christian movement has been on the side of the strong and the powerful and against the weak and oppressed—this, despite the gospel."[52] He laments: "The crucial question, then, is this: Is there any help to be found in the religion of Jesus that can be of value here?"[53]

Thurman teaches us that we cannot develop a discipleship for the well-heeled, the privileged. We need discipleship for those who were called, that is, those most in need of the call, those with their backs against the wall.

Thurman draws much from an understanding of the historical Jesus by noting: "The Christian Church has tended to overlook its Judaic origins, but the fact is that Jesus of Nazareth was a Jew of Palestine when he went about his Father's business, announcing the acceptable year of the Lord."[54] Thus Thurman insists on grasping three historical facts: Jesus was a Jew,[55] a poor Jew,[56] and a "member of a minority group in the midst of a larger dominant and controlling group."[57]

In light of these facts, we need to realize that Rome stole Israel from the Jews. They were the disinherited. Thurman writes: "No Jewish person of the period could deal with the question of his practical life, his vocation, his place in society, until first he had settled deep within himself this critical issue. This is the position of the disinherited in every age."[58]

Then he adds:

> The basic fact is that Christianity as it was born in the mind of this Jewish teacher and thinker appears as a technique of survival for the oppressed. That it became, through the intervening years, a religion of the powerful and the dominant, used sometimes as an instrument of oppression, must not tempt us into believing that it was thus in the mind and life of Jesus. "In him was life; and /the life was the light of men." Wherever his spirit appears, the oppressed gather fresh courage; for he announced the good news that fear, hypocrisy, and hatred, the three hounds of hell that track the trail of the disinherited, need have no dominion over them.[59]

The grace of discipleship redounds to the disciples. Themselves. Though most of the original twelve lost their lives painfully, the accounts that we have from the Acts of the Apostles is that without a doubt they grew in grace exponentially as disciples of Christ.

Thurman looked for how those with their backs against the wall could hear the call to discipleship if their inheritance of the Gospel call has been taken by a religion that brings Good News solely to the privileged. So as to help those with their backs against the wall, he insists that "a profound piece of surgery has to take place in the very psyche of the disinherited before the great claim of the religion of Jesus can be presented. The great stretches of barren places in the soul must be revitalized, brought to life, before they can be challenged."[60]

Thurman turns to excise "fear, hypocrisy, and hatred, the three hounds of hell that track the trail of the disinherited," dedicating three of the five chapters to these self-harming vices.

In the final chapter he argues that the "religion of Jesus makes the love-ethic central."[61] He writes, "The religion of Jesus says to the disinherited: 'Love your enemy.' Take the initiative in seeking ways by which you can have the experience of a common sharing of mutual worth and value. It may be hazardous, but you must do it."[62]

I think what Tillmann and Lohfink miss is that the call to discipleship is redemptive for the one called. The message that Thurman seeks to find is the message of relief for the captive, or relief for the sick soul that we saw from William James. The one called is not only called to follow Jesus and promote the Kingdom but called, paradoxically, for her or his own sake, for indeed the call to discipleship is itself redeeming for the one who follows the Lord. Ironically, one cannot pursue one's own redemption; one needs instead to pursue Jesus who redeems us. By becoming vulnerable to Jesus, we become vulnerable to ourselves, those who journey with us, and those we serve along the way.

Of course, I do not mean this in some jejune way. Certainly, Peter was crucified upside down, Paul executed, and Edmund Campion hung, drawn, and quartered. But in each the call was, as Thurman was among the first to note, liberating. By answering the call, each became someone that otherwise they could not have been. A Mother Theresa and Dorothy Day could experience trials and tribulations, a long loneliness even, yet the tangible experience of rebirth and redemption is itself healing and life-giving.

Thurman, the mentor of the Reverend Dr. Martin Luther King Jr.,[63] leads us to see another reason why Jesus called fishermen, tax collectors, and others to be his disciples and why he does the same today. Liberation is constitutive of the call to discipleship.

CHAPTER 5

THE MAN BORN BLIND

On March 5, 1989, Gustavo Gutierrez preached at Blackfriars here in Oxford on the "Liberating of the Man born blind," talking of how the man was liberated from his illness, his poverty, and his alienation, and how he and those around him were freed from "an arrogant and false idea of what religious knowledge is."[64]

It might be good to remember that in the man born blind (Jn 9:1–41), Jesus's disciples see the man and ask Jesus whose sin caused his blindness, the man's or his parents'? Jesus responds that it was neither; but that God's work might be shown, Jesus heals the man by putting mud on his eyes and telling him to wash in the temple pool. When the man is cured and returns to the temple, neither Jesus nor his disciples are present. People are confused when they see the man; could this, they ask, be the same man born blind who has been begging at the temple? He insists that he is the same man and that the one who healed him is Jesus. As he is questioned by the crowd, investigated by the Pharisees, abandoned by his parents, and finally rejected from the temple, in each instance he confesses that Jesus was his healer and adds that Jesus could not be a sinner because only an agent of God could do this miracle. He progressively becomes more articulate in witnessing what Jesus has done and effectively becomes Jesus's witness. This witnessing leads to him being denounced by literally everyone to whom he was ever related, and now, outside the temple, the man is found a second time by Jesus. They speak together; Jesus discloses to him that he is the Son of Man, and the man worships him.

This is easily my favorite pericope in the Scriptures. I love it because of the way the man grows, without the presence of Jesus, in strength, freedom, and abandon as he answers his interrogators. The absence of Jesus occurs on other occasions in John, as when Jesus delays upon hearing the news about Lazarus's illness (Jn 11:6) or when Jesus "slips out" after the healing of the paralytic man (Jn 5:13). In each of these instances, Jesus eventually arrives or returns. No healing, however, leaves us with such an articulate witness. Here, because of Jesus's absence the man born blind has to defend himself and Jesus. As the interrogation goes forward, he is more interested in protecting Jesus's reputation than his own well-being: he progressively marshals from his own depths, what I think of as, a Spirit-filled testimony. He speaks with the force we will later see in the Apostles after the Pentecost. Like them, he knows what Jesus has unequivocally accomplished in him and he speaks like them, full-throated. It is classic parrhesia, a remarkably bold proclamation, and John gives us in the man born blind what Luke gives us in Acts.[65]

I also love the story because his own healing is a part, if you will, of his own call to discipleship. Finally, I love it because he grows in vulnerability as he grows in his recognition of Jesus.

In this light I would like to emphasize several points in the account, while taking exegetical comments from a commentary on John by Karoline M. Lewis, the Marbury E. Anderson Chair in Biblical Preaching at Luther Seminary in St. Paul, Minnesota.[66]

The first point is to understand that the healing of the man is intimately linked to the discourse on the Good Shepherd in chapter 10. Lewis writes:

> In the discourse, Jesus depicts himself as both the door and the shepherd, and these images are meant to unpack key themes presented in chapter 9. In other words, the blind man and Jesus have already acted out Jesus' words in 10:1–18. As a result, to separate the sign from the discourse is to dislodge the full meanings of Jesus as both door and shepherd and to reduce the healing and witness of the blind man to just one more fantastical miracle of Jesus.[67]

Second, the healing of the man happens without the man's own request. Of course, we need only to think of Paul's own conversion to realize that Jesus's calling of disciples is sometimes, what I call, "an unsolicited interruption." Still, Lewis highlights what many overlook: Jesus's recognition of the man whom he sees first. The healing, she argues, is really a call to discipleship. The man is healed because Jesus recognizes in the man a disciple. She writes: "At first, the man born blind appears to be only a pawn or a prop in a plan about which he has no knowledge. . . . Yet this is not Jesus' first reaction to the blind man. As Jesus is walking along, he sees the blind man. . . . In this man blind from birth, Jesus sees a disciple, a witness, just as he did with the Samaritan woman at the well."[68] There is at the outset an act of recognition.

Third, verses 6–7 narrate the sign itself. Jesus's "making of mud recalls how this Gospel begins, in the recollection of creation. While not the same word, 'dust' in Genesis, 'mud' in John 9, the allusion to the creative act of God is unquestionably at work."

Fourth, integral to the sign is the man's listening. Lewis makes a "critical note: the blind man listens to Jesus' voice and follows Jesus' directions." Lewis wants us to see that it is not about seeing but about listening! The man is the one who listens, a command that we hear time and again in John's Gospel as what Jesus's mother first directs the wine stewards to do at the wedding feast or as the royal official asks Jesus to simply utter his command rather than come and touch his servant. In each pericope, the call to hear and act accordingly is constitutive of the miracle. Lewis comments: "The blind man first hears Jesus, just as Jesus' sheep hear his voice in chapter 10."[69]

Fifth, the man's growth in understanding of who Jesus is progresses just as the Samaritan woman at the well did (Jn 4:19). It is noteworthy that the man's "sight" is progressing without Jesus being present, a significant theme throughout this Gospel: "Blessed are those who do not see and yet come to believe" (Jn 20:29). "The blind man will develop in his belief in Jesus not with Jesus being present but by witnessing to Jesus's presence in his life. The actual act of testimony has everything to do with the capacity to believe."[70]

Sixth, as he grows in faith, he begins to live out his discipleship rather quickly: this emerges when the man takes the upper hand in the discourse in verse 27 and responds to the Pharisees' insistence that he repeat the account of his being able to see. He answered, "I have told you already and you did not listen. Why do you want to hear it again? Do you want to become his disciples too?" Lewis writes: "'Do you also want to become one of his disciples?' is the theme at the heart of this entire passage: what it means to be a disciple, what discipleship is, and what the characteristics of a disciple are. The blind man names what is at stake in these two chapters—hearing and discipleship."[71] I would add it is also growing vulnerable in responsive recognition of Jesus.

Seventh, the hearing and listening between Jesus and the disciple are mutual. Lewis first comments on how in verse 35 Jesus hears that the Pharisees have thrown out the man born blind and notes "the mutuality between Jesus and his disciples who hear him." She focuses on how "to find" is the same verb used when Jesus calls the first disciples, by first finding Philip and then calling him to "Follow me" (Jn 1:43). In the calling of Philip, Andrew, and Simon "the verb 'to find' is used five times in only five verses." Lewis notes: "It is against this backdrop and thematic focus that we are to read and interpret the implications of Jesus finding the man born blind. As a result, the blind man is now a disciple, found by Jesus, a sheep in the fold."[72]

Like the man born blind we are blessed because though we do not see him, we hear his voice and follow him. The call to discipleship is one that we hear personally and collectively; it is a call in which we are found by Christ and invited to vulnerably recognize him.

The entire account ironically ends with the comment (Jn 10:20), "Why listen to him?" which takes us back to the very beginning of chapter 9. The question is not to be answered, I think, for those who do not hear the call but, precisely, for those who do.[73]

Thank you.

NOTES

1. Lohfink, *Jesus of Nazareth*.
2. Burridge, *Imitating Jesus*.
3. Thurman, *Jesus*.
4. Preceding quotes from Ratzinger, *Relationship between Magisterium and Exegetes*. I am grateful to Lúcás Chan Yiu Sing, whose research on Tillmann led me to this essay as well as to the reviews of Tillmann's books.
5. Tillmann, *Der Menschensohn*; Tillmann, *Die Wiederkunft Christ*; Tillmann, *Das Selbstbewusstsein des Gottessohnes*.
6. Tillmann, *Persönlichkeit und Gemeinschaft*.
7. Steinbüchel, *Die philosophische Grundlegung*; Müncker, *Die psychologische Grundlegung*; Tillmann, *Die Idee der Nachfolge Christi*.
8. "Als Formalprinzip, bzw. Wie man richtiger sagen sollte Moralgrundprinzip, stellte Fritz Tillmann die 'Nachfolge Christi' heraus. Andere folgten diesem Beispiel." Kleber, *Historia Docet*, 89.
9. Tillmann, *Der Meister ruft*.
10. Congar, "Der Meister ruft," 641.
11. Thalhammer, "Der Meister ruft," 451.
12. Reiter, "Die Katholische Moraltheologie Zwischen," 231–42.
13. Tillmann, *The Master Calls*, 3.
14. Tillmann, *The Master Calls*, 4–7.
15. Tillmann, *The Master Calls*, 9–10.
16. Tillmann, *The Master Calls*, 15.
17. Keenan, "The Bible and Ethics," 2120–37.
18. Chan, *Biblical Ethics in the 21st Century*.
19. Chan, "Biblical Ethics: 3D," 112–28.
20. Gilleman, *Le Primat de la charité*; Gilleman, *Primacy*. Later, see Spicq, *Charity and Liberty*; Spicq, *Agape*.
21. For more on Tillmann, see, Chalmers, "Fritz Tillmann, Discipleship," 352–69; Keenan, *A History of Catholic Moral Theology*, 83–110.
22. Harrington and Keenan, *Jesus and Virtue Ethics*; *Jesus e a ética*; *Paul and Virtue Ethics*.
23. Lohfink, *Jesus of Nazareth*, 39.
24. Lohfink, 58.
25. Lohfink, 73.
26. Lohfink, 74.
27. Lohfink, 75.
28. Lohfink, 76.
29. Lohfink, 85.
30. Lohfink, 86.
31. Lohfink, 86.
32. Lohfink, 87.
33. Lohfink, for a list, see 89.
34. Lohfink, 89.
35. Lohfink, 97.
36. Lohfink, 99.
37. Harrington and Keenan, *Jesus and Virtue Ethics*; *Jesus e a ética*.
38. Harrington and Keenan, *Jesus and Virtue Ethics*, 52–53.

39. "In hoc quippe mundo humana anima quasi more navis est contra ictum fluminis conscendentis: uno in loco nequaquam stare permittitur, quia ad ima relabitur, nisi ad summa conetur" (Gregory, Reg. Past. p. III. c. 34: ML 77, 118c).
40. "In via vitae non progredi regredi est" (Bernard, Serm II in festo. Purif., n. 3: ML 183, 369 C).
41. "In via Dei stare retrocedere est." Thomas attributes the quote to Bernard in In III Sen d29, a8, qla2, la, and to Gregory in ST II–II,24,6 ob3.
42. Carol Glatz, "Pope Francis: Christians Wanting to Go Backward 'Does So Much Harm to the Church,'" *America*, May 13, 2022. https://www.americamagazine.org/faith/2022/05/13/pope-francis-amoris-laetitia-conference-242986.
43. Burridge, *What Are the Gospels?*
44. Chan, "Biblical Ethics: 3D," 115.
45. Burridge, *What Are the Gospels?*, 61, 68.
46. Burridge, *Imitating Jesus*, 325–26.
47. Thurman, "Good News for the Underprivileged."
48. Cone, *The Cross*; Jennings, *The Christian Imagination*; Copeland, *Enfleshing Freedom*; Massingale, *Racial Justice*.
49. Thurman, *Jesus*, 1.
50. Thurman, 3.
51. Thurman, 19.
52. Thurman, 20.
53. Thurman, 36.
54. Thurman, 6.
55. Thurman, 5.
56. Thurman, 7.
57. Thurman, 8.
58. Thurman, 12.
59. Thurman, 18–19.
60. Thurman, 58.
61. Thurman, 79.
62. Thurman, 90.
63. See the thoughtful chapter, "Howard Washington Thurman and Martin Luther King Jr.: Critical Resources in the Development of Ethical Leadership," in Fluker, *Ethical Leadership*, 11–32.
64. Gutierrez, "Gutierrez on the Liberating of Man Born Blind," 158–60, at 160.
65. On parrhesia, see LaCouter, *Balthasar and Prayer*; Regan, "The Criteria of 'Authentically' Catholic Theology," 1071; Miller, "Christian Communal Parrhesia and the Case of the 1965 Bloody Sunday March," 9–28; Boland and Clogher, "A Genealogy of Critique," 116–132. For a related study, see Kaveny, *Prophecy without Contempt*.
66. K. Lewis, *John*, 123–49.
67. K. Lewis, 124.
68. K. Lewis, 126.
69. K. Lewis, 127.
70. K. Lewis, 128.
71. K. Lewis, 130.
72. K. Lewis, 131.
73. K. Lewis, 146.

6

GRACE AND SIN

At the end of my last lecture on discipleship, I was left with a sense that I had not taken the lecture further forward enough. In the question-and-answer session, my host, Nicholas Austin, SJ, the Master of Campion Hall, asked two separate questions, as if prompting me to consider more matters of the imagination and asceticism. Friends from the United States, Gina and Steve Wolfe, had come up from London for the lecture, and Steve asked afterward if I could have brought in more the practical side of how to be a disciple, for instance, how to be vulnerable and how to be more inclined to give recognition.

The lecture expressed well, I thought, the major theological insights and claims for discipleship today, but at the end I felt somehow that the urgency of the call to discipleship was missing. After I left the lecture, I read about the awful attack in Uvalde, Texas, that left nineteen children and two teachers dead. This was only ten days after another mass killing in Buffalo, New York, of ten Black Americans, by another eighteen-year-old white male. Clearly, in the United States, we do not yet have a solution to the use of deadly force against innocent people.[1] Can a disciple of Christ not sense the urgency of this matter there?

During the evening, I kept looking to discover what I needed to find.

I woke up the next morning thinking of Dietrich Bonhoeffer, and then in prayer I saw in the day's Gospel reading (John 16:12) the need to heed the Spirit of Truth. I wanted to be open to the Spirit of Truth, the Advocate, and realized then that in my lecture I had spoken of discipleship without Bonhoeffer, without attending to the most critical theological figure of the twentieth century who wrote on discipleship and witnessed to Christ in the midst of unspeakable violence. His twin admonitions regarding religion and cheap grace brought discipleship closer, more immediately into ordinary life during the war years and in a manner of speaking into our contemporary world.

At breakfast the next morning, a fellow Jesuit, Fr. Rob Marsh, SJ, asked me whether I was satisfied with my lecture and I responded, "Actually, no." After breakfast, I ran into Nick and said, "I realize now what I missed in the last lecture, the invitation to encounter discipleship as a meaningful response now, today!" And then I added, "And so, I will start next week's lecture with Bonhoeffer." He laughed and said, "Maikki Aakko (a graduate student at Campion and my host for the fifth lecture) and Joel Rasmussen (an Oxford Professor at Mansfield College) both wondered aloud after your lecture why you had not spoken on Bonhoeffer!"

I start then this lecture with a nod to Bonhoeffer and hopefully aim for a collective discipleship that pursues Christ aided by the post-Pentecostal Advocate of Truth. Then I turn to the matters of grace and sin in the light of vulnerability and recognition.

DIETRICH BONHOEFFER

Turning to Bonhoeffer after having considered Howard Thurman's dichotomy between religion and the Gospel is such a natural move. That dichotomy is alive in the writing of Dietrich Bonhoeffer, who in his later works, particularly in his *Letters and Papers from Prison*, imagined the possibility of a "religionless Christianity."[2]

Clearly, Bonhoeffer was not suggesting that there be no church; rather, he wanted to strip away the accretions of religion that take us away from a more direct reception of the Gospel. Religion mediates the Gospel, but that mediation can take us down pathways that are less true than the Gospel itself. Bonhoeffer highlighted the compromise by inviting us to consider a "religionless Christianity" so as to let the Gospel of Jesus refract with fewer filters. In a way he wanted to let the Gospel come through just as Thurman wanted it to burn away "that fear, hypocrisy, and hatred, the three hounds of hell that track the trail of the disinherited." But as Thurman turned to the Gospel, free of religion, to heal and liberate the souls of the disinherited, Bonhoeffer turned to religionless Christianity to hear the Gospel call to be other-directed, to respond to the neighbor in need, to heed the Gospel summons to work in the vineyard with him who lays his life down for us. Bonhoeffer would do that when he was executed on April 9, 1945, after eighteen months in the prison of Tegel and another six months in the Flossenbürg concentration camp, where he was hanged.

Significantly, these two contemporary voices, one known for his opposition to racism and the other for his opposition to Nazism, had similar interests.

In fact, David Robinson helps us understand how the antiracism articulated by Black theologians in the United States influenced the theology of Dietrich Bonhoeffer.[3]

Robinson emphasizes how Bonhoeffer, "writing as a refugee in New York in the summer of 1939," recognized that US churches had "racial lines drawn between churches."[4] In that year, Bonhoeffer published "Protestantism without Reformation," in many ways an argument for a religionless Christianity, where he recognized how the churches in the United States masked racial segregation.[5]

Living in the Harlem community, Bonhoeffer recognized in the white Christ the "theological problem of whiteness" that "camouflages" itself.[6] He also observed that the "young, forward-looking generation of Negroes are turning away from the faith of their elders" and "that today the 'black Christ' is pitted against the 'white Christ,'" revealing "a destructive rift within the church of Jesus Christ."[7] Bonhoeffer considered "the figure of a black Christ is not so much innovation as provocation in order to show the racialized representation—the default assumption that Christ is white—hidden behind claims to 'color-blindness' or being 'beyond race.'"[8] In 1939, while noting that "many white Christians through influential organizations do whatever they can to improve the relations between the races and that discerning Negroes recognize the serious difficulties," Bonhoeffer recognizes nonetheless: "But today the general picture of the church in the United States is still one of racial fragmentation. Blacks and whites come separately to word and sacrament. They have no common worship."[9]

Bonhoeffer learns that this whiteness "marginalizes the person and work of Jesus Christ,"[10] and sadly concludes, "Christendom in American theology is essentially still religion and ethics. Hence, the person and work of Jesus Christ recedes into the background for theology and remains ultimately not understood, because the sole foundation for God's radical judgment and radical grace is at this point not recognized."[11]

Where then is Bonhoeffer's hope? Bonhoeffer finds hope precisely in the churches where he worshipped in New York, for "nowhere else is revivalist preaching still so alive and widespread as it is for Negroes; here the gospel of Jesus Christ, the Savior of sinners, is truly preached."[12] When Bonhoeffer writes: "The issue of the Negro is one of the most decisive future tasks for the white churches,"[13] he clearly wants the white churches to stop their exclusion of Blacks because of its oppressive impact on Blacks; but he also recognizes that the only way whites in white churches can ever survive is if they recognize their Black fellow Christians, drop their own whiteness, and embrace the Christ preached in the Black churches, "the Savior of Sinners."

Astutely Robinson writes: "Bonhoeffer's treatment of America's racialized and denominated history leads to the ethical task of "confession," a form of acknowledging what I referred to earlier as collective guilt.[14] Robinson adds that "the renunciation of such habit can renew the confessions of the global body of Christ, setting a dialectic of incarnation and cross against a pallid Christology of Western glory."[15]

In short, religion gave sanction to white supremacy, and the dismantling of white supremacy belongs as a task not only because such supremacy gives license to individuals and collectives to brutalize African Americans but because it removes whites themselves from hearing and witnessing to the good news of redemption by the Gospel of Jesus Christ.[16]

The obscurantism of Christian preaching particularly in hiding structural racism is raised then as a challenge and a need for particular populations. Thurman suggests it, and here Bonhoeffer names it.

Bonhoeffer's prompt on "religionless Christianity" couples here beautifully I think with his admonition against cheap grace. Still, it is good to recognize that the term "cheap grace" was first coined by the Reverend Adam Clayton Powell (1865–1953), the pastor of the largest Black church in the United States, the Abyssinian Baptist Church in Harlem, where Bonhoeffer lived. Powell, not Bonhoeffer, generated the term. Bonhoeffer came in contact with it as he worshipped at the church where he also taught Sunday School.[17]

Two quotes from Bonhoeffer capture his understanding of cheap grace, both from his *Cost of Discipleship*. And both lead us I hope to consider now, in the next section, how grace serves to animate our preparation for the moral life as disciples of Jesus Christ, or as Bonhoeffer concludes his text "Through fellowship and communion with the incarnate Lord,"[18] "Cheap grace is the preaching of forgiveness without requiring repentance, baptism without church discipline. Communion without confession. Cheap grace is grace without discipleship, grace without the cross, grace without Jesus Christ, living and incarnate." A few lines later, he writes: "Costly grace confronts us as a gracious call to follow Jesus, it comes as a word of forgiveness to the broken spirit and the contrite heart. It is costly because it compels a man to submit to the yoke of Christ and follow him; it is grace because Jesus says: 'My yoke is easy and my burden is light.'"[19]

Through religionless Christianity and cheap grace, Bonhoeffer helps us see the immediacy and urgency of the call to discipleship. Indisputably, along with Thurman, he helps us to not only hear the call of discipleship but to vulnerably recognize the context in which we live as rife with inequity and injustice, obstacles that need to be removed as we learn to follow in the footsteps of the one who calls.

GRACE

I began my last lecture telling you about one of the great Catholic reformers of the twentieth century, Fritz Tillmann. Here I want to begin with a story about another reformer, the Redemptorist, Bernhard Häring. But then I turn to yet two other reformers who in the shadows of World War II bring us into the world of grace and, in so doing, prompt the moral life to be more connected to systematic and ascetical theology. I think knowing this history provides us then with a better understanding that there have been some changes, even, dare I suggest, progress, but it also reminds us that there is still so much more at stake.

When asked to consider the study of moral theology for his future ministry, Häring describes his response to his superior: "I told my superior that this was my very last choice because I found the teaching of moral theology an absolutely crushing bore."[20] As he began actually studying, he became even more repelled. "In 1936 when I came to study moral theology under the guidance of a professor who was a canon lawyer, he used the manual of Aertnys-Damen; we students found ourselves in crisis and even disgusted. For my personal-in-depth development I found other ethical writers of great value. Thus, I created a deviation between the official morality for the preparation of the office of confessor and the personal work for a morality to live and to announce."[21]

In 1954, Bernhard Häring published in German his deviation, the 1,600-page, three-volume magisterial manual, *Das Gesetz Christi*.[22] In 1961, the English translation, *The Law of Christ: Moral Theology for Priests and Laity*, was published.[23] The first paragraph of the first chapter of the first volume captured the positive call to moral theology. It was riveting:

> The moral theology of Jesus is contained in its totality in the glad tidings of salvation. The tremendous *Good News* is not actually a new law, but the Sovereign Majesty of God intervening in the person of Christ and the grace and love of God manifesting itself in Him. In consequence, all the precepts of the moral law, even the most sacred, are given a new and glorious orientation in divine grace and a new focus, the Person of the God-man. There is nothing novel in the call to repentance for all sin. What is new is the glad tidings announcing that *now* the time for the great conversion from sin and the return to God is at hand.[24]

Häring summoned the reader: the moment of kairos is now. "We understand moral theology as the doctrine of the imitation of Christ, as life in, with, and through Christ . . . the point of departure in Catholic moral theology is Christ, who bestows on man a participation in his life and calls on him to follow the Master."[25]

In treating the topic of grace now, I want to first highlight the work of two contemporaries of Tillmann, Dom Odon Lottin and Gerard Gilleman, who brought us the reform of moral theology that was eventually expressed by Häring's *The Law of Christ*, more the seventy years ago. We need to recognize that Roman Catholic theological ethics went through a period of enormous transition in the twentieth century, abandoning its classic textbooks, the so-called moral manuals, which were singularly centered on sins derived from the Decalogue. The twentieth-century reformers developed a so-called revisionist moral theology that attempted to reintegrate moral theology with both systematic and ascetical theology. They revised the tradition by looking to the Scriptures and to more grace-filled moments in the tradition. In terms of grace, I argue here that these revisionists moved grace from its peripheral connection to the sacrament of confession, where grace kept us from sin and absolved us when we failed, to a much more robust engagement of grace as the very foundation of the moral life for empowering Christians to becoming disciples of Christ. When grace was used by moral theologians before the revisionists, it was preeminently so as to avoid sin and the punishment of purgatory or hell. With the revisionists grace was preeminently so as to follow Christ. Still, I will argue that it is precisely in a discipleship ethics that we become even more attentive to and honest about not just grace but the reality of sin in our lives.

Thus, I begin with the gift of grace and the dynamism of the call in that context, and in that way, I can subsequently focus on sin. I do not see sin as the antithesis or outside of grace but rather sin as human failing within the context of the call to discipleship and therefore within the context of a life of grace. Here I will especially recall the emergence of the Irish Penitentials not as standalone sin texts but as guides for the *anamchara*, the Irish spiritual directors who helped medieval monks and nuns in their lifelong struggles to follow Christ. I will argue that sin invariably is a failure to be vulnerable and to recognize or, as I say, a failure to bother to love. Sin is effectively the refusal of charity.

I conclude with a coda on culpable ignorance so as to leave us all a little uncomfortable.

DOM ODON LOTTIN

I have argued in my new book, *A History of Catholic Theological Ethics*, that to understand the syntheses of Häring, Josef Fuchs, Charles Curran, Lisa Sowle

Cahill, and others, we need to appreciate the contributions of their predecessors.[26] Having seen Tillmann's call of discipleship, we now turn to Odon Lottin's historical study of moral theology and then Gérard Gilleman's proposal on the role of charity in sustaining our deep tendency toward the moral life.

Odon Lottin's contributions shaped and animated the shifts that we see over the twentieth century.[27] From 1942 to 1960 he wrote a four-volume study (roughly 3,000 pages) on the development of scholasticism through the twelfth and thirteenth century.[28] Here he revolutionized our understanding of scholasticism in general and Thomas Aquinas in particular, emphasizing not the unchangeableness of scholasticism but, on the contrary, the incredibly dynamic form of inquiry it engaged that prompted regular revisions in theologians' own claims and sustained debates among the scholastics themselves. Change, development, and history entered into our understanding of the tradition; these concepts that once highlighted uncertainty and precarity now were seen as aids for attaining truth.

In postwar Europe, Lottin presented a scholasticism that was very attractive at suggesting how one could go forward from the rubble. In 1946, he published his first moral theological synthesis, the two-volume work *Principes de morale*. Rather than being a text for hearing confessions, the first volume was a theological foundation for the formation of conscience, and the second volume reported historical debates on twenty-eight topics such as synderesis, erroneous conscience, the connection of the virtues, the gifts of the Holy Spirit, and so on. Here, Lottin was reintegrating moral theology into what was then called dogmatic theology but today is known as systematic theology.[29]

In 1954, he published his revolutionary *Morale fondamentale*. On the first page of the text proper, he insisted that moral theology ought not to be categorized by the sins against the Decalogue but rather according to the moral and theological virtues. He also argued that moral reasoning ought to follow the inductive logic of prudence rather than the deductive legalistic casuistry of the moral manuals.[30] There he broke completely from the manualists, criticizing the wretched past of moral theology and blaming the parish priest for having no interest in moral theology except that which directly affected his being a confessor.

He also critiqued canon law's influence on moral theology, which, he believed, caused moral theology to lose its moorings in dogmatic theology and in the biblical and patristic sources of theology. Moreover, the manualists' singular interest in avoiding sin not only took Christians away from their Christian vocation to follow Christ in holiness and service, but moral theology itself lost its deep connection to ascetical and mystical theology.[31] Finally, he critiqued some of his more liberal colleagues, who seemed more interested in excusing Christians from certain sins than in urging mature, challenging virtuous living that a true Christian should pursue.[32]

Later, in *Au cœur de la morale chrétienne*, he critiqued the numerous mediocre Christians who asked their confessors to give them minimalist expectations for the moral life and lamented the terrible decline of moral theology after Aquinas. He added that moral theology "separated itself from its living sources, Scripture and dogmatics; it amputated its limbs of ascetical and mystical theology; it introduced a number of canonical questions which sought no solution in biblical texts; and it became much more interested in sin than in virtue."[33] Clearly, Lottin wanted to kick the dust of the manuals from his shoes as he covered new terrain on the pathway of the Lord.

To get moral theology to its proper home, Lottin argued, morality was deeply dependent upon dogmatics. "Dogmatics, in a word, presents us God's part in the work of our salvation, morals organizes our part."[34] Lottin saw the end of morality as the right realization of the person and the community in and according to God's salvific plan. For this reason, the entirety of Lottin's *Morale fundamentale* aimed at the formation of the Christian conscience: what all ministers should look to do is to help the members of the church to lead conscientious lives.[35]

His striking break with the manualists is most evident in the hermeneutical context in which he establishes the conscience as foundational to the moral life. In the moral manuals, the Christian conscience was often treated as sick and weak. In Lottin, we no longer find the manualists' pathologies of conscience, categorized as doubtful, laxed, scrupulous, uncertain, erroneous, and so on. Lottin wanted to start afresh with the Christian conscience as capable of hearing the call to discipleship. In forming the conscience, he turned to the virtues acquired, developed, and maintained by learning through prudence.[36]

By turning to prudence, Lottin liberated the Christian conscience from its singular docility to the confessor priest. He instructed church members to become mature self-governing Christians and insisted that Christians have a lifelong task, a "progressive one" he called it,[37] toward the ideals of both the natural and supernatural virtues. By turning to prudence, Lottin urged his readers to find within themselves, their community, their faith, and the Scriptures the mode and the practical wisdom for determining themselves into growing as better Christians.

This emphasis on personal responsiveness to the call to discipleship was not a move away from community. While the moral manuals simply prohibited certain forms of activity and never guided us into becoming better neighbors (though they did aim to keep us from becoming worse ones), Lottin argued from Thomas that our personal good was derived from the common good.

Finally, this Benedictine monk's writing style was at once highly academic yet also fairly forthright and prophetic. He was calling out theologians, priests, and laity, telling them to wake up, get with the agenda, and stop their whining about their struggle with confessing sins. With their introverted examination of their sinfulness, they were missing the call of the Lord who was summoning them to, in a way, forget about their guilt (after all it was Jesus Christ redeeming them, not themselves) and get on with the work of promoting the Kingdom of God, which is the person of Jesus Christ. One could say Lottin's own summons was laced with parrhesia, for, indeed, he sounded as bold as the man born blind or as the disciples after the outbreak of the Spirit in the Upper Room on the Pentecost.

GÉRARD GILLEMAN

In 1947, the Belgian Jesuit Gérard Gilleman defended his dissertation on the role of charity in moral theology at the Institut Catholique in Paris under the guidance of the French Jesuit René Carpentier.[38] Shortly after submitting his dissertation, Gilleman was assigned to teach dogmatic theology at St. Mary's Theological College in Kurseong, India. He never returned, and left his mentor the task of publishing a French edition of the revised dissertation.[39]

If Lottin awakened in moralists the need for a deeper connection with fundamental or systematic theology, then Gérard Gilleman awakened the need for ascetical theology. As he wrote: "The task of Christian morality and of asceticism which is intimately linked to it, is to render the intention and exercise of charity in us always more and more explicit."[40]

This more positive, interior, and integrated direction for finding moral truth was of extraordinary moment. Gilleman examined the most internal and gracious of all virtues, charity. I want to note here that Gilleman's pursuit of charity as a virtue perfecting a tendency or inclination parallels my own pursuit of vulnerability needing also to be realized. I am looking for that which ontologically precedes all else, including conscience, that makes me capaciously, ethically responsive. I argue that we are made human by God, and in our humanity we discover that we are ontologically vulnerable; but that vulnerability needs to be realized, developed, and perfected, and from Gilleman we will see that charity is the virtue that prompts the right realization of our vulnerability. As Gilleman explains, charity informs the form of all of our actions yet unites us to the last end. Significantly, as Gilleman notes, for Thomas, charity was the mother of the virtues: "Charity is the mother and root of all the virtues, in as much as it is the form of them all"

(*ST* I–II.62.4.corpus).[41] Inasmuch as I have already identified humility as the first virtue for vulnerability, I think that humility makes possible the needed virtue of charity, which realizes and develops our vulnerability as capacious.

The achievement of a moral theology integrated with ascetical theology was major, precisely because the moral manualists refused any interest for three centuries in the pursuit of the good, focusing solely on the avoidance and confession of sin. For moral theologians only the avoidance of sin was necessary for salvation; the pursuit of Christ was only for those few so chosen. Thus, they left to the field of ascetical theology the pursuit of spiritually developing a relationship with God. But just as moral theology avoided the ascetical, so too did ascetical theology avoid the moral.

One might think this an exaggeration, but it is not. For instance, in the preface of the first manual published in English in the twentieth century, *A Manual of Moral Theology for English-Speaking Countries* (1906), the English Jesuit Thomas Slater noted that the manuals "should not be censured for not being what they were never intended to be."[42] Rather, they are "technical works that are necessary for the Catholic priest to enable him to administer the sacrament of penance and to fulfill his duties."[43]

In remarkably stark terms, he famously described the manuals of moral theology "as technical as the text-books of the lawyer and the doctor. They are not intended for edification, nor do they hold up a high ideal of Christian perfection for the imitation of the faithful. They deal with what is of obligation under the pain of sin, they are books of moral pathology."[44] Slater acknowledged that if readers were looking to learn how to become better disciples, they should look elsewhere: to the manuals of ascetical, devotional, or mystical theology, where they would find the "high ideal of Christian perfection." Finally, Slater concludes his stunning preface by bisecting the natural law's fundamental principle, "do good and avoid evil." He writes, instead, that "the first step on the right road to conduct is to avoid evil."[45]

If the manualists identified morality as solely the avoidance of evil and ascetical theology as the pursuit of the good, then by being reintegrated, the first principle of the natural law—to do good and avoid evil—finally emerged again on Gilleman's watch as under the one discipline of moral theology, though one now informed by charity.

To do this Gilleman aimed for a moral theology that was primarily about the interior life. From that interior life, each Christian could discover what each person shares with the other, that is, the tendency for union with God through charity. Gilleman refers to a tendency within every human being.[46] Indeed, throughout the question on natural law, I.II.94, Thomas uses a common term, *inclinatio* (inclination), to describe within us a natural, compelling desire for the good, for completion, and inevitably for union with God.⁴⁷ Both terms, "tendency" and "inclination," point to the human desire for flourishing and both terms suggest at once what is and what is not yet. You can see, I hope, that the concept of vulnerability functions in my writings in an analogous way as that internal capacity prior to the moral life that actually prompts us to the moral life. Thus, Gilleman's "tendency" infused with charity is the possible foundation for every human moral vulnerable action.

This tendency within the interior life is not primarily for private use but is that by which we are and seek to be connected to God and to one another. Here we engage what the modern person seeks: an objective for the longing for interior fulfillment. For Gilleman, charity infuses that tendency with enormous capabilities: "By introducing charity as the pivot of its formulation, moral theology will not only come into closer contact with Christ but will also meet the best aspirations of the modern conscience." He added, "By its insatiable demands it liberates all the generous impulses of the individual without minimizing precise duties; without diminishing the importance of his own person, it drives a man into the society of other men."⁴⁸

Arguing that charity perfects that tendency, Gilleman showed that charity acts as the first mover, as prior to all other movements. Most moral intentions can be based on some previous intention. For instance, one could act generously so as to deepen a friendship or another could act courageously in the pursuit of justice. For an act of charity, however, there can be no previous intention. Charity is not one virtue among others but rather the form of the form of the virtues or the first mover of all graced human activity. Only charity allows us to be in union with God, ourselves, and our neighbor. In union with God, we can act out charity and perform acts of justice, temperance, and fortitude. Thus, if I act out of the love of God, I cannot claim that I do so for another intention because then I would no longer be acting out of charity.⁴⁹

Gilleman concluded that for Thomas, "charity is, in a very real sense, the soul of the moral life; it is everywhere present in our activity."⁵⁰ This echoes an earlier claim of his that the purpose of his study was "to apply to the formulation of each and every question of moral theology the universal principle of St. Thomas: *Caritas forma omnium virtutum* ('charity is the form of all the virtues')."⁵¹ As form, charity would direct the rest of the moral life, giving it shape and purpose.

Finally, Gilleman aimed to reconstruct a charity-centered moral theology, arguing that just as charity marked the beginning of the moral life, that which was prior to any moral action, so too charity was the end of the moral life, our union with God.

In the ordering of love, Gilleman claimed, the love of God precedes the love of self because in charity we are closer to God than even to ourselves. He wrote: "There is no way of escaping the fact that the ontological cohesion of any being is possible only through actual participation in Being. Our love for God is a more intimate constituent of ourselves than love for our own selves!"[52] We ought not, therefore, separate the love of God from God. Gilleman writes: "Jesus Christ came to reveal something entirely new concerning love in God. Not only does God have love, but He is *agapè* (1 John 4.8), which Thomas interprets in saying '*Ipsa essentia divina caritas est*' (II.II.23.2.ad1)."[53] Gilleman notes that when Thomas writes that "charity is the divine essence itself," he adds that "the charity whereby formally we love our neighbor is a participation of Divine charity." Gilleman writes: "Charity commands the powers now that they are divinized. . . . For the Christian in the state of grace, all good voluntary action is necessarily elicited by a divinized will, that is to say, by charity-love."[54] Charity is truly grace building upon grace.

Through the concept of a tendency infused by the grace-filled virtue of charity, Gilleman captured the dynamic tension between what we seek and what we will actually encounter lastingly in the kingdom. In the meantime, he proposed that we seek, through sustained reflective exercises, to develop within us the acquired virtues that further realize other dimensions of our selves. The subject of the seventh lecture, the virtues, then, expresses the exigencies of charity.[55] Gilleman writes: "Our moral life, the result of liberty creating our spiritual person, appears at last in its naked reality: it is a work of love springing at once from God's heart and from ours."

SIN

For the longest time, we have thought of the Irish Penitentials as standalone texts that helped abbots to ascertain fair penances for similar sins in the different abbeys. But then Hugh Connelly investigated the practice. In his study *The Irish Penitentials*, Connolly notes the originality in the Celtic practice of confessing sins in that it shows no familiarity with the earlier canonical penances or the "order of penitents."[56] Instead, these "confessions were usually made to a spiritual guide known as an *anamchara*, a Gaelic word that literally means a soul-friend, who was recognized within the monastic system. An ancient Irish saying comments that "anyone without a soul-friend is like a body without a head." Every monk was expected to have an anamchara to whom he could make a manifestation of his conscience (*manifestation conscientiae*).[57]

Connolly's study remarkably shifted the understanding of the Penitentials by showing us that the manuals were effectively aids for what today we would call spiritual directors, not confessors, people who accompany others not primarily in their avoidance of sin but in their pursuit of promoting the Kingdom of God.

The role of the soul-friend was not, then, a judicial one; rather, the *anamchara* was a guide to accompany the individual through the trials of life. The encounter between the soul-friend and the individual aimed at a dialogue that "was neither contractual nor constraining but which bore testimony, instead to a God who was always willing to forgive." The dialogue therefore was a "healing" one.[58] For this reason the anamchara was to be hospitable, welcoming the weary nun or monk on her or his journey so that the individual could manifest her or his conscience. Thus, the anamchara is a fellow pilgrim on the "same pilgrim path."[59] The hospitality that the anamchara offered was solidarity, so that the pilgrim maintained the journey. In many ways the anamchara was one who "comes through the fire of real suffering and self-sacrifice while at the same time, growing ever more open to the saving forgiving grace of Christ, and one who always reserves in his heart, a sincere hospitality for the stranger, the fellow-pilgrim, the fellow-sufferer."[60]

I think this is how we need to understand sin, in the context of responding in grace to the call to discipleship. In the attempt to follow, we sin but in order to discern our way forward, we need to be accompanied.

The first matter we need to face about sin is, as we saw in the lecture on conscience, we sin not out of weakness but out of strength. This overriding insight is key for any theology of sin. It is for this reason that for years I have defined sin as the failure to bother to love. In a vulnerability ethics in which charity so effectively perfects our vulnerable tendency to recognize and respond to the other, sin is that failure to bother to recognize and respond, the same failure that we see in Matthew 25 or in Dives and Lazarus (Lk 16:19–31).[61] That failure to bother is all the more a sign of the dynamism of our call to follow Christ. We must be vigilant of all those to whom we are called to vulnerably recognize and respond. Moreover, this call to accountability is healthy. Nearly fifty years ago, in 1973 in *What Became of Sin?*, the psychiatrist Karl Menninger summoned readers to recognize that the language of sin within the context of moral accountability and responsibility was a true guide to healthy self-understanding.[62]

So much of our manualist theology of sin, without a theology of conscience, made sin seem inevitable and our own selves look weak, living in a world without virtue and grace. In that context we confessed sins that we could not have avoided, pleading that other conditions made us do what we did. In this context, confessors infantilized many of the laity, thinking of their consciences as pathologically weak. Learning to confess our sins in the light of Christ, we realize in grace that the chance of acting otherwise is usually there and that the excuses we proffer are just, well, excuses. The true confession of sin that Franz Böckle and Lottin wrote about makes us realize that the trajectory of our personal and social history can be otherwise.

Moreover, in the illumination of our sinfulness, we see just how sinful we are. We might do well to remember contemporary figures like Dorothy Day and Pope Francis, who remind us of their own sinfulness.[63] That insight brings with it a redemptive humility, a humility not burdened with self-deprecation but rather with an unabashed self-understanding of what grace and freedom are.[64] William Cavanaugh reminds us that the only reason why believers can be witnesses to the world is that "they have been enabled to name sin truthfully through the revelation of the living God."[65]

Some argue that sin is not only failure but sometimes an actual desire to do harm.[66] But these sins of "malice," as they are called (*ST* I.II.78), ought to be seen as subsequent to the antecedent failure to respond to the call to love. Sinful hearts become hardened and, on occasion, turn to malice.

In all this we need to remember from Gilleman, from Thomas, from Paul, and from Jesus that the first movement is from God, who through Christ invites us to walk with him along the way by his grace. Christ calls us forth. Therein, goodness is our first response; badness is simply a failure to respond. As Aquinas noted, "To stand in the way of God is to withdraw." Sin or badness is the failure to respond to the Lord who calls us to move forward.

Sin is not fundamentally choosing the wrong or even the failure to choose the right, but the failure to be bothered in the first place. In *The Spiritual Exercises*, Saint Ignatius made this clear. In the colloquy with Jesus on the cross, the exercitant is asked to consider three questions: "What have I done for Christ?", "What am I doing for Christ?", and "What ought I to do for Christ?" These questions are not posing what right things ought one to do versus what wrong actions ought one to avoid. Rather, the questions concern whether one is trying to do anything at all for Christ. The underlying question is, whether I bother myself about Christ or not.[67] Sin is the failure to bother, in the first place. It is the failure of Dives and the goats.

We could tarry with sin longer, but let us attend to three concluding issues: naming specific sins, collectively acknowledging guilt and confessing sinfulness, and culpable ignorance.

Regarding specificity, Darlene Fozard Weaver wonders how we can "take sin seriously enough without attending to sins."[68] She reminds us that "attention to sins and their expression in moral acts is essential if we are to understand and respond to the full reality of sin in a way that befits the person as subject and agent."[69] I think she is completely right. We might, however, ask how we name, what we name, and where we name these specific sins. Here I think that as anyone who has worked with an anamchara knows, our true sinfulness resists identification. For this reason and for our own moral laziness, we fail to name those sins of ours that most affect ourselves and others; such is the power of sin to obscure.

I think we catch our real sinfulness out of the corner of our eye. As we follow Christ, we capture glimpses of those inclinations within ourselves, deeply embedded, resisting discovery that harm us personally and collectively by their amiably deceptive familiarity when in fact they are nothing but longstanding unnatural resistances to the gift of grace.

The shame of the present era is that we have taken a long pause to confessing sin. We need to confess sin again but not as an end in itself, not as if by doing that alone we will be free of sin and therefore damnation. We have already been saved and called. We are already on the pathway of discipleship. But we have gone from more than three centuries of defining ourselves by sin to the opposite end of the spectrum, wherein a theology of cheap grace is patently too evident.

We need to let consciences indict. We need to get out of our seats and ask the usher to get out of our way. But we cannot do that directly. For we only see sin indirectly. We need to get out of the reach of the usher to see all that we have been kept from seeing. We need to learn to see what we need to find. Only when we dare to pursue the good itself, only when we develop the virtues one after another, only when we set our mind to run Paul's race with a willingness to receive the gift of grace, will we discover the games we play that keep us from recognizing what we need to see. We need to not go backward to a world of sin manuals, but we need to go forward in humility and charity to be vigilant about learning how best to respond to the call of Christ. As we pursue the virtues as ways of realizing our vulnerable tendencies for the good, we will begin to see, as Block and Vasko want us to see, the ways we excuse ourselves from bothering to focus on the other. Its only in the dynamism of grace that we encounter the seductive slothfulness of sin. It is why it is so easy to sit in our seats and watch the show.

Second, hopefully we will find ways of confessing anew what we find personally and collectively on the way. We saw the brothers of Joseph collectively confess. It is not as rare a phenomenon as we think, though in the United States it is. Still, we confess collectively every time we gather for the liturgy; following Thurman, Bonhoeffer, and others, churches have begun to acknowledge their guilt in being racist; dioceses and religious orders have confessed their guilt over their handling of sex abuse; and, assuredly, local communities throughout the United States are asking how they are responsible for the mass killings that we witness with ever greater frequency. Collective confessions of guilt may *seem* new, but I think we need, as in the issue of specificity, more attempts and reports on the ever-expanding collective acknowledgment of sins.

Finally on culpable ignorance let us turn, for a moment, to Thomas. He dedicates two articles to the issue. First, Thomas asks, do we sin when we do not obey what conscience presents? He answers in *ST* I.II.19.5: "absolutely speaking, every will at variance with reason, whether right or erring, is always evil." That is, we sin always, without exception, whenever we fail to heed what our consciences direct us to do.

But how do we assess if one follows one's conscience and later one realizes that their conscience was mistaken. Are we responsible for that error? Thus, Thomas asks in the next article (*ST* I.II.19.6) *"whether an erring conscience excuses?"* Here, he makes a distinction between whether the ignorance that caused the error was directly or indirectly voluntary. Directly voluntary is the deliberate refusal to know; indirectly voluntary, he explains, "is due to negligence, by reason of a man not wishing to know what he ought to know."[70] Neither excuses us. But the latter one concerns that matter of not bothering to know, dare we say, not bothering to recognize what we need to recognize.[71] Of course, we recognize what the goats, the rich man, the priest and the Levite needed to recognize but did not. Still if they are guilty for not knowing what they should have known, so are we when we fail to recognize. But how then do we recognize our culpable ignorance?

Thomas does not say much more on this. Curiously the most inquisitive and investigative theologian in history does not help us figure out not only what we need to know but how we suspect that we do not know what we need to know. That was after all the reason why Niebuhr, Wilkerson, and even Menninger wrote reminding us about the forces that help lull us into a culpable ignorance that calms us when we are prompted to be vigilant and insists on teaching us that we cannot but act otherwise. In short, indirect voluntary ignorance is, I think, the price we pay to keep our own cheap grace. Indirect voluntary ignorance is what lets us follow the usher to our seats.

How then can we learn to be vigilant about our propensity to cooperate with indirect voluntary ignorance? How do we, in a word, bother to recognize what we have not yet recognized? I think the answer to that is in our next lecture, on the virtues. For only by actually pursuing the good will we ever know what we need to know and therein we will find how much, in fact, we did not believe could ever be known. Only by going forward can we see how much is at stake.

Thank you.

NOTES

1. With all the different data emerging these days, I found this the most helpful: BBC, "America's Gun Culture."
2. Bonhoeffer, *Papers from Prison*; Hooton, *Bonhoeffer's Religionless Christianity*; Pugh, *Religionless Christianity*.
3. Robinson, "Confessing Race," 121–39.
4. Robinson, 121.
5. Robinson. See Bonhoeffer, "Protestantism," 568–92.
6. Robinson, "Confessing Race," 126. Robinson notes (on 136) that James Cone argues, "White liberal preference for a raceless Christ serves only to make official and orthodox the centuries-old portrayal of Christ as white." From Cone, *Black Theology and Black Power*, 68.
7. Bonhoeffer, "Protestantism," 586–87. Please note so as to capture how Bonhoeffer was affected by his Harlem experience, I have retained his use of the term "Negro," which was common at the time.
8. Robinson, "Confessing Race," 126.
9. Bonhoeffer, "Protestantism," 587.
10. Bonhoeffer, "Protestantism," 587.
11. Bonhoeffer, "Protestantism," 591.
12. Bonhoeffer, "Protestantism," 588.
13. Bonhoeffer, "Protestantism," 588.
14. Robinson, "Confessing Race," 129.
15. Robinson, 135. For Bonhoeffer's recognition of the truth of Christianity in the black churches, see Williams, *Bonhoeffer's Black Jesus*. See also Mawson and Ziegler, *The Oxford Handbook*.
16. See here Grimes, *Christ Divided*.
17. Clingan, *Against Cheap Grace in a World Come of Age*.
18. Bonhoeffer, *The Cost*, 301.
19. Bonhoeffer, *The Cost*, 44–45.
20. Häring, *My Witness*, 19.
21. Häring, *Teologia morale verso il terzo millennio*, class notes, the last course Häring offered.
22. Häring, *Das Gesetz*.
23. Häring, *The Law*.
24. Häring, *The Law*, 3.
25. Häring, *The Law*, 61.
26. Keenan, *A History*. See also Keenan, "Virtue, Grace and the Early Revisionists," 365–80; *A History of Catholic Moral Theology in the Twentieth Century*. On the other hand, to predict how things might unfold, one can see students' tributes to their professor; for an

excellent example, see the recent festschrift to Lisa Sowle Cahill: Choi, Moses, and Vicini, *On Lisa Sowle Cahill's Contributions to Christian Ethics*.
27. See Iozzio, *Self-Determination and the Moral Act*.
28. Lottin, *Psychologie et morale*.
29. Lottin, *Principes de morale*.
30. Lottin, *Morale fondamentale*, vi.
31. Lottin, *Morale fondamentale*, 23–25. He entitles this section "Causes de l'infériorité actuelle de la théologie morale."
32. Lottin, *Morale fondamentale*, 331.
33. Lottin, *Au cœur de la morale chrétienne*, 6.
34. Lottin, *Morale fondamentale*, 13: "Le dogmatique, en un mot, nous présente la parte de Dieu dans l'œuvre de notre sanctification, la morale organiste la parte de l'homme."
35. Lottin, *Morale fondamentale*, 297–339.
36. Lottin, *Morale fondamentale*, 363–69, 379–81, 448–52.
37. Lottin, *Morale fondamentale*, 54–56.
38. Gilleman, *Le rôle de la charité*.
39. In the editor's note, Carpentier modestly wrote that due to an appointment, Gilleman was "unable to do himself the considerable work of revision, completion and even recomposition that he judged necessary for the publication of his work." Carpentier added, "I performed this work of revision in full agreement with him—agreement made easy by friendship and a profound kinship of thought." See Gilleman, *Primacy*, v.
40. Gilleman, *Primacy*, 82.
41. See Harrington and Keenan, *Jesus and Virtue Ethics*, footnote 4, for where Gilleman talks about this.
42. Slater, *A Manual of Moral Theology*. On the manuals, besides Keenan, *A History of Catholic Moral Theology*, see Mahoney, *The Making*.
43. Slater, *A Manual of Moral Theology*, 6.
44. Slater, 5–6.
45. Slater, 5–6.
46. Gilleman, *Primacy*.
47. The secondary literature on inclination in Thomas is remarkable. Three classic instances include Bourke, "Is Thomas Aquinas?" 52–66; Gallagher, "Desire for Beatitude," 1–47; Jean-Pierre Torrell, "Nature et grâce," 167–202.
48. Gilleman, *Primacy*, xxxiv.
49. Gilleman, *Primacy*, 34.
50. Gilleman, *Primacy*, 49.
51. Gilleman, *Primacy*, xxxvi.
52. Gilleman, *Primacy*, 132.
53. Gilleman, *Primacy*, 135.
54. Gilleman, *Primacy*, 156.
55. Cf. Gilleman, *Primacy*, 180–82.
56. Connolly, *The Irish Penitentials and Their Significance*, 14.
57. Connolly, 14.
58. Connolly, 15, 16.
59. Connolly, 178.
60. Connolly, 181.
61. Keenan, "Sin," 45–67.

62. Menninger, *What Became of Sin?*
63. Stephen Bullivant, "'I Am a Sinner': The Deep Humility of Pope Francis," *America*, September 25, 2013, www.americamagazine.org/faith/2013/09/25/i-am-sinner-deep-humility-pope-francis.
64. See Paulinus Odozor on Bernhard Häring and Karl Rahner on sin in his *Moral Theology in an Age of Renewal*, 94–98.
65. Cavanaugh, "Pilgrim People," 88–105, at 95.
66. Langan, "Sins of Malice," 19–198.
67. Azpitarte, "Ignatius' Meditations on Sin," 97–113.
68. Weaver, *Acting Person*, 45.
69. Weaver, *Acting Person*, 59. See also Weaver, "Intimacy with God and Self-Relation in the World," 143–63; Weaver, "Taking Sin Seriously," 45–74.
70. Keenan, "Can a Wrong Action Be Good?" 205–19.
71. McKenna, "The Possibility of Social Sin," 125–140; see also his dissertation from Fordham University: "Evil and the Possibility of Social Sin: A Theological Anthropodicy."

7

THE VIRTUES

In these lectures I am developing a more biblically based, grace-filled theological ethics within a hermeneutics of vulnerability and recognition. I do this mindful that not only are we in the image of God but that our destiny is God. Toward that end, I posit the Imago Dei as primarily and necessarily Trinitarian, since we really cannot follow Jesus unless we appreciate his relation to the Father and to the Spirit. I am not interested, therefore, in a discipleship ethics that disconnects Jesus from the divine relations that he has revealed to us. Indeed, we human beings are very much a collective of persons as the Trinity is. In fact, the very notion of person as used to talk of the Father, Son, and Holy Spirit is hardly an emphasis on autonomy but on relationality. I am not a modalist. But the mystery of the Trinity affirms clearly that there is one God. Simply put, the mystery of Trinity leads us immediately to understand that to be a person of the Trinity is to be very much connected to the other two persons.

I begin, therefore, this lecture on the virtues by asking, How vulnerable is the Trinity? By considering the matter of the image of God, I want to critically examine the vulnerability of God by arguing that we are vulnerable because God is vulnerable. The vulnerability of Jesus Christ that we saw earlier prompts us to recognize that vulnerability as belonging to the nature of the Triune God. Toward that end I shall examine first the Son, then the Spirit, and, finally, the Father.

Then, in the second part of this lecture, in light of the constitutive vulnerable relationality of the Trinity, I will first explain why we theological ethicists write in the key of virtue today, and then I will propose a set of virtues for us as made in the image of God's relationality.

ASKING IF THE TRINITY IS VULNERABLE

At the beginning of my claims, let me first assert the incomprehensibility of God, an insight that nearly forty years ago Elizabeth Johnson emphasized rather brilliantly. God's incomprehensibility, she wrote, is "total." She added that "if we claim to comprehend God, then what we have comprehended is simply not God."[1]

In our attempt through analogy to talk about God and to acknowledge the tradition that we are made in God's image, I want to ask can we imagine God as vulnerable since we are arguing here not only that we are ontologically vulnerable but in striving to realize our end, we believe our destiny is to be vulnerable? Is our vulnerability rooted in our God as vulnerable? Let me reiterate that from the first two lectures: I am understanding vulnerable as not meaning having been wounded but rather the capacity for responsiveness even to the point of being wounded. That is, the question of vulnerability and God's vulnerability does not necessarily assume that God suffers or has suffered.

Here I want to acknowledge that we do well as Christians to see the model of vulnerability as *not primarily* in our humanity but rather in the revelation of Jesus Christ. As the alpha and omega, it is his vulnerability upon which we are modeled. Thus, here I want to ask, by extension, if you will, can we talk of the members of the Trinity as vulnerable?

I am not the first to pursue this inquiry. As we saw in the second lecture, Enda McDonagh and others suggested that our vulnerability is based on the vulnerability of God, and therefore our understanding of ourselves very much depends on our understanding of God. If God is vulnerable, then we are by nature and destiny to be vulnerable.

Thus, when many today think of the image upon which the human is made, they think of the face of Adam in the Creation on the Sistine Chapel ceiling, which has the same face as Christ at the Last Judgment. That is, the image out of which the human is made is singularly Jesus Christ. But we should think on Genesis 1:26: "Then God said, 'Let us make humankind in our image, according to our likeness.'" We do well to remember that the dominant image of God upon which the human is made has, until recently, been the Trinity.[2] Thomas Aquinas, for instance, in question 93, article 5 of the Pars Prima of the *Summa Theologiae*, asks whether we are made in the image of God as Trinity. In answering the question positively, he also notes in agreement that Augustine rejects the idea that the human being is made in the "image of the Son only."³

Though Thomas describes how the human being is in the image of the Triune God using the procession of memory, understanding, and love, my interests in the language of image are much more modest. I am only positing that if we are in the image of God, then we need to be relational. If so, we could never have been in the divine plan a singular stand-alone figure, if the Triune God meant to make us in God's image.

Of course, others have asked these types of questions. Interestingly, both Miroslav Volf and Leonardo Boff have looked at the image of God as Trinity and found there remarkable ways to imagine the blueprint for the church as a community of grace for Volf and as a perfect community for Boff.⁴ I want to ask how the Triune God affects our understanding of ourselves collectively and personally and how it affects our naming of the appropriate virtues for right humanity.

If God is relational, then our virtues must perfect or realize that relationality. Therefore, I want to look at the virtues not as solely for me or solely for a person but rather for us in our relationality, that is, with the ontological precedence of vulnerability that makes us open to responsiveness and connectedness before even discussing our self-understanding as personal and social. It is for this reason that I want to ask here, Is the God of the Trinity vulnerable?

But I wonder how comfortable are we with a vulnerable God? Certainly, Christ crucified reveals very much the vulnerability of God. Can we say the same for the rest of the Trinity or even for the Trinity itself? Let us look at the vulnerability of first the Son, then the Spirit, and then the Father.

HOW VULNERABLE ARE THE PERSONS OF THE TRINITY?

I find three considerations helpful for exploring the vulnerability of the Son: first, Jesus as the *autobasileia*, that is, the Kingdom itself; then Jesus in the Throne of Grace and in the Pietà; and finally, Jesus as our "wisest and dearest friend" in Thomas Aquinas.

I first came upon the insight of Origen that Jesus Christ is the autobasileia, the Kingdom of God itself, in the writings of Stanley Hauerwas.⁵ I found the identification compelling, since all the expectations that we have of the Kingdom are embodied in Jesus Christ. As we saw in the lecture on discipleship, it is not primarily the teachings of Jesus Christ that convict us to follow him but Jesus himself. How then could we separate, asked Origen, the Kingdom of God from Jesus?[6] Indeed, affirming Jesus as the autobasileia shares analogous heuristic interests with the claim that the church is the Body of Christ. If the Kingdom of God is not the life in Christ revealed, then what else could it be?

Through this concept, Hauerwas develops his ecclesiology, which is the core of his overall theological interests. He wants his readers to embrace the Kingdom as they would Christ, to be as faithful and hospitable to its members as Jesus is to us.[7] Another theologian, Terrence Tilley, in *The Disciples' Jesus: Christology as a Reconciling Practice* expanded the notion of the autobasileia toward the reconciling practices of Jesus as needing to be embodied by the church.[8] Here again, Jesus's vulnerable responsiveness is modeled for the church: Tilley looks at whether the church is vulnerably reconciling, for instance, in upholding doctrinal teaching, leading him to ask whether the way the church teaches promotes the reconciliation of Jesus.

These are good first steps, but I want to go further and insist that Jesus, from his birth in Bethlehem to his resurrection in Jerusalem, is the quintessential incarnation of vulnerability. If Jesus is the incarnation of vulnerability, then can we not ask whether the Kingdom is as well, and whether the church appreciates that that is what it is called to be? I might add that whenever Pope Francis refers to the church as a field hospital, he is very much highlighting the capaciously responsive vulnerability of the Body of Christ.

Let me add that I am not talking of solely the historical Jesus. I am mindful of images of the Trinity, from the Andrei Rublev icon from the fourteenth century to the Ignatian Contemplation at the start of the Second Week of the Exercises, where we are invited to contemplate the Trinity considering the need to save humanity, a very vulnerable Trinitarian "moment."[9] In fact, we even hear the Trinitarian vulnerability to our experience in that contemplation as Ignatius invites us to hear the Trinity say, "Let us work the redemption of the whole human race; let us respond to the groaning of all creation." Indeed, the whole contemplation is precisely to enter into consideration, I think, of the Trinity's vulnerable responsiveness to humanity.

Tangibly it is in art that the vulnerability of Jesus is most often caught and in particular in the Crucifixion or the Pietà.[10] One motif is the famous Throne of Grace, taken from Hebrews 4:15–16,[11] which depicts the Father and the Spirit presenting the vulnerable body of Christ Crucified on the cross. I might add that the motif of Jesus's resurrection wherein Christ in glory is seen embodied with the wounds of his crucifixion captures further that vulnerability in glory, a vulnerability that like Piero della Francesco's Risen Christ continues to bleed. I will return to the Throne of Grace shortly.

Finally, Jesus's vulnerability as capaciously responsive shines through in Aquinas's definition of Christ as "our wisest and dearest friend "*Sed Christus maxime est sapiens et amicus*'" (ST I–II.108.4.sc). Thomas Ryan in his splendid essay "Jesus—'Our Wisest and Dearest Friend': Aquinas and Moral Transformation" explains that "for Aquinas, friendship is the best model to express our relationship with God."[12] Ryan's argument resonates with what we already saw from Gilleman, that Thomas repeatedly describes charity as union, a union that captures the intimacy with which God enters us to be closer to us than we are to ourselves. Not surprisingly, the vulnerability of friendship emerges as the proper way of describing our relationship with him. Indeed, "friend" is precisely how Jesus calls his disciples and because he considers them his friends, he explains: "Everything I have learned from my Father, I made known to you" (Jn 15:15). Let us note again that in that revelation of friendship, Jesus insists on bringing the Father into it.

Additionally, when Aquinas explains Jesus's Passion he writes: "He suffered both out of love of the Father, according to John 14:31: *That the world may know that I love the Father, and as the Father hath given Me commandment, so do I: arise, let us go hence*—namely, to the place of His Passion: and out of love of His neighbor, according to Galatians 2:20: *He loved me, and delivered Himself up for me*" (ST.III.47.2.ad1). In the Passion Jesus expresses his vulnerable love for us and for the Father. He is our wisest and dearest friend.

Just as there are multiple ways for considering the vulnerability of the Trinity in the Second Person of the Trinity, I think there are multiple expressions for the Third Person. Indeed, if vulnerability is measured by responsiveness, then the Spirit who "intercedes with sighs too deep for words" seems very much at home in our own very limited vulnerability (Rom 8:26).

Moreover, if charity perfects our own vulnerability, it is the Spirit precisely who prompts us to recognize others in light of that vulnerability. In his new book, *The Holy Spirit and Moral Action in Thomas Aquinas*, Jack Mahoney notes that the idea of the Holy Spirit "prompting" (*instinctus Spiritus Sancti*) was a phrase often used by Thomas.[13] Prompting is not simply being led or guided, it is an internal awakening, a counsel to take heed, to act, to respond, that is, I dare suggest, to recognize.

Remembering that recognition is the first act that causes us to cross the threshold of moral responsiveness, we can appreciate that Mahoney notes how Thomas asserts that "in every action of the spiritual person, it is the initiative of the Holy Spirit which is the source and the principle of the action and that God's children are truly acted upon" though in such a way that "they themselves act."[14] Noting the principle which Thomas regularly observes that "no habit proceeds to act spontaneously; it needs to be aroused by some agent,"

I think we can see that the pivotal act of recognition is prompted in us by the counsel of the Spirit opening our eyes to the other.[15] The Spirit helps us to recognize again and again. The vulnerable Spirit is our prompting to recognize the other. Our vulnerability is rooted in the Trinity's, and here precisely in the work of the Spirit. Indeed, the Pentecost is the prompting of the Spirit to recognize and witness Jesus as risen Lord.

In his *Commentary on Romans*, Thomas also writes that "the Holy Spirit does not just teach us what ought to be done by enlightening our mind on what we should do; he also inclines our desires to act rightly."[16] That original vulnerable inclination, that *synderesis*, that tendency, when prompted by the Spirit, is the act of recognition. The vulnerability of the Spirit helps us realize our own vulnerability.

Let us turn now to God the Father. The Milanese priest Federico Cinocca asks in his dissertation, entitled "We Believe in God, the Father Almighty: Liturgy, Ethics, Dominance, and Vulnerability," whether we could confess that we believe in God the Vulnerable Father. His "thesis is that a patriarchal language and iconography depicting God as primarily an omnipotent monarch, eclipses other biblical images and inhibits our ability to speak of God as vulnerable."[17]

Indeed, it is precisely as a monarch that God the Father often appears in the various expressions of the icon known as the Throne of Grace. In the *Roman Missal* used in the United States, for instance, on the page opposite the second Eucharistic prayer, and therein arguably the most used page of the entire missal, there is the picture of the Throne of Grace, where the Father lifts up for all to see the sacrificial offering of his son crucified. While the Spirit hovers between the faces and, more specifically, the mouths of the Father and Son, the Father in that particular icon wears a papal tiara. As Sara Jane Pearman explains in *The Iconographic Development of the Cruciform in the Throne of Grace from the Twelfth-Century to the Sixteenth-Century*, it is the role of the Father in the Throne of Grace motif that continues to undergo change.[18] In its classic form the Father is enthroned, holding up the cross on which the body of the Son hangs, while the Spirit hovers between both. A constant image throughout its history is that the Father's holding up of the cross of his Son highlights all three as involved in the sacrifice of the death of the son wherein we locate the Throne of Grace.

Among the most significant changes is the depiction of the Father. When the Throne was first depicted in the twelfth century, the Father was represented as much younger, looking almost like Christ as in the *Maejestas Domini*. But later the Father takes on the appearance of the Ancient of Days, the now more familiar bearded Father.[19] Adding the triple-tiered tiara to the Father's head is an early fourteenth-century creation of the Avignon popes. At the same time the Father's clothes become papal as well, with copes replacing robes. By 1450, and first in German lands, the tiara becomes replaced by a secular crown, clearly an attempt to distance the Father from papal extravagances.[20] Yet a variable throughout the depictions is the Father's face. In some, like the one in the missal, his face is without expression; in others, the Father visibly grieves. Noticeably earlier depictions of the Father in the throne of grace show his face as grievous. Often, with the tiara and robes, the face loses its visible connection to the death of the Son. Certainly, among theologians today, Jurgen Moltmann, who has written on the suffering of the God, would concur with this earlier depiction.[21]

I find this depiction of grief to be very rich and provocative. It needs to be noted, first, that whether the Father suffers or not does not necessarily depend on Sabellianism, a heresy that does not respect the distinctive personhoods of the Trinity but instead endorses each as a modality of one person. Such insistence of a necessary connection between the suffering of God and modalism only came from critics who used the term "Patripassianism," a pejorative word used by Tertullian deriding Praxeas that basically means not that the Father suffered when the Son died on the cross but that the Father, through modalism, himself died on the cross.[22] I am not endorsing such heresy. We need, however, to recognize that there is no necessary connection between acknowledging the "grief" of the Father and the pejorative game.

While recognizing the distinctiveness of each person, does not John's Gospel suggest time and again that if the Son is vulnerable then the Father would be as well? Would not the one who submitted his vulnerable offering be vulnerably received by the Father? I am not looking to withdraw from the mystery of the Trinity but to enter it.

Here Elizabeth Johnson in another work helpfully suggests that the Father does suffer but in a divine way, and the divinity is not in any way diminished by suffering.[23]

Still, I am not even equating vulnerability with suffering. I am only asking whether we can acknowledge that the Father is capaciously responsive to Jesus's death.

Clearly, I am not interested in compromising the aseity of God, who is sufficient and has no need, but we are compelled by the Scriptures to look more favorably on those depictions of the Father in the Throne of Grace, or in analogous depictions of the Trinity in the Pietà, wherein the Father (not those of Mary, the Mother of Jesus) holds up the collapsed and lifeless body of His Son, or in the Mourning Trinity motif, where the Father conveys himself not as dominant but as a vulnerable witness to the Son, whose body he holds. Those depictions may be captured by a sadness in his face, the openness of hands, the affectionate gesture of his face drawing near to the face of the Son, or by his shoulders being arched to support the heavy weight of his Son's body. Indeed, from Robert Campin's *Mourning Trinity* (1433) to El Greco's *Holy Trinity* (1577) and Paolo Veronese's *The Trinity* (1582), we see such signs of vulnerability in the Father.

I think these gestures in these works of art attempt to capture the vulnerable offering and the vulnerable reception. And I add that the impassible face of God together with the tiara and cope are in fact more theologically problematic than some other scholars suggest. In fact, as I have argued elsewhere, images and practices of dominance that derive from our hierarchy need very much to be replaced by ones of vulnerability, not only because they corrupt our episcopacies and our church but also our ability to receive the revelation of God.[24] In short, we need to draw near to these attempts to convey the Throne of Grace to see how vulnerability, as a capacious responsiveness, is seen not only in the Son and the Spirit but is also captured in the Father in whose Trinitarian image we are made. In the interest of a vulnerability ethics that captures both the source of our morality and the end of it, I think we would do we well to investigate further the vulnerability of the Trinity.[25]

INTRODUCING VIRTUE ETHICS

Renewed interests in virtue ethics arose in the late 1970s and early 1980s out of a dissatisfaction with the way of doing ethics, which focused primarily on policies regarding major controversial actions or quandaries, as they were called, think here abortion, gay marriage, gene therapy, et cetera.[26] Virtue ethicists have more fundamental concerns. We believe that the real discussion of ethics ought to be not what actions are morally permissible but rather who ought we to become in light of a moral agenda that we as agents of moral courses of action set.

Indeed, virtue ethics tries to develop further the basic theological anthropology that it invokes.[27] In the *Nicomachean Ethics*, Aristotle gives us eleven different virtues that are necessary for citizens to engage. Friendship, magnanimity, and practical wisdom are some of these. In the "Second Part" of the *Summa Theologiae*, Thomas Aquinas takes from Plato, Cicero, Ambrose, Gregory, and Augustine the four cardinal virtues: prudence, justice, temperance, and fortitude. Together with these he adds the three theological virtues: faith, hope, and charity. He states that we can acquire the first four through deliberately willed and enjoyed habitual exercises; the latter three are gifts from God. These seven virtues help us to answer the question of whom ought we to become.

We use the virtues, therefore, to set the personal goals that we encourage one another to seek. In fact, the word "cardinal" comes from *cardo*, the word for hinge. If we think of the cardinal virtues as a way to develop the theological anthropology that we posit, they are then the hinges upon which our eventual vision of the full human being depends or hangs. For Thomas, this would mean the seven virtues that give us the vision of the type of people we ought to become.

But the actual pathway for attaining the virtues requires one of these very virtues: prudence. It is hard to underestimate the importance of prudence. Still, for many years prudence has had a terrible reputation. The exhortation "be prudent" meant "watch out," "hesitate," "be extra careful," or "I wouldn't do that if I were you."

For Aristotle and Thomas, prudence is not simply caution. Prudence is rather the virtue of a person whose feet are on the ground and who thinks both practically and realistically. Prudence belongs to the person who not only sets realistic ends but sets out to attain them. The prudent person is precisely the person who knows how to achieve ends, in particular the end to be the person they aim to become.[28] For instance, when I teach prudence, I use as an exemplar the Reverend Martin Luther King Jr.'s *Letter from A Birmingham Jail*, in which he admonishes fellow and sympathetic white pastors to understand why they need to be part of the Civil Rights Movement.[29] On this point, let me commend to you Linda Hogan's significant essay "Moral Leadership: A Challenge and a Celebration," in the year 2021's *Theological Studies*.[30]

Being prudent is no easy task. Pseudo-Dionysius set the bar high when he declared that any action is called "right only when it is so in every way but wrong by a single defect" ("Bonum est ex integra causa, malum ex quocumque defectu").[31] From the medieval period until today, we recognize that it is far easier to get something wrong than to get it right. From parking a car correctly to making a pasta Bolognese, one simple error makes the entire enterprise wrong.

Prudence is even more complicated when we try to figure out the appropriate ways of becoming a more virtuous person or group of persons. One must be attentive to personal and social details, anticipate difficulties, and measure rightly. Moreover, as anyone who has watched children knows, we are not born with prudence. Instead, we acquire it through a very long process.

Prudence is attained by finding the middle point, that is, the "mean" between extremes. As Aristotle and Aquinas remind us repeatedly: "Virtue is the mean" (*NE* II.6; *ST* I.II.64.1–3). The mean is located where there is adequate tension for growth, neither too little nor too much. That mean is not fixed. The mean of virtue is not something set in stone: rather, it is the mean by which only specific persons or communities can grow. This is another reason why prudence is so difficult: no two means are the same.

Finding the mean of the right tension depends on who the persons or communities are. In a matter of speaking, a virtue ought to fit a person the way a glove fits one's hand. There is a certain tailor-made feel to a virtue, which prompts Aquinas to call virtue "one's second nature" (*ST* I.II.58.1).

Virtue ethics is, therefore, a proactive system of ethics. It invites us to see whom we believe we are to become and to design prudential pathways for realizing those dimensions of ourselves. Moreover, it invites us to see that we set the agenda not only of the end but also of the means to accomplish that end.

Virtuous actions, like temperate drinking or courageously facing our fears, are the prudential means for achieving the end of becoming more virtuous persons. Virtue ethics encompasses our entire lives. It sees every moment as the possibility for acquiring or developing a virtue. To underline this point, Thomas held that "every human action is a moral action" (ST I.II.18.9.ad2). He uses, as an example, the simple human act of going to bed (ST I.II.18.9.ad3). A human action for Thomas was simply any action that we knowingly perform; it is a moral action because it affects us in becoming moral persons. Whatever we do helps us become what we do. Thomas invites us to see every moment as a possible opportunity for further growth, for further passage on the way of the Lord.

Thomas saw every human action as an *exercitium*, or "exercise" (*ST* I.II.65.1.ad1). Though some of us go through life never examining the habits we engage, Thomas suggests to us that we ought to examine our ways of acting and ask ourselves: Are these ways making us more just, prudent, temperate, and brave? If they are, they are virtuous exercises.

When we think of exercise, we think of athletics. The person who exercises herself by running eventually becomes a runner just as the one who dances becomes a dancer. From that insight, Thomas like Aristotle before him sees that intended, habitual activity in the sports arena is similar to other arenas of life. If we can develop ourselves physically, we can develop ourselves morally by intended, habitual exercises.

Virtue ethics sees, therefore, the ordinary as the terrain on which the moral life moves. While most ethics makes their considerations about rather controversial material, virtue ethics often engages the commonplace. It is concerned with what we teach our children and how; with the way we relate with friends, families, and neighbors; and with the way we live our lives day by day. Moreover, it is concerned not only with whether a physician maintains professional ethics, for instance, whether she keeps professional secrets or observes informed consent with her patients. It is equally concerned with her private life, with whether she knows how to respect her friends' confidences or her family members' privacy. In a word, before the physician is a physician, she is a person. Virtue ethics is specifically concerned with her life as a person and as a social participant in professions.

Virtue ethics looks at the agency of the personal or collective, seeing the agent as actor with critical self-knowledge looking to find ways for growing in assessment and realization, while setting the agenda of personal and communal ends and means in both the ordinary and the professional life.

The virtues are therefore traditionally teleological (i.e., end-oriented), trained dispositions that collectively aim for the further right realization of human agency, both personal and collective. As such, the virtues need to be continually realized and redefined; their final expression remains outstanding. The mature person is constantly growing in the virtues: the more we grow in virtue, the more we are able to recognize our need for further growth.

This type of growth ought not to be seen as a cycle or a circle but as a spiral moving us forward through history. The nature of virtue is, then, historically dynamic; being in themselves goal-oriented, virtues require being continually considered, understood, acquired, developed, and reformulated.[32]

Underlying the teleological nature of the virtues is then an implicit belief in the progress of ethical thought, both in the individual and in the community. This plays out in the lives of both individual persons and moral communities.

For this reason, ethicists and moralists have several tasks: to critically reflect on the contemporary situation to see whether existing anthropologies and the corresponding constellations of virtues inhibit or liberate members of our global community; to perceive new horizons of human possibility; to express the possible ways that virtue can attain those horizons; and to make politically possible the actual new self-understanding and self-realization. This final task is often overlooked: too often ethicists and moralists think that our work ends with written proposals, but inasmuch as ethical insight *to be ethical* must end in action, similarly the task of the ethicist must end in political action, an insight that Aristotle routinely affirmed.

Finally, virtue ethics works itself out within the natural law. Natural law is the universally accessible study through human reason of a normative anthropology. Articulating that normative anthropology is problematic, however, since we each perceive the natural law from our own context. Christian ethicists perceive the *humanum* with the eyes of faith. Thus, we believe that our perception will be prompted by our faith and that what we see will have a particular urgency because of the narrative of salvation history.[33] This is the reason why we look for agreement on the vulnerability of God as the Imago Dei before we name and profess the virtues for the human. As Klaus Demmer puts it simply: "Genuine theology leads to a fundamental change in our way of thinking."[34] Thus, virtue ethics is the stuff, the articulation, of the normative anthropology of the natural law. In short, in developing my argument I am attempting a theological anthropology of a virtue ethics that helps us grow vulnerably in responsive recognition.

THE VIRTUES FOR THOSE MADE IN THE IMAGE OF THE VULNERABLE TRIUNE GOD

Our hermeneutical investigations into the nature of the human person, the horizon of our anthropological vision, and the corresponding virtues we need to realize that vision depends then where we are in history. Hopefully, we become more able to see what or rather whom we should become as we mature. If we continue to think of history as a spiral, then we see that we are always being challenged to discover a more correct anthropology of human personhood and community.

For where we are in history today, I have been suggesting that Judith Butler helpfully puts forward our point of departure: vulnerability as capacious responsiveness. Axel Honneth advances recognition as integral to that responsiveness because it is so needed for human flourishing, yet as Reinhold Niebuhr and Isabel Wilkerson highlight, ironically, recognition is the one action that collectives most often try to eclipse. Still, theologians like Tillmann, Gilleman, and Lottin have been moving us toward a grace-filled, biblically based discipleship ethics that promotes charity and other virtues and that awakens our vulnerability toward recognition and conscience responsiveness.

How do we get there?

We have already established three critical virtues: charity, humility, and prudence. Charity gives us union with God, self, and neighbor and perfects that vulnerable inclination in ourselves. Humility lets us understand our place in God's world. It is a virtue that constantly informs how we perceive ourselves both in our own histories and in God's world. Both virtues are about our relationality: charity informs our desires for connectedness and humility our understanding of ourselves in that connectedness.

Here now I develop more on humility. When a conscience acknowledges its guilt, it develops its capacity by the epistemic virtue of humility, as Lisa Fullam calls it, a virtue integral to conscience formation.[35] This virtue is animated by what Margaret Farley calls the grace of self-doubt.[36] Together they help us to see that the work of realizing ourselves as disciples of Christ is a formidable lifelong task fraught with misperceptions and yet possible precisely because of that epistemic humility and grace of self-doubt. Certainly, conscience does not us make us infallible; quite the contrary, as *Gaudium et spes* reminds us, we frequently err. But we cannot get to the truth except through conscience. Humility then is constitutive of the Christian quest for moral truth, but humility arises when conscience admits its guilt.

Farley describes "epistemic humility" as "the basic condition for communal as well as individual moral discernment."[37] All the more, we can see how collectives themselves need to acknowledge their mistakes and guilt as well, so as to recognize the need for such a virtue. Farley is concerned that often people become unquestionably self-reliant and self-assured. The grace of self-doubt is not, however, some hyperactive neurotic stance that questions every fundamental conviction we hold. Rather, she writes: "It is a grace for recognizing the contingencies of moral knowledge when we stretch toward the particular and the concrete. It allows us to listen to the experience of others, take seriously reasons that are alternative to our own, rethink our own last word. It assumes a shared search for moral insight, and it promotes (though it does not guarantee) a shared conviction in the end."[38]

A third virtue is prudence, a virtue that never stands alone. Indeed, Aristotle departed from Socrates on the point that prudence is sufficient for self-realization and self-determination. Prudence, Aristotle warned us, depended upon the other virtues and those virtues were dialectally dependent upon prudence (*NE* VI.13). Thomas posited, for instance, that we grow in prudence as we grow in justice, temperance, and fortitude and vice versa. For this reason, the competency of prudence is deeply imbedded in the historic nature of human beings such that human beings can only perceive well the horizon of their possibilities to the extent that they have rightly realized themselves through the virtues.

If we take the cardinal virtues as they are proposed in Thomas Aquinas (*ST* I.II.61), we find that the four cardinal virtues—prudence, justice, temperance, and fortitude—perfect four corresponding powers: the practical reason, the will, the concupiscible, and the irascible, respectively.

These virtues inhere in a particular hierarchy. Temperance and fortitude are predominantly at the service of justice. Prudence determines the right choice of means for each of the virtues, but it especially looks to recommend the just action since justice governs all exterior principles. In a manner of speaking, the anthropological identity of the virtuous person is basically the just one.

We need to note that Thomas *developed* the Patristic agenda on the virtues. For instance, Augustine held that all real virtues were rooted in charity, without which there was no real virtue; Thomas modified Augustine's claim: while acknowledging that justice without charity is not perfect justice, for Thomas justice without charity is nonetheless virtue (*ST* 55.4). This is one of the ways that Thomas used Aristotle to develop his own Augustinian theology.

These classical cardinal virtues and their overarching structure are, however, no longer adequate and in fact endorse an anthropology that inhibits the present theological agenda. As far as I see it, there are now four reasons for replacing them. First, contemporary writers repeatedly express dissatisfaction with the insufficiency of justice. For the most part, they offer hyphenated constructs, the most famous being "love-justice," which attempts to acknowledge that while working for the equality for all persons through justice, we still maintain specific loving relationships that need to be nurtured and sustained.

I find the hyphen distracting, however. Rather than reducing one to the other or eliding the two together, Paul Ricœur places them in a "tension between two distinct and sometimes opposed claims."[39] Ricœur's insight that the virtues are distinct and at times opposing stands in contrast with Aquinas's strategy of the cardinal virtues, where justice is supported by fortitude and temperance and neither is shaped nor opposed by these two auxiliary virtues. Only when another virtue stands as a fully equal heuristic guide can there be a dialectical tension wherein the virtues challenge and define one another and, as Ricœur suggests, "may even be the occasion for the invention of responsible forms of behavior."[40] Therefore, I suggest that Ricœur and others are proposing a virtue other than justice that stands with justice as preeminent.

Second, the modern era insists that moral dilemmas are not based on the simple opposition of good and evil but, more frequently, on the clash of goods. Thus, a constellation of virtues acting as heuristic guides ought not resolve the priority of one virtue over another by a preconceived hierarchal structure that preempts realism. We cannot propose heuristic guides that prefabricate solutions when the concrete data are still forthcoming. Thus, we need virtues that go beyond protecting the single good of justice and that allow us to interpret in each instance which of the primary virtues ought to be in play.

Third, the primary identity of being human is not an individual with powers needing perfection but rather a relational rational being whose modes of relationality need to be rightly realized. On this last point we can begin proposing a set of cardinal virtues that allow us at once to try talking cross-culturally and that cover our main objections.

Fourth, these insights prompt us then to take into account that we need to realize ourselves as, like the Trinity, defined by our relationships, as vulnerably responsive. Thus, we ask not what virtues do I need, but what do we need? How do we together grow as a people, both personally and socially?

I propose that our identity is relational in three ways: generally, specifically, and uniquely. Each of these relational ways of being demands a cardinal virtue: as a relational being in general, we are called to justice; as a relational being specifically, we are called to fidelity; and, as a relational being uniquely, we are called to self-care. These three virtues are cardinal. Unlike Thomas's structure, none is ethically prior to the other; they have equally urgent claims, and they should be pursued as ends in themselves: we are not called to be faithful and self-caring in order to be just, nor are we called to be self-caring and just in order to be faithful. None is auxiliary to the others. They are distinctive virtues with none being a subset or subcategory of the other. They are cardinal. The fourth cardinal virtue is prudence, which determines what constitutes the just, faithful, and self-caring way of life for an individual. The older two virtues, fortitude and temperance, remain auxiliary and exist to support the realization of the other four.[41]

Let me explain how these four virtues work: Our relationality generally is always directed by an ordered appreciation for the common good in which we treat all people as equal. As members of the human race, we are expected to respond to all members in general equally and impartially.

Thomas argued that justice was the virtue by which we give each their due. Kant later argued that we needed to operate by a principle of impartiality so as to guarantee our objectivity in giving each their due. Modern conceptions of justice insist on impartiality and equity,[42] and suggest such devices as blindly reading proposals so as not to be influenced in any way by one's relationship with the other or others.

If justice urges us to treat all people equally and impartially, then fidelity makes distinctively different claims. Fidelity is the virtue that nurtures and sustains the bonds of those special relationships that humans enjoy, whether by blood, marriage, love, citizenship, or sacrament. If justice rests on impartiality and universality, then fidelity rests on partiality and particularity.

Fidelity here is like love in the "just-love" dialectic. It is also like the claim that Carol Gilligan made in her important work *In a Different Voice*. Gilligan criticized Lawrence Kohlberg for arguing that full moral development was found in the person who could reason well singularly about justice as impartial and universal. She countered that the human must aim both for the impartiality of justice *as well as* the development of particular relational bonds.[43]

Neither of these virtues, however, addresses the unique relationship that each person has with oneself. Care for self enjoys a considered role in our tradition, as, for instance, the command to love God and one's neighbor as oneself. In his writings on the order of charity, Thomas Aquinas, among others, developed this love of self at length.[44] I dare say, though I have not asked her this, that Hille Haker's moral autonomy within a vulnerability ethics looks like it would accommodate this virtue and the other three virtues—prudence, justice, and fidelity—so as to maintain the balance she proposes.

Finally, prudence has the task of integrating the three virtues into our relationships, just as it did when it was among the classical list of the cardinal virtues. Thus, prudence is always vigilantly looking to the future, trying not only to realize the claims of justice, fidelity, and self-care in the here and now but also calling us to anticipate occasions when each of these virtues can be more fully acquired. In this way, prudence is clearly a virtue that pursues ends and effectively establishes the moral agenda for the person growing in these virtues. But these ends are not in opposition to nor in insolation of one another. Rather, prudence helps each virtue to shape its end as more inclusive of the other two.

Inasmuch as all persons in every culture are constituted by these three ways of being related, by naming these virtues as cardinal, we have to some very modest extent a device for talking cross-culturally. Of course, what we call prudence, justice, fidelity, and self-care will invariably have other titles and definitions elsewhere. In a manner of speaking, we could identify these three ways of relatedness heuristically so as to diminish any attempts at colonizing virtue.

The cardinal virtues do not purport to offer a picture of the ideal person, nor do they exhaust the entire domain of virtue. Rather than being the last word on virtue, they are among the first, providing the bare essentials for right human living and specific action. As "hinges," the cardinal virtues provide a skeleton of both what human persons should basically be and at what human action should basically aim. Other issues of virtue might hang on the skeletal structures of both rightly integrated dispositions and right moral action, though as we saw with humility and charity they are prior to the cardinal virtues.

Still, we could cautiously discuss how these *thin* and skeletal virtues become *thickened* and enfleshed in different cultures in different ways.[45] For instance, some understanding of justice (the willingness to be impartial and to give to each their due) is presumably present in every culture. Justice in the United States, however, is affected considerably by its esteem of personal autonomy and its respect of personal rights. Autonomy thickens justice inasmuch as we would not give "the due" to any persons without their consent. This understanding of justice differentiates itself from justice in the Philippines, where an emphasis on "smooth interpersonal relationships" governs most social relationships. Similarly, through autonomy, American understandings of fidelity depend on the importance of mutual consent. In the Philippines, its strong emphasis on cohesion, unity, and peace clearly provides the yeast for translating fidelity very differently into ordinary life.[46] In a manner of speaking, I propose these so-called cardinal virtues so as to promote some international discourse that allows for descriptions about normative directives not only for acting but also for becoming. Moreover, I am doing it also for the sake of correcting the claim of the singular priority of justice. I am insisting that in preparing for the moral life, we aim not only for justice for all but fidelity to our particular relations and self-care for ourselves. It is very much an ethical agenda.

Cultures give flesh to the skeletal cardinal virtues. This thickening differentiates, then, one virtue in one culture from a similar one in another. Justice, fidelity, and self-care in a Buddhist culture have somewhat similar and somewhat different meanings than they do in a liberal or Confucian context.[47]

Finally, when it comes to thickening in Catholic culture, we need to turn to the virtue of mercy, which I have argued over the years is the trademark of Catholicism.[48] In Catholic cultures, mercy thickens our understanding of the virtues. Inasmuch as mercy is, as I argue, the willingness to enter into the chaos of another so as to respond to the other, mercy thickens justice by taking into account the chaos of the most marginalized. Mercy does not temper justice as so many believe; rather, mercy prompts us to see that justice applies to all, especially those most frequently without justice, those abandoned to the chaos of the margins. In Catholic cultures, mercy prompts justice both to recognize the neglected, the persecuted, and the oppressed and to bring them into the solidarity of humanity by assisting them in the pursuit of their rights.[49]

Similarly, fidelity in the many relationships we enjoy is enfleshed by mercy. Mercy helps Catholics to see from the start that no relationship is without its chaos and that every relationship requires the merciful practice of reconciliation. In Catholic marriages, for instance, the balm of mercy prompts spouses to enter one another's chaos and to forgive each other not once or twice but seventy times seven times.[50]

Finally, the Catholic practice of self-care urges each person, through mercy, to enter into the deep chaos of one's own distinctively complicated life. By the examination of conscience, we believe that the loving, merciful light of Christ illuminates every dimension of the soul and helps us to see what we need to do in the care of ourselves.

It is on mercy that I close and look forward to the next lecture which will begin with mercy and magnanimity as the key to understanding the communion of saints, the works of mercy, and, finally, the beatitudes.

Thank you.

NOTES

1. Johnson, "The Incomprehensibility of God and the Image of God Male and Female," 441–65.
2. See Bynum, "Did the Twelfth Century Discover the Individual?" 1–17.
3. On Aquinas's development of his interpretation of Augustine's *De Trinitate*, see Merriell, *To the Image of the Trinity*; Nieuwenhove, "In the Image of God," 227–37.
4. Volf, *After our Likeness*; Boff, *Holy Trinity, Perfect Community*.
5. See Lampe, "Some Notes on the Significance of *basileia tou theou, basileia christou*, in the Greek Fathers," 58–73. Additionally, see the thoughtful essay by Brinkmann, "The Humanity of Christ II: Christ and Anxiety," 136–45.
6. Viviano pursues the legacy of Origen's claim in "The Kingdom of God in Albert the Great and Thomas Aquinas," 502–22.
7. Hauerwas, "Jesus: The Story of the Kingdom," 36–52. See the helpful Lorrimar, "Church and Christ in the Work of Stanley Hauerwas," 306–26.
8. Tilley, *The Disciples' Jesus: Christology as a Reconciling Practice*.
9. Puhl, *The Spiritual Exercises of St. Ignatius*, sections 101–34.
10. Babka, "Sensibility to Vulnerability in the Form of Art," 89–119.
11. Hebrews 4:15–16 (New Revised Standard Version Catholic Edition). "For we do not have a high priest who is unable to empathize with our weaknesses, but we have one who has been tempted in every way, just as we are—yet he did not sin. Let us then approach God's throne of grace with confidence, so that we may receive mercy and find grace to help us in our time of need."
12. Ryan, "Jesus—'Our Wisest and Dearest Friend,'" 575–90; see also Long, "The Way of Aquinas," 339–56.
13. Jack Mahoney, *The Holy Spirit and Moral Action in Thomas Aquinas*, 49.
14. Mahoney, 58.
15. Mahoney, 68. See *De Virtutibus* 1. ad 14.
16. Mahoney, *The Holy Spirit and Moral Action in Thomas Aquinas*, 83. See *In Rom* 8, lect. 1.
17. Cinocca, "We Believe in God, the Father Almighty: Liturgy, Ethics, Dominance, and Vulnerability," 2. On a related issue, Autiero has investigated the vulnerability of St. Joseph as an exemplar of fatherhood in "Giuseppe: Un'altra morale è possibile," 182–99.
18. Pearman, "The Iconographic Development of the Cruciform in the Throne of Grace from the Twelfth-Century to the Sixteenth-Century"; see also Babka, "The Trinity in the Gnadenstuhl Motif," 17–37.
19. Pearman, "The Iconographic Development of the Cruciform in the Throne of Grace from the Twelfth-Century to the Sixteenth-Century," 41.
20. Pearman, 45.
21. Chopp, *The Praxis of Suffering*; Feske, "Christ and Suffering in Moltmann's Thought," 85–104.
22. Sarot, "Patripassianism, Theopaschitism and the Suffering of God," 363–75; Sarot, "Patripassianism and the Impassibility of God," 73–81.
23. Johnson, *She Who Is*.
24. Keenan, "Vulnerability and Hierarchicalism," 129–42.
25. See Iozzio, "Radical Dependence and the *Imago Dei*," 234–60.
26. Pincoffs, *Quandary Ethics*.

27. MacIntyre, *After Virtue*; Meilaender, *The Theory and Practice of Virtue*; Kekes, *The Examined Life*; Porter, *The Recovery of Virtue*; Spohn, "The Return of the Virtues," 60–75; Keenan, *Virtues for Ordinary Christians*; Keenan, "Virtue Ethics," 84–94; Kotva, *The Christian Case for Virtue Ethics*.
28. Nelson, *The Priority of Prudence*; Keenan, "The Virtue of Prudence (IIa IIae 47–56)," 259–71.
29. King, *Letter from a Birmingham Jail*.
30. Hogan, "Moral Leadership," 138–54.
31. Pseudo Dionysius, De divinis nominibus, IV, 30 (PG 3, 729).
32. Kopfensteiner, "The Metaphorical Structure of Normativity," 331–46; Patrick, "Narrative and the Social Dynamics of Virtue," 69–80.
33. For other insights on natural law, see Porter, *Natural and Divine Law*; *Nature as Reason*.
34. Demmer, "Die autonome Moral—eine Anfrage an die Denkform," 262.
35. Fullam, *The Virtue of Humility*.
36. Farley, "Ethics, Ecclesiology, and the Grace of Self-Doubt," 55–77.
37. Farley, 69.
38. Farley, 69.
39. Paul Ricœur, "Love and Justice," 196.
40. Ricœur, 197.
41. I began working on this proposal thirty years ago: Keenan, "Proposing Cardinal Virtues," 709–29. Reprinted in *The Historical Development of Fundamental Moral Theology in the United States*, 281–306. See also Keenan, "Virtue and Identity," 69–77; Keenan, "Virtue Ethics and Sexual Ethics," 183–203; Keenan, "Riscoprire la via delle virtù," 119–34. See, as well, Zacharias, "Virtue Ethics as a Framework for Catholic Sexual Education."
42. Ricœur, "Love and Justice," 195.
43. Gilligan, *In a Different Voice*.
44. Pope, "Expressive Individualism and True Self-Love," 384–99; Vacek, *Love, Human and Divine*.
45. Walzer, *Thick and Thin*. See also Nussbaum, "Non-relative Virtues," 32–53.
46. Jocano "Rethinking 'Smooth Interpersonal Relations,'" 282–91.
47. Yearley, *Mencius and Aquinas*; Sing and Keenan, "Bridging Christian Ethics and Confucianism through Virtue Ethics," 74–85; Sing, "Bridging Christian and Confucian Ethics," 49–73.
48. Harrington and Keenan, *Jesus and Virtue Ethics*; Keenan, *Moral Wisdom*; Keenan, *The Works of Mercy*. See also Burggraeve, "Une éthique de miséricorde," 281–96; Burggraeve, "From Responsible to Meaningful Sexuality," 303–16; Spohn, *Go and Do Likewise*.
49. Despite some attempts to argue that rights language is inimical to virtue or even theological language, see Tierney, *The Idea of Natural Rights*.
50. See Pope Francis, *Amoris Laetitia*.

8

THE COMMUNION OF SAINTS, THE WORKS OF MERCY, AND THE BEATITUDES

I want to start this final lecture with two personal stories. First, I have wonderful memories of growing up in Brooklyn, where I went to a Catholic Grammar school in my parish, St. Thomas Aquinas. We had separate boys' and girls' grammar schools, with Sisters of Mercy teaching the girls and Brothers of the Holy Cross teaching the boys. There were two classes for each grade in each school and upwards of seventy or even eighty to a class. That could mean over 300 pupils per grade. Still, we got a great education.

In our almost entirely Catholic neighborhood made up of working-class families living in their own semidetached homes, we children could walk safely to our school.

One day of the year, anybody driving through our neighborhood would get an exceptional treat: All Saints. We each went to school dressed as our namesakes. We knew we belonged early, vicariously, to the communion of saints. Our families not only knew the saints; they knew what they would have worn. I was dressed with white robes, a walking staff, and beard; my brother Bob was dressed in brown robes like a monk, whom my mother somehow knew was bald. I went, I remember to this day, with two of my friends: Peter also in white robes with a dark beard who carried these huge keys (made out of aluminum foil), and George, who kept wielding his sword. Just imagine driving through a neighborhood where several hundred children from three to four feet tall were all in proper iconographic costume walking to school. If you were Catholic, you would have been able to recognize each saint in the group.

We knew our saints, and though we knew them collectively, we also recognized their trademarks that identified them personally; that distinctiveness gave the communion of saints a variegated spectrum that made it spectacular.

The second story is from 1987, and I am now a Jesuit priest finishing my doctorate in Rome and trying to buy a keepsake: a sketching of a sixteenth-century confraternity that built hospitals for those infected with syphilis throughout Europe. The hospitals were called, *Ospedali degli incurabili* (Hospitals for the Incurables). Specifically, I was looking for the one at the Church of St. James on the Via Flaminia just a few hundred meters from the main Roman entry gate at the Piazza del Popolo, where all pilgrims to Rome entered, including those infected with syphilis. I found a major shop on the same street and asked the young owner if she could help me find an etching of the *ospedale*, and she gasped, "Sono nata là" (I was born there!). She told me that it was still standing today, 477 years after its founding, as a major obstetrics hospital. Together we marveled at the spirit that animated building such a hospital in the sixteenth century.

As we begin to enter into a reflection on the communion of saints, the works of mercy, and the Beatitudes, we encounter the fairly relational and traditional insights and practices that very much form our identities. Indeed, this chapter is really about how we are socially directed not by Wilkerson's usher nor Niebuhr's brutal collectives, but rather in an entirely new mode, to recognize those that others keep us from seeing: first the communion of saints; then the naked, the hungry, and the imprisoned; and, finally, the poor in spirit. These three practices prompt a new recognition, transform and perfect our vulnerable selves both collectively and personally. They keep us away from the influence of the egotistical herd and their ushers. Indeed, while they spring out of our faith and are animated by charity, they take us further into the moral life and in so doing teach us hope. Finally, I believe that together they provide us the three stages of growing to be disciples of Christ by providing three particular schools of recognition. Through the fellowship of the saints, we recognize exemplars who train us in their ways of recognizing Christ in the other who is in our midst. Through the works of mercy, we are trained to recognize the other whom our societies have carefully marginalized and removed from the secular, cultural gaze. Through the Beatitudes we learn to develop an interiority that enables us, as Søren Kierkegaard would say, to will one thing, to vulnerably respond to the poor in spirit.[1]

THE COMMUNION OF SAINTS

In *Friends of God and Prophets: A Feminist Theological Reading of the Communion of Saints*, Elizabeth Johnson reports that in the early centuries of the church the communion of saints was a "companionship of friends" who offered "lessons of encouragement" to the People of God. There was an intimacy then among the saints both dead and living, with the former offering counsel to the latter by the wisdom of their own lives. This friendship was made through the Spirit who formed the community thus.[2]

Later, between the third and fifth centuries, the communion of saints developed into a new model "of patron and petitioner," which reflected in many ways the authority and governance of the Roman empire. In time, papal power also developed similarly, hierarchically, and the image of God subsequently reflected a sovereign much like the pope, where God the Father dominated, becoming effectively a stern judge. Here the saints became intermediaries for us, while even their entry into the heavenly court became regulated by a canonization process ultimately determined again by the pope. In this patronage system, while saints moved from friend to intermediary advocate, the Spirit too shifted migrating "from nave to sanctuary."[3]

Johnson retrieves and develops the earlier circle of friends and prophets. She writes that the communion of saints should not be seen "as a static doctrine but as a dynamic symbol of the company of friends of God and prophets, thanks to the life-giving work of the Spirit."[4] By retrieving this earlier model, she directs our gaze to recognize the saints as friends and companions, as vulnerable to us and we to them. They engage us too by their example, offering us lessons like an *anamchara*, if you will.

Moreover, these friends are different from each other; the singular saint is not absorbed by the collective but remains distinctive yet included. Bonhoeffer, for instance, investigated the communion of saints as a sociological collective in which the individual remained as such in his dissertation in 1927.[5] Since Bonhoeffer and Johnson, many more theologians follow in their footsteps.

More recently, my friend Antonio Autiero writes:

> In the past the theological notion "communion of saints" was considered from an ecclesiological perspective, thus indicating the "ecclesia triumphalis" and expressing more of an eschatological sense than a sense of reference to the present; the theological reflexion today considers this notion from a predominantly "soteriological" perspective.
>
> It helps to understand that the salvation that God gives is always a communal gift, and not a gift to the individual. The community of human beings receive the gift of salvation from God, and each person shares in this salvation by standing in solidarity with others.
>
> The theological notion of the communion of saints emphasises this communitarian, solidaristic sense of salvation, although this must not be understood in such a way that the individual person disappears. On the contrary, the theological notion tends to hold the communitarian

sense and the personal-individual commitment to salvation in a right and fruitful tension.

Autiero also sees salvation as a gift rather than as a negotiation based on merit. This leads him to recognize that the gift "is also available to those who may fail in their actions, if they keep themselves open to the desire for salvation and the hope of having a share in it . . . because the community of those who do good extends to and includes even those who fail."

He concludes, "The change of perspective towards the soteriological horizon is full of fruitful implications."[6]

This fellowship is the antithesis of the social forces that Niebuhr and Wilkerson named. The saints, participating in their friendship with God, turned their gaze invariably not to themselves or their kind but to those who were specifically overlooked or excluded. Entering into friendship with the saints led to a practice of recognizing those whom they turned to, that is, those in need of mercy. Moreover, their response was often fairly extravagant.

Years ago, I read but can no longer remember where, how one hagiographer remarked that if you really knew a saint, you needed to appreciate how profligate their love for God and neighbor was. The writer went so far as to say that the true lives of the saints should not be shared with children simply because their actions could terrify a child or worse suggest the child should imitate them! Saints were too dangerous for that! Still, I think the saints are exemplars but extravagant ones.

In her presidential address to the American Historical Association entitled "Wonder," Caroline Walker Bynum captures our stance as she refers to the long-standing traditional practice that in offering the saints as exemplars, the People of God "were urged to wonder at, not imitate, the power and extravagant asceticism of holy men and women."[7] I think this wonder means: be like them, but be original and do not be a copy.

This extravagance is found in the *Summa Theologiae*, where Thomas famously argued that while the end of all the acquired virtues is to attain the mean between extremes, there is no mean to be observed in the theological virtues: "Never can we love God as much as He ought to be loved, nor believe and hope in Him as much as we should. Much less therefore can there be excess in such things. Accordingly, the good of such virtues does not consist in a mean but increases the more we approach to the summit" (I.II.64.4).[8]

I would like to conclude these insights by turning to a recent essay by the theologian, Nicholas Austin, the Master of Campion Hall, my host. He writes on magnanimity, which he describes as "the quality by which we lean on others' friendship and God's help to attain a steep moral good, rising above the minimal requirements of the moral law."[9] Like Thomas and Johnson, Austin approaches both the saintly and the divine through friendship.

Underlining the steep moral good of saintliness, Austin locates magnanimity by comparison and contrast with other virtues and vices. For instance, at the outset, he focuses on Aquinas's suggestion that magnanimity is a surprisingly worthy companion to humility. He writes:

> Aquinas brilliantly places the apparently opposed virtues of magnanimity and humility in mutually interpretive dialectic. These two habits work in contrariwise directions: humility tempers the will for an arduous good; magnanimity fosters it. Yet they meet in the rational mean, since both rest on self-knowledge, whether of weakness or worth. The marriage of this unlikely couple corrects both the self-effacement that masquerades as humility and the presumptuous pride with which magnanimity is easily confused. "Humble magnanimity," therefore, names a dynamic tension between contrasting moral qualities that cannot rightly be conceived without each other.[10]

Later, Austin posits that magnanimity is "the well-ordered hope for excellent moral agency."[11] To make the turn to hope, Austin investigates Thomas Cajetan's sixteenth-century commentary, who develops Thomas's own understanding by asserting that "magnanimity's aim is for moral greatness,"[12] and is primarily located in "the intrinsic and immanent acts of the virtues."[13] Unlike magnificence that is seen by its external acts, magnanimity functions internally, provoking all the virtues to their greatest expression. As Cajetan writes: "Magnanimity has for its formal object and end *the great* in the work of any virtue."[14]

Austin highlights how the virtue prompts us to climb these extravagantly steep ascents: "Christian magnanimity is implicit here as the vocational virtue opposed to the prideful refusal of God's call. The altitude to which God calls a person gives rise to a vertiginous queasiness. The humble awareness of one's own limitations may therefore slide into stubborn resistance to vocation that paradoxically blends pusillanimity with pride. The corrective to such small-heartedness is a magnanimous confidence in God."[15]

This confidence is itself an expression of hope. Austin explains: "Magnanimity participates in theological hope because it hopes in divine help to attain its arduous and great good."[16]

Finally, Austin underlines how cooperative this hope is by returning to the exemplars as collectives, the very theme of this chapter. The saints work with the help of one another, the central point of both Johnson and Autiero as well as Bonhoeffer. I give Austin the last word here: "Far from being a virtue of pride-filled self-sufficiency, magnanimity is a cooperative virtue. The tuning fork for her *animus* is her self-image as someone gifted and helped by God. Magnanimity hopes to do a great work by confidence in the self's bestowed goodness, the friendship of others, and in the first place, the help of God. Aquinas's magnanimity imitates its big sister, theological hope."[17]

THE CORPORAL WORKS OF MERCY

If the communion of saints calls us to recognize their vulnerable responsiveness to God by their extravagant love of neighbor, the works of mercy provide us with a recognition agenda of ways we can respond to those neighbors so long overlooked or hidden.

The agenda of mercy defines the early church. Indeed, mercy is not simply a disposition; it is an active set of practices. In Matthew 25, the saved are those who performed what we later called the corporal works of mercy—feed the hungry, give drink to the thirsty, shelter the homeless, clothe the naked, visit the sick, visit the imprisoned, and bury the dead. While the first six are in Matthew 25, by adding the seventh, bury the dead, the church created an easier pedagogical device that would in turn later generate other lists of seven, like the seven deadly sins, the seven virtues, the seven spiritual works of mercy, and the seven sacraments.

In following Jesus, we find that he set the agenda of mercy by recognizing the needs of those overlooked. The inauguration of Jesus's ministry was marked, in fact, by many healings (Mk 1:32–33; Mt 4:23; Lk 4:40–41). Not surprisingly, then, like Jesus, disciples of Jesus have the same instinct: Mary's visit to Elizabeth is the first expression of Mary's own discipleship: she promptly responds to the Annunciation by attending to her cousin in need. Likewise, after the Pentecost, the disciples' ministry is immediately marked by the physical and spiritual care of those in need.

In the early church, attending to the sick is a fairly common Christian practice. Cyprian, bishop of Carthage, leads his congregation to respond to victims of the plague in 252. Bishop Dionysius provides a narrative of his community's response to the plague in Alexandria in 259: from Eusebius we read: "Most of our brethren, in their surpassing charity and brotherly love did not spare themselves and clinging to one another fearlessly visited the sick and ministered to them. Many, after having nursed and consoled the sick, contracted the illness and cheerfully departed this life. The best of our brethren died in this way, some priests and deacons, and some of the laity" (Eusebius, *Hist. Eccl.* 7.22.9).

Perhaps the most interesting of the works of mercy is the last. While belief in the resurrection is, as Augustine notes, what separates Christians from others, the emperor Julian contended that one of the factors favoring the growth of Christianity was the great care Christians took in burying the dead. Though individuals often performed the task, the church as a community assigned it to the deacons, and, as Tertullian tells us, the expenses were assumed by the community. Lactantius reminds us further that not only did Christians bury the Christian dead, but they buried all of the abandoned: "We will not therefore allow the image and workmanship of God to lie as prey for beasts and birds, but we shall return it to the earth, whence it sprang: although we will fulfill this duty of kinsmen on an unknown man, humaneness will take over and fill the place of kinsmen who are lacking."[18]

The Christian community accompanied the dead to their resting place, and their care for the dead extended not only to burying them but also to making offerings for the repose of their souls. The significance of burying the dead is then rooted in the profound respect that Christians have for the human body. The human body created and redeemed by God is to be raised up by God in glory.

In my book on the *History of Catholic Theological Ethics* I emphasize that from the early Church on, Christians seek in their way to follow Christ by recognizing, responding to, and accompanying those who are discarded in the broader society, and in most instances this activity was done collectively. One instance that is fairly remarkable is the development of the Confraternities in the sixteenth century.

Generally speaking, these associations were formed as a collective response to an urgent need. They were not first formed after which members looked for a charitable practice to engage; rather, they were formed precisely to collectively respond to concrete urgent issues. Still, to fortify both their response and the collective itself, they also gathered in fellowship to pray. This twofold movement, of collective service and communal prayer, repeated itself time and again, putting the agenda of service at the forefront of the life of discipleship. Wedding spiritual devotion to the practice of mercy, they had an enormous influence on the moral formation of Roman Catholics.[19]

Of the hundreds of confraternities dedicated to specific works of mercy, my favorite cared for those with syphilis. Syphilis was a very sixteenth-century illness, deeply connected to commerce in general but in particular to the conquests of Christopher Columbus, who probably imported the virus along with the gold. By 1495 there was an epidemic in Europe.[20] From its inception, syphilis, as contagious, was often associated with foreigners: the first European report of it was in Naples, but because the disease entered Naples at the same time that French soldiers invaded it, syphilis became known as the French disease by the people of Naples. In 1497, the Compagnia del Divino Amore (Confraternity of Divine Love) was founded in Genoa, a port city, by Chancellor of the Republic Ettore Vernazza as a group of laity and clergy committed to working for those suffering from shame: the poor, the prostitute, and the syphilitic. Victims of syphilis, having been abandoned both by their families because of shame and by hospitals because of fear of contagion, found a welcome in the confraternity's Ospedali degli incurabili (Hospitals for the Incurables). In 1499, the confraternity built the first hospital in Genoa. In 1517, Gaetano da Thiene (1480–1547) together with the confraternity built "Hospital of Mercy" in Verona. Shortly thereafter, Gaetano went to Vicenza to reorganize the Hospital of Mercy, there to serve again the person with syphilis. In 1521, the Ospedale degli incurabili was opened in Brescia. In 1522, Gaetano opened a hospital in Venice. In the same year, a confraternity chapter was founded in Padova, and within four years they opened their hospital. In 1572, a hospital opened in Bergamo and in 1584 another in Crema.[21]

Of all the ospedali, the most compelling one is the one built in 1510 by the Confraternity of Divine Love for pilgrims arriving in Rome. One can only imagine the horrendous experience of those pilgrims arriving in Rome with syphilis, fearing rejection, stigma, alienation, and a horrible death precisely as an unworthy foreigner. Instead, the care and hospitality of the Hospital of the Incurables were offered to these people at the pilgrim Church of Saint James on the Via Flaminia, only a few hundred meters from the main entry gate of Rome at the Piazza del Popolo. Moreover, like the hospital in Venice, these institutions were built to last: while I mentioned at the start of this lecture that St. James's ospedale is today a major obstetrics hospital, Venice's enormous ospedale sitting in the Dorsoduro, built in 1522 by Thiene, is today the Accademia di Belle Arti di Venezia.[22]

To locate just how expansive these confraternities were, let us look at one corporal work of mercy, visiting the prisoner. This corporal work has been practiced consistently throughout the life of the church. No less than Christ had been a prisoner. Thus, like Peter, Paul, and many of the Apostles, the imprisoned were perceived as not only people in need but also people of courage and holiness. Early church members visited their imprisoned brothers and sisters, worked to liberate them, and sought their blessing as well. About their liberation, for instance, Clement of Rome (35–99) wrote to Corinth in his Epistle, chapter 55, that many ransomed others by offering themselves in exchange for the one held hostage.[23] In the late twelfth century and into the thirteenth century, charitable institutions were established for the release of prisoners. The Trinitarians (Order of the Most Holy Trinity for the

Redemption of the Captives) founded by Saint John of Matha (1160–213), were singularly dedicated to ransoming prisoners and laboring to alleviate the conditions of those who remained in slavery. Similarly, the Royal, Celestial, and Military Order of Our Lady of Mercy and the Redemption of the Captives was founded by Saint Peter Nolasco (1189–256) for the same task.[24]

Later in the sixteenth century, religious orders were founded, and their members worked along with other ministries for the care and release of prisoners. The Jesuits, for instance, provided a variety of services. The Jesuit historian John O'Malley reminds us first that these prisoners were either debtors or those awaiting trial, sentencing, or execution. In Rome, for example, over half the imprisoned were debtors from the poorer classes; the others, awaiting trial, had not yet had their guilt established. Jesuits took care of the imprisoned by preaching, catechizing, hearing the confessions of the imprisoned, and bringing them food and alms. In Italy and Spain, Jesuits spent a great deal of time raising funds through begging so as to pay off the prisoners' creditors. Elsewhere they begged for money to ransom back prisoners taken by the Turks. Likewise, they preached against slave-taking raids. Sometimes the Jesuits worked to improve the plight of prisons. In Palermo, for instance, a confraternity was founded based on one Jesuit's work to improve the sanitary conditions of prisons. Another confraternity organized by the Jesuits, the Confraternity of the Imprisoned, was founded for laypersons in Rome, and it generated other confraternities in six other cities throughout Italy.[25]

Other confraternities of the laity also dedicated themselves to those in prison. In Rome, the Archconfraternity of Charity was specifically for those in captivity, as was the Confraternity of Pietà and Our Lady of Loreto in Milan. In France, confraternities such as the Work of Prisons in Marseilles and the Confraternity of Mercy in Lyons were solely dedicated to prisoners' needs, while the White Penitents and the Sisters of the Dominican Third Order were singularly dedicated to the needs of women prisoners.[26] Another confraternity, in Naples, was dedicated to prisoners awaiting execution, most of whom were political prisoners. They would visit the prisoners and spend the night with them before the execution, praying with them and helping them to identify with Jesus as a condemned prisoner. The following day, a priest confraternity member dressed in white, hence known as the "Bianchi," would walk to the gallows with each prisoner, walking ahead of him and holding a painted panel of the suffering Christ in front of his face so that the condemned man could keep his gaze fixed on Jesus instead of on the crowds or the executioners.[27] Subsequently, the confraternity attended to the needs of the widows and orphans. Later, in 1775 and 1777, Alphonsus Liguori published a set of instructions, *Advice for Priests Who Minister to Those Condemned to Death*,[28] noting that such men merited the "greatest sympathy" among any about to die, because of "four anxieties": the fear of eternal punishment for their crimes; the dread of the execution itself, cutting short their lives; the public shaming of the execution itself; and the profound regret of leaving family, wives, parents, and children without benefit of support and protection.

These confraternities recognized the prisoners and in turn focused on the need to recognize their plight. Of course, the confraternity helped all the members to first recognize the prisoners and then their plight. From their experiences of the prisons, there grew subsequently numerous critical voices that protested prison conditions and started movements of reform to correct conditions among the imprisoned in Spain, Italy, France, and England.[29]

These sixteenth-century confraternities highlight the imaginative ways that Christian collectives, out of their own experiences of having received mercy, tried to accompany those whose lives were deeply precarious. In all the innovative developments of the sixteenth century, the confraternities were clearly the ones most focused on recognizing and responding humanely to those experiencing overwhelming struggles.

Today, remarkably, people refer to lay leadership as if it were a new phenomenon in the church. Yet, with the earlier guilds, lay associations, and, subsequently, the confraternities we find instead robust and enduring lay leadership across Europe in these centers of mercy where Christians concretely worked out their response to the call to "come, follow me." A variety of historians, having worked on confraternities in their research, have significantly shown how the relations between clergy and laity were complicated and that the confraternities were "as social spaces where laity and clergy met, mediated, and sometimes competed and fought."[30] But, above all, their engagement was prompted by the recognition of others in need and then by the recognition of the causes that prompted their condition.

THE BEATITUDES

In November 2017, I was invited to a conference on homelessness that was hosted by Mark McGreevy, founder of the Institute of Global Homelessness. At the conference of about thirty people, of whom fifteen were Catholic theological ethicists, McGreevy told us about a staffer who was pursuing a PhD in theological ethics on homelessness who could find not one essay written by a Catholic ethicist on homelessness. This was remarkable because ethicists are precisely in the business of recognition, and here we were learning that a population that remains unseen by millions of urban pedestrians remained also unrecognized by ethicists themselves.

In response to the conference, McGreevy and I edited a collection of essays, *Street Homelessness and Catholic Theological Ethic*.[31] In that collection, I published an essay, "Blessed Are the Poor in Spirit: A Response to Homelessness by a Reading of Matthew's Beatitudes."[32] Here I abridge that essay to introduce you concretely to a way of understanding the Beatitudes developmentally through the lens of collectivity.

Let me first offer two introductory comments. As I often noted in the first three lectures, the threshold that takes us into the moral life is crossed when one in recognition responds. Getting to that threshold has been the entire goal of these lectures, and so I conclude with the Beatitudes, a veritable training ground for developing an internal life capable of vulnerable and responsive recognition in mercy.

Second, I am completely indebted here to the work of the late Yiu Sing Lúcás Chan, SJ, and, in particular, his study of the Beatitudes that he developed in *The Ten Commandments and the Beatitudes: Biblical Studies and Ethics for Real Life*.[33]

Chan writes that the attributes in the Beatitudes were key features of the identity of Jesus. They make sense only if we see them as filling out the image of the one we wish to follow. They are the eschatological attributes for those who want to enter the Kingdom of God, for the Kingdom of God is, as we saw in the last lecture, no other than Jesus himself. These attributes for the disciple are the very identifying traits of the master who, like the Good Samaritan, recognizes and responds to those wounded on the road.

Chan highlights the broad moral relevance of the Beatitudes in history. Augustine claimed that the Sermon was the complete, perfect teaching of Christian morality. In *Veritatis splendor*, Pope John Paul II called the Sermon on the Mount "the *magna carta* of Gospel morality,"[34] and added that the Beatitudes are "a sort of *self- portrait of Christ*."[35]

In their eschatological orientation, Matthew's Gospel proposes the Beatitudes as a way of following Jesus Christ, who is preparing us for the Kingdom of God: he is giving us a blueprint, both personally and communally, of the attributes we need to enter the Kingdom that Jesus is bringing in.

Moreover, the Beatitudes have a much greater coherence than is normally acknowledged. Chan helpfully insists that they need to be read dynamically in that each macarism builds one upon another until finally one realizes that one is climbing a ladder of ascent into the Kingdom. From the beginning, they look perfectionistic, but once we begin to take the first few steps, we realize that each step, in a way, empowers the other. The steps, as Chan notes, are internally transformative. Like any notion of personal or communal growth, until we begin the program, we really are not able to see where the program is taking us.[36] And, it is only by heeding Chan's admonition to climb the ladder that we begin to see their internal connectedness and logic.

With this in mind, let us begin the steep ascent as Austin would say.

The First Beatitude, Matthew 5:3

Blessed are the poor in spirit, for theirs is the kingdom of heaven.

Chan tells us that the term "poor" refers not only to those who are poor with few possessions but especially those who are socially and economically needy and dependent, such as those being forced to beg.[37] These poor, whose economic and spiritual poverty has left them in a state of complete alienation, are, in a word, the homeless. They are the poor in spirit, the least recognized people on earth.

Recognizing a virtue for each of the Beatitudes, Chan argues that to be "poor in spirit" is the equivalent of having the virtue of humility, a spiritual emptying out: "Humility means accepting the complete poverty of our human condition."[38] This is what the poor in spirit experience: only in God do they find their needs met. Discarded by all in society, reduced to begging, they have only God as their hope and to God they come supplicant. That stance, that humility, is the foundation of any Christian anthropology.

Yet Chan insists that it is these poor in spirit whom we must gaze upon as we ascend the ladder. They, Chan argues, are the first and ultimate subjects whom we need to keep our eyes on in this. The Beatitudes are effectively, as both Chan and Elizabeth Sweeney Block would say, about our recognition of them.

The Second Beatitude, Matthew 5:4

Blessed are they who mourn, for they shall be comforted.

For the second Beatitude, Chan wants us to understand who are these blessed mourning? He turns to exegetes who write that the grieving in the second Beatitude is in fact directed to the poor in spirit in the first.

Chan is mindful of those other ethicists and preachers who think otherwise and try to claim that the Beatitude is a summons to mourn our losses; sounding like grief counselors, they suggest that if one denies one's own grief, one will never know the comfort and happiness that follow.

But the object of the Beatitude's mourning is not our own losses but those of the poor in spirit. Those in the second Beatitude in our community are mourning the condition of the poor in spirit; and we are called to emulate them in their empathetic solidarity.[39] Clearly, we are not mourning those who elect a poverty of spirit but rather those whose condition is so bereft of any human good that they are poor in spirit.

Chan writes, "The object of mourning is not so much one's own suffering or sins, but rather the concrete human experience of poverty and suffering encountered by community members. Mourning points to an other-oriented moral value."[40] Then emphatically he adds: "Such is the lot of the disciples of Christ—when our brothers and sisters suffer, we cannot help but mourn." He adds, the Beatitude "is about a certain disposition that genuine disciples have with one another, such that if one suffers, the other mourns as well."[41]

There is much to be learned by this practice of a studied mindfulness of another's condition.[42] Chan writes: "In mourning the self tries to identify with the other. Mourning is then the ready subordination of one's own comfort and well-being to the suffering of others." He adds, "In this way, one allows one's private life to be touched by the pain and suffering of the other."[43] Not until I fully grasp the loss of the homeless can I resonate with the condition of my sibling who is homeless. By this mourning, we grow in vulnerability to our neighbor and move to the third Beatitude.

The Third Beatitude, Matthew 5:5

Blessed are the meek, for they shall inherit the earth.

At the third Beatitude, Chan surveys the work of biblical theologians and uncovers how inclusive the term "meek" is. It appears often in the Septuagint as a word for the *anawim*, the poor, the remnant, those completely left behind, that is, effectively the poor in spirit. But meekness is also an attribute of biblical leadership, both of Jesus and others in the community (Mt 11:29; Lk 7:36–50; 1 Peter 3:4; Ti 3:2).[44]

Chan sees meekness as a transformative virtue that tempers those who having mourned the poor in spirit are inclined to use their power to save the poor in spirit. Meekness finds its correlative in gentleness and in this sense, Chan writes: "The virtue of meekness helps transform our desire to dominate into a vital force to serve."[45] In this way we can see how we can "emphasize it as a virtue for the poor and the powerful." It helps make the powerful meet the poor as the poor are and as the powerful need to be.

Here Chan turns to Monika Hellwig's astute observation that the powerful "need to unlearn those patterns of behavior that control and dominate others" even when they want to help another.[46] Chan and Hellwig argue that meekness helps the mighty to become capable of accompanying the poor in spirit. In a fairly remarkable application to social context, Chan also explores how meekness could look in the corporate world.

When the powerful become champions of justice, they need to develop interiorly a new modesty, an ability to stand as one among others, as one not expecting the head place at the table. Meekness allows the powerful to enter the community as a member instead of as its leader; it allows the powerful to use their assets gently, not narcissistically but compassionately, that is, truly in an other-directed way. Meekness tames the powerful so that their work is truly righteous. Without meekness, they are not able to inherit the earth.

This Beatitude seems to be addressed to those who want to serve the homeless but whose own positions of self-importance keep them from being able to enter into true solidarity with the poor. They inevitably "condescend" in their assistance; they want to assist, but they do so from their positions of importance. They try to accompany, but they continue to think of themselves as morally superior. The third Beatitude calls all those who want to assist the homeless to spend some time in learning meekness. Here then, we begin to see that this ladder of ascent helps us to become trained in the way of the Lord. The ascent becomes empowering but through an inversion: we grow in power as we surrender it.

The Fourth Beatitude, Matthew 5:6

Blessed are those who hunger and thirst for righteousness, for they will be filled.

The notion of the ladder of ascent leads us to see that the Beatitudes are a training school for Christian discipleship; the exercises of fasting here, then, are not public fasts to protest something but rather private actions that aim to transform the one who wants to mourn for the poor in spirit and who struggles to become meek. In order to pursue these virtues, the disciple is now instructed to practice asceticism so as to become more capable of these virtues. By fasting, we try to see the righteousness of empathy and meekness; this asceticism aims to develop within the exercitant a deeper hunger for God's righteousness.[47]

This fasting is notably to be accompanied by prayer. Chan writes, "Praying (with the Lord's Prayer in particular) helps focus on social transformation; as we pray, we are invited by God to bring God's kingdom on earth and to deliver others from all forms of indebtedness."[48]

The Fifth Beatitude, Matthew 5:7

Blessed are the merciful, for they will receive mercy.

Having recognized the poor in spirit, having mourned their condition, having sought to be meek in our encounter, and having practiced prayer and fasting for their account, now at the fifth Beatitude we are called to act. Mercy is the call, as I define it, to enter the chaos of another.[49] Having ascended the ladder, we are at the point where we are finally capable of encountering the chaos of the poor in spirit.

Mercy is the way we understand the actions of God toward humanity. Chan writes: "Creation is God's merciful act that brings order into the chaos of the universe; the incarnation is God's entry into the chaos of human existence; and the redemption is God's mercy that delivers us from the chaos of slavery to sin.... Mercy is emphasized by Scripture as the condition for salvation. In short, God who is mercy first shows mercy to us."[50] Mercy is therefore the way of participating in God's works, of being most like God in God's ways, as Aquinas argues (*ST* II–II.30.4). By entering into affinity with God, by entering into the chaos of the poor in spirit, we enter into the world of God where mercy is exchanged. Thus, being merciful we receive mercy. Mercy is, if you will, its own reward.

The Sixth Beatitude, Matthew 5:8

Blessed are the pure in heart, for they will see God.

The move from the practice of mercy in union with God leads to a new level of capacity in the ever-ascending disciple, growing in magnanimity. Being primarily other directed, a new level of integration has been given to the disciple such that the reconciling work of mercy lives now in an ongoing way in the disciple.

For this reason, Chan points rather quickly to the comprehensive significance of "purity of heart." Chan argues that "pure in heart" "points to neither external purity nor single-heartedness alone but a sense of *integrity* between one's interior life and external actions."[51] He adds, "The pure in heart emphasizes the integrity of one's whole being and understands such an attitude as a fundamental, all-encompassing virtue."[52] In this integrity, one experiences a reconciliation within oneself.

How does one maintain this integrity? Chan suggests, "one growing popular practice," the daily "examen of conscience," as suggested in the *Spiritual Exercises of St. Ignatius*. This is a prayer exercise where "one tries to find the movement of the spirit in one's daily life and through it, to identify the incongruence between one's inner movements and external actions. Examen helps us to be more sensitive to the longings and sources of our own spirit and hence becomes more open to God."[53]

The Seventh Beatitude, Matthew 5:9

Blessed are the peacemakers, for they will be called children of God.

Purity of heart is nothing short of the reconciliation of the conflicting motivations we may have had in attending to the poor in spirit. This seventh Beatitude follows the sixth, then: Making peace within oneself, one now can become a peacemaker among others. This one can reconcile others to act together for the poor in spirit.

Chan notes that it is through peace that one can work for justice, for the peace that Christ speaks of is not simply the absence of conflict or the stability of order but more importantly capacity to reconcile others, so that they together can work for justice.[54] In effect, the peacemaker is the one whose integrity leads others in the work of justice for the poor in spirit. Chan notes that "an exegesis of the Greek and Hebrew terms for peace shows that peace is paralleled with 'justice'" and is closer to the concept of righteousness than to that of tranquility or order.[55]

Chan provides a helpful summary of how the seventh Beatitude expresses the fullness of the achievement of all the previous Beatitudes. Arguing that it is mistaken to view that peace and justice are incompatible, he writes:

> Genuine peace is built upon justice. Thus, the cultivation of the virtue of peacemaking implies the simultaneous attainment of the virtue of justice at the same time. Moreover, since genuine peace is achieved by means of neither force nor passive acceptance of injustice at any cost, the virtues of meekness and fortitude are called into place respectively: meekness insists on patience and the rejection of violence, while fortitude demands active seeking of peace and endurance. In this way, the third and the seventh Beatitudes are closely connected to each other.[56]

Chan concludes: since peacemakers inevitably encounter opponents in the process of making peace, peacemaking can lead not only to eventual reconciliation but also to restoring rightful relationships.[57]

The Eighth Beatitude, Matthew 5:10–12

> *5:10 Blessed are those who are persecuted for righteousness' sake,*
> *for theirs is the kingdom of heaven. Blessed are you when people revile you*
> *and persecute you and utter all kinds of evil against you falsely on my account.*
> *Rejoice and be glad, for your reward is great in heaven, for in the same*
> *way they persecuted the prophets who were before you.*

Remembering that it is Christ who first aims our attention at the poor in spirit, Chan notes that the phrase ἕνεκεν ἐμοῦ (on account of me) "states clearly that the proper cause of persecution is Jesus and his teaching."[58] Additionally, he notes that the promise of the eighth Beatitude is the same as that of the first. He concludes that 5:10–12 "tells us that those who suffer from various kinds of physical and/or verbal persecution for the sake of righteousness as the prophets did and as the disciples do now, on account of Jesus and his teaching, will be rewarded greatly in the eschatological coming of the kingdom of Heaven."[59]

By forming an *inclusio* with the first Beatitude, Chan notes that this expanded eighth Beatitude "sums up the basic thoughts and forms a high point for the ethical teaching of the whole Beatitudes."[60] Able now to stand with the poor in spirit, we can now experience their world and Christ's.

In sum, the Beatitudes help us to recognize the internal agenda that we need to address if we want to address the external agenda of practicing the works of mercy. The call to serve the homeless is a call to become truly able to serve them precisely by becoming like them, so as to serve them in fellowship.

The argument of this lecture series has been that an ethics of vulnerability would bring us to the threshold of recognition. I hope that these three different sets of practices highlight how, through a vulnerability ethics, we have within our own way of proceeding the tools for a new mindfulness about vulnerability and recognition as we prepare for the moral life.

Thank you!

NOTES

1. Kierkegaard, *Purity of Heart Is to Will One Thing*.
2. Johnson, *Friends of God and Prophets*, 79.
3. Johnson, *Friends of God and* Prophets, 86. Johnson later returned to the topic through her study of Mary, *Truly Our Sister*.
4. Elizabeth Johnson, "Circle of Friends: A Closer Look at the Communion of Saints," *U.S. Catholic*, January 27, 2011, https://uscatholic.org/articles/201101/circle-of-friends-a-closer-look-at-the-communion-of-saints/.
5. Bonhoeffer, *The Communion of Saints*. See the review by Gustafson, "The Communion of Saints," 527–29.
6. Antonio Autiero, from a private communication, June 4, 2022. See also Autiero, "Salvezza nella 'drammatica' della storia," 223–40.
7. Bynum, "Wonder."
8. Keenan, "Distinguishing Charity as Goodness and Prudence as Rightness," 407–26.
9. Austin, "Moral Hope," 820.
10. Austin, 818.
11. Austin, 819.
12. Austin, 833.
13. Austin, 834.
14. Austin, 835, from Cajetan, *Commentary on ST*, q. 129, a. 4, no. 5.
15. Austin, 849.

16. Austin, 850–51
17. Austin, 851.
18. Lactantius, "Of the Kinds of Beneficence, and Works of Mercy."
19. See Keenan, "Pathways To Modernity II." Also, Black, *Italian Confraternities in the Sixteenth Century*; Terpstra, *Lay Confraternities and Civic Religion in Renaissance Bologna*; Terpstra, *Cultures of Charity*. That these confraternities were not without their own problems, see Terpstra, *Lost Girls*.
20. Rothschild, "History of Syphilis," 1454–63.
21. Camillocci, "I devoti della carità. Le confraternite del Divino Amore nell'Italia del primo Cinquecento"; Fois, "La Risposta confraternale alle Emergenze sanitarie e sociali della prima metà del Cinquecento Romano," 83–107.
22. Insidecom, "Hospital for the Incurable in Venice Zattere Pavement."
23. Clement, "Letter to the Corinthians."
24. Brodman, *Ransoming Captives in Crusader Spain*.
25. O'Malley, *The First Jesuits*.
26. See Black on the imprisoned in *Italian Confraternities*, 213–33.
27. Giovanni Romeo, *Aspettando il boia*. See also Guido, "Confraternita dei Bianchi sede presso Ospedale Incurabili."
28. Jones, "Advice for Priests Who Minister to Those Condemned to Death," 330–36. Six hundred years later, Sister Helen Prejean provides the same support in her accompaniment of those who are sentenced to death for capital crimes: she attends their executions, telling them to look on her face and see the face of Christ, see her *Dead Man Walking*.
29. Liguori is not the first to author such a manual. Much has been written on its prototype, the late fifteenth-century *Bologna Comforters' Manual*, used by the Bolognese confraternity of Santa Maria della Morte, but shared with other confraternities throughout the peninsula, including Ravenna, Ferrara, Padua, and Genoa. See Terpstra, "The Bologna Comforter's Manual," 183–292; Terpstra, "Piety and Punishment," 679–94; Prosperi, *Crime and Forgiveness*. Special thanks to Shaun Slusarski for introducing me to this text.
30. Terpstra, Prosperi, and Pastore, *Faith's Boundaries Laity and Clergy in Early Modern Confraternities*. See also Eisenbichler, *A Companion to Medieval and Early Modern Confraternities*.
31. Keenan and McGreevy, *Street Homelessness and Catholic Theological Ethics*. See also Pontifical Justice and Peace Commission, *What Have You Done to Your Homeless Brother?*
32. Keenan, "Blessed Are the Poor in Spirit," 176–86.
33. Chan, *The Ten Commandments and the Beatitudes*. This book was later published in India and then translated into Chinese and published in China.
34. John Paul II, *Veritatis splendor*, sec. 15, quoted in Chan, *The Ten Commandments and the Beatitudes*, xvi.
35. John Paul II, *Veritatis splendor*, sec. 6.
36. Chan, *The Ten Commandments and the Beatitudes*, 153, 164.
37. Chan, *The Ten Commandments and the Beatitudes*, 161
38. Chan, *The Ten Commandments and the Beatitudes*, 164.
39. Chan, *The Ten Commandments and the Beatitudes*, 171.
40. Chan, *The Ten Commandments and the Beatitudes*, 171.
41. Chan, *The Ten Commandments and the Beatitudes*, 171.
42. Clark, *The Vision of Catholic Social Thought*.
43. Chan, *The Ten Commandments and the Beatitudes*, 172.
44. Chan, *The Ten Commandments and the Beatitudes*, 178–80.

45. Chan, *The Ten Commandments and the Beatitudes*, 180.
46. Hellwig, "The Blessedness of the Meek, the Merciful, and the Peacemakers," 193, qtd. in Chan, *The Ten Commandments and the Beatitudes*, 181.
47. Chan, *The Ten Commandments and the Beatitudes*, 188.
48. Chan, *The Ten Commandments and the Beatitudes*, 189.
49. Keenan, *The Works of Mercy*.
50. Chan, *The Ten Commandments and the Beatitudes*, 196.
51. Chan, *The Ten Commandments and the Beatitudes*, 202.
52. Chan, *The Ten Commandments and the Beatitudes*, 203.
53. Chan, *The Ten Commandments and the Beatitudes*, 205.
54. Chan, *The Ten Commandments and the Beatitudes*, 210.
55. Chan, *The Ten Commandments and the Beatitudes*, 211.
56. Chan, *The Ten Commandments and the Beatitudes*, 213.
57. Chan, *The Ten Commandments and the Beatitudes*, 213.
58. Chan, *The Ten Commandments and the Beatitudes*, 221.
59. Chan, *The Ten Commandments and the Beatitudes*, 221.
60. Chan, *The Ten Commandments and the Beatitudes*, 222. See also Mattison, *The Sermon on the Mount and Moral Theology*.

BIBLIOGRAPHY

Ad Hoc Committee for Religious Liberty. "Our First, Most Treasured Freedom." Last modified April 12, 2012. Accessed August 6, 2022. https://www.usccb.org/committees/religious-liberty/our-first-most-cherished-liberty.

Alexander, Michelle. *The New Jim Crow: Mass Incarceration in the Age of Colorblindness*. New York: New, 2012.

Alison, James. *Faith beyond Resentment: Fragments Catholic and Gay*. New York: Crossroad, 2001.

Aquinas, Thomas. *Summa Theologiae*. 2nd and rev. ed., literally translated by Fathers of the English Dominican Province. London: Burns Oates and Washbourne, 1920–22.

Augustine. *Quaestiones Evangeliorum*.

Austin, Nicholas. "Moral Hope: Aquinas and Cajetan on Magnanimity." *Nova et vetera* 18, no. 3 (2020): 817–52. https://doi.org/10.1353/nov.2020.0044.

Autiero, Antonio. "Il compimento della salvezza nella 'drammatica' della storia. Una lettura prospettica." In *Dio e la sua salvezza: Il dramma della storia e il compimento della libertà*, edited by Lucio Casula, 223–40. Milan: Glossa, 2019.

———. "Giuseppe: Un'altra morale è possibile." In *Maschilità in questione. Sguardi sulla figura di san Giuseppe*, edited by Antonio Autiero and Marinella Perroni, 182–99. Brescia, Italy: Queriniana, 2021.

Azpitarte, Eduardo López. "Ignatius' Meditations on Sin: From Guilt to Gratitude." *Way* 47 (2008): 97–113.

Babka, Susie. "Sensibility to Vulnerability in the Form of Art." In *Through the Dark Field: The Incarnation through an Aesthetics of Vulnerability*, 89–119. Collegeville, MN: Liturgical Press, 2017.

———. "The Trinity in the Gnadenstuhl Motif: Illustrating the Cross as Event of the Triune God." In *God's Grandeur: The Arts and Imagination in Theology*, edited by David Robinson, 17–37. Maryknoll, NY: Orbis, 2007.

Baert, Barbara. "The Gaze in the Garden: Mary Magdalene in *Noli me tangere*." In *Mary Magdalene, Iconographic Studies from the Middle Ages to the Baroque*, edited by Michelle Erhardt and Amy Morris, 187–221. Leiden, Netherlands: Brill, 2012.

Bailey, Kenneth. *Finding the Lost: Cultural Keys to Luke 15*. St. Louis, MO: Concordia, 1992.

BBC News Staff. "America's Gun Culture—In Seven Charts." *BBC*, May 26, 2022. https://www.bbc.co.uk/news/world-us-canada-41488081.

Becker, Ernest. *The Denial of Death*. New York: Free Press, 1997.

Bede. *Lucae Evangelium Expositio*.

Benjamin, Jessica. *Beyond Doer and Done to: Recognition Theory, Intersubjectivity and the Third*. New York: Routledge, 2017.

———. *The Bonds of Love: Psychoanalysis, Feminism, and the Problem of Domination*. New York: Pantheon, 1988.

Betz, Hans Dieter. *The Sermon on the Mount*. Edited by Adela Yarbro Collins. Minneapolis: Fortress Press, 1995.

Black, Christopher. *Italian Confraternities in the Sixteenth Century*. New York: Cambridge University Press, 1989.

Block, Elizabeth Sweeney. "A Call to Action: Global Moral Crises and the Inadequacy of Inherited Approaches to Conscience." *Journal of the Society of Christian Ethics* 37, no. 2 (Fall/Winter 2017): 79–96. https://www.jstor.org/stable/44987552.

———. "Conscience." In *T&T Clark Handbook of Christian Ethics*. Edited by Tobias Winright. London: T & T Clark, 2021.

———. "Embodied Formation, Embodied Cognition: Incorporating Neuroscientific Findings into Conscience Formation." In *Conscience and Catholic Education*, edited by David DeCosse and Kevin Baxter, 45–60. Maryknoll, NY: Orbis Press, 2022.

———. "Moral Intuition, Social Sin, and Moral Vision: Attending to the Unconscious Dimensions of Morality and Igniting the Moral Imagination." *Religions* 12, no. 5 (2021): 292. https://doi.org/10.3390/rel12050292.

———. "White Privilege and the Erroneous Conscience: Rethinking Moral Culpability and Ignorance." *Journal of the Society of Christian Ethics* 39, no. 2 (Fall/Winter 2019): 357–74. https://www.jstor.org/stable/48617081.

Böckle, Franz. "Theological Reflection about Guilt and Sin." In *Fundamental Moral Theology*, 87–124. Dublin: Gill and Macmillan, 1980.

Boff, Leonardo. *Holy Trinity, Perfect Community*. Maryknoll, NY: Orbis Books, 2000.

Boland, Tom, and Paul Clogher. "A Genealogy of Critique: From *Parrhesia* to Prophecy." *Critical Research on Religion* 5, no. 2 (2017): 116–32. https://doi.org/10.1177/2050303217690896.

Bonhoeffer, Dietrich. *The Communion of Saints: A Dogmatic Inquiry into the Sociology of the Church*. New York: Harper and Row, 1963.

———. *The Cost of Discipleship*. New York: Simon and Schuster, 2018.

———. *Letters and Papers from Prison*. Minneapolis: Fortress, 2009.

———. "Protestantism without Reformation." In *The Bonhoeffer Reader*, edited by Clifford J. Green and Michael P. DeJonge, 568–92. Minneapolis: Fortress Press, 2013.

Boopalan, Sunder John. *Memory, Grief, and Agency: A Political Theological Account of Wrongs and Rites*. New York: Palgrave Macmillan, 2017.

Bourdieu, Pierre. *Outline of a Theory of Practice*. Translated by Richard Nice. New York: Cambridge University Press, 1977.

Bourke, Vernon J. "Is Thomas Aquinas a Natural Law Ethicist?" *Monist* 58, no. 1 (1974): 52–66. http://www.jstor.org/stable/27902343.

Brinkmann, Bruno. "The Humanity of Christ II: Christ and Anxiety." *Way* 16, no. 3 (1976): 136–45.

Brodman, James William. *Ransoming Captives in Crusader Spain: The Order of Merced on the Medieval Spanish Frontier*. Philadelphia: University of Pennsylvania Press, 1986.

Brooks, Claire Vonk. "Psalm 51." *Interpretation* 49, no. 1 (1995): 62–66. https://doi.org/10.1177/002096439504900107.

Brown, Brené. *Daring Greatly: How the Courage to Be Vulnerable Transforms the Way We Live, Love, Parent, and Lead*. New York: Avery Publishing, 2015.

Brown, Dee. *Bury My Heart at Wounded Knee: An Indian History of the American West*. New York: Holt, Rinehart and Winston, 1970.

Burggraeve, Roger. *The Awakening to the Other: A Provocative Dialogue with Emmanuel Levinas*. Leuven, Belgium: Peeters, 2008.

———. "From Responsible to Meaningful Sexuality: An Ethics of Growth as an Ethics of Mercy for Young People in This Era of AIDS." In *Catholic Ethicists on HIV/AIDS Prevention*, edited by James Keenan, assisted by Lisa Sowle Cahill, Jon Fuller, and Kevin Kelly, 303–16. New York: Continuum, 2000.

———. "Une éthique de miséricorde." *Lumen Vitae* 49 (1994): 281–96.

———. *The Wisdom of Love in the Service of Love: Emmanuel Levinas on Justice, Peace, and Human Rights*. Milwaukee: Marquette University Press, 2003.

Burridge, Richard A. *Imitating Jesus: An Inclusive Approach to New Testament Ethics*. Grand Rapids: Eerdmans, 2007.

———. *What Are the Gospels? A Comparison with Graeco-Roman Biography*. Grand Rapids, MI: Eerdmans, 2004.

Bush, George W. "A Nation Challenged: President Bush's Address on Terrorism before a Joint Meeting of Congress." Transcribed at Capitol Hill, Washington, DC, September 21, 2001. https://www.nytimes.com/2001/09/21/us/nation-challenged-president-bush-s-address-terrorism-before-joint-meeting.html.

Butler, Judith. *Frames of War: When Is Life Grievable?* London: Verso, 2008.

———. *Giving an Account of Oneself*. New York: Fordham University Press, 2005.

———. *Notes toward a Performative Theory of Assembly*. Cambridge, MA: Harvard, 2015.

———. *Precarious Life: The Powers of Mourning and Violence*. New York: Verso, 2004.

———. "Precarious Life, Vulnerability, and the Ethics of Cohabitation." *Journal of Speculative Philosophy* 26, no. 2 (2012): 134–51.

Butler, Judith, Zeynep Gambetti, and Leticia Sabsay, eds. *Vulnerability in Resistance*. Durham, NC: Duke University Press, 2016.

Bynum, Caroline Walker. "Did the Twelfth Century Discover the Individual?" *Journal of Ecclesiastical History* 31, no. 1 (1980): 1–17. https://doi.org/10.1017/S0022046900036186.

———. "Wonder." *American Historical Association*. January 3, 1997. https://www.historians.org/about-aha-and-membership/aha-history-and-archives/presidential-addresses/caroline-walker-bynum.

Cajetan. Commentary on *ST*. II.

Camillocci, Daniela Solfaroli. "I devoti della carità. Le confraternite del Divino Amore nell'Italia del primo Cinquecento." *Comitatus: A Journal of Medieval and Renaissance Studies* 35 (2002): 198–99. https://doi.org/10.1353/cjm.2004.0011.

Carey, Holly J. *Jesus' Cry from the Cross: Towards a First-Century Understanding of the Intertextual Relationship between Psalm 22 and the Narrative of Mark's Gospel*. Vol. 398 of *The Library of New Testament Studies*. New York: Bloomsbury Publishing, 2009.

Cavanaugh, William T. "Pilgrim People." In *Gathered for the Journey: Moral Theology in Catholic Perspective*, edited by David Matzko McCarthy and M. Therese Lysaught, 88–105. Grand Rapids, MI: Eerdmans, 2007.

Chalmers, Stuart. "Fritz Tillmann, Discipleship and the Renewal of Moral Theology." *Irish Theological Quarterly* 86, no. 4 (2021): 352–69.

Chan, Yiu Sing Lúcás. *Biblical Ethics in the 21st Century: Developments, Emerging Consensus, and Future Directions*. Mahwah, NJ: Paulist Press, 2013.

———. "Biblical Ethics: 3D." *Theological Studies* 76, no. 1 (2015): 112–28. https://doi.org/10.1177/0040563914565290.

———. "Bridging Christian and Confucian Ethics: Is the Bridge Adequately Catholic and East Asian?" *Asian Christian Review* 5, no. 1 (Summer, 2011): 49–73.

———. *The Ten Commandments and the Beatitudes: Biblical Studies and Ethics for Real Life*. Lanham, MD: Rowman and Littlefield, 2012.

Chan, Yiu Sing Lúcás, and James Keenan. "Bridging Christian Ethics and Confucianism Through Virtue Ethics." *Chinese Cross Currents* 5, no. 3 (2008): 74–85.
Chan, Yiu Sing Lúcás, James F. Keenan, and Shaji George Kochuthara, eds. *Doing Catholic Theological Ethics in a Cross Cultural and Interreligious Asian Context*. Bangalore: Dharmaram Press, 2016.
Chan, Yiu Sing Lúcás, James F. Keenan, and Ronaldo Zacharias, eds. *The Bible and Catholic Theological Ethics*. Maryknoll, NY: Orbis Books, 2017.
Choi, Ki Joo. *Disciplined by Race: Theological Ethics and the Problem of Asian American Identity*. Eugene: Cascade Books, 2019.
Choi, Ki Joo, Sarah M. Moses, and Andrea Vicini, eds. *Reimagining the Moral Life: On Lisa Sowle Cahill's Contributions to Christian Ethics*. Maryknoll, NY: Orbis Books, 2020.
Cholbi, Michael. *Grief: A Philosophical Guide*. Princeton, NJ: Princeton University Press, 2021.
Chopp, Rebecca. *The Praxis of Suffering: An Interpretation of Liberation and Political Theologies*. Maryknoll, NY: Orbis Books, 1986.
Cinocca, Federico. "We Believe in God, the Father Almighty: Liturgy, Ethics, Dominance, and Vulnerability." Theology Department, PhD diss. proposal, Boston College, 2021.
Clark, Meghan J. *The Vision of Catholic Social Thought: The Virtue of Solidarity and the Praxis of Human Rights*. Minneapolis: Fortress Press, 2014.
Clark, Patrick. "Reversing the Ethical Perspective: What the Allegorical Interpretation of the Good Samaritan Parable Can Still Teach Us." *Theology Today* 71, no. 3 (2014): 300–309. https://doi.org/10.1177/0040573614542308.
Clement. "Letter to the Corinthians." New Advent. Accessed August 8, 2022. https://www.newadvent.org/fathers/1010.htm.
Climacus, John. *The Ladder of Ascent*. Mahwah, NJ: Paulist Press, 1988.
Clingan, Ralph Garlin. *Against Cheap Grace in a World Come of Age: An Intellectual Biography of Clayton Powell, 1865–1953*. New York: Peter Lang, 2002.
Cloutier, David J. "Cavanaugh and Grimes on Structural Evils of Violence and Race: Overcoming Conflicts in Contemporary Social Ethics." *Journal of the Society of Christian Ethics* 37, no. 2 (Fall/Winter 2017): 59–78. https://www.jstor.org/stable/44987551.
Cochran, Clarke. "Joseph and the Politics of Memory." *Review of Politics* 64, no. 3 (2002): 421–44. https://doi.org/10.1017/S0034670500034963.
Cochran, Elizabeth Agnew. "Faith, Love, and Stoic Assent: Reconsidering Virtue in the Reformed Tradition." *Journal of Moral Theology* 3 (2014): 199–227. https://doi.org/10.5040/9780567671387-003.
Cone, James. *Black Theology and Black Power*. Maryknoll, NY: Orbis Books, 1997.
———. *The Cross and the Lynching Tree*. Maryknoll, NY: Orbis Books, 2011.
Congar, Yves M-J. "Der Meister ruft." In "Bulletin de Théologie." *Revue des Sciences Philosophiques et Théologiques* 27 (1938): 641.
Connolly, Hugh. *The Irish Penitentials and Their Significance for the Sacrament of Penance Today*. Dublin: Four Courts Press, 1995.
Copeland, M. Shawn. *Enfleshing Freedom: Body, Race, and Being*. Minneapolis: Fortress, 2010.
———. "Revisiting Racism: Black Theology and a Legacy of Oppression." *America* 211, no. 1 (July 2014): 21–24.
Crenshaw, Richard. "Saint Mary Magdalene or The Weeper." *PoetryNook*. https://www.poetrynook.com/poem/saint-mary-magdalene-or-weeper.
Daly, Daniel. *The Structures of Virtue and Vice*. Washington, DC: Georgetown University Press, 2021.

Darr, Ryan. "Social Sin and Social Wrongs: Moral Responsibility in a Structurally Disordered World." *Journal of the Society of Christian Ethics* 37, no. 2 (2017): 21–37. https://www.jstor.org/stable/44987549.

Davies, William, and Dale Allison, Jr. *A Critical Exegetical Commentary on the Gospel According to Saint Matthew*. Vol. 1, *Matthew: 1–7*. New York: Continuum, 1988.

De Anda, Neomi. "Spirit of Community: Forced Vulnerability, the Little Details as Realized Hope and Lament as Prophetic Protest." Lecture at Duquesne University, October 5, 2021.

DeCosse, David, and Kristin Heyer, eds. *Conscience and Catholicism: Rights, Responsibilities, and Institutional Policies*. Maryknoll, NY: Orbis Books, 2015.

Demmer, Klaus. "Die autonome Moral—Eine Anfrage an die Denkform." In *Fundamente der theologischen Ethik*, edited by Adrian Holderegger, 261–76. Freiburg im Breisgau, Germany: Herder, 1996.

DiFransico, Lesley. "Distinguishing Emotions of Guilt and Shame in Psalm 51." *Biblical Theology Bulletin* 48, no. 4 (2018): 180–87. https://doi.org/10.1177/0146107918801511.

Dworkin, Andrea. "I Want a Twenty-Four-Hour Truce during Which There Is No Rape." In *Letters from a War Zone*, 162–71. New York: E. P. Dutton, 1988.

Ehle, John. *Trail of Tears: The Rise and Fall of the Cherokee Nation*. New York: Double Day, 1988.

Eisenbichler, Konrad, ed. *A Companion to Medieval and Early Modern Confraternities*. New York: Brill, 2019.

Equal Justice Initiative. "The National Memorial for Peace and Justice." Accessed May 20, 2021. https://museumandmemorial.eji.org/memorial.

———. *Reconstruction in America: Racial Violence after the Civil War*. Montgomery, AL: Equal Justice Initiative, 2020. https://eji.org/report/reconstruction-in-america/.

Evon, Dan. "Did Obama Apologize for Dropping the Atomic Bomb on Japan?" *Snopes*. Accessed August 6, 2022. https://www.snopes.com/fact-check/obama-apology-hiroshima/.

Farley, Margaret. "Ethics, Ecclesiology, and the Grace of Self-Doubt." In *A Call to Fidelity: On the Moral Theology of Charles E. Curran*, edited by James J. Walter, Timothy E. O'Connell, and Thomas A. Shannon, 55–77. Washington, DC: Georgetown University Press, 2002.

Feske, Millicent C. "Christ and Suffering in Moltmann's Thought." *Asbury Theological Journal* 55, no. 1 (2000): 85–104. https://doi.org/10.7252/Journal.01.2000S.07.

Finn, Daniel K., ed. *Moral Agency within Social Structures and Culture: A Primer on Critical Realism for Christian Ethics*. Washington, DC: Georgetown University Press, 2020.

———. "What Is a Sinful Social Structure?" *Theological Studies* 77, no. 1 (2016): 136–64. https://doi.org/10.1177/0040563915619981.

Fleming, Daniel J. *Attentiveness to Vulnerability: A Dialogue between Emmanuel Levinas, Jean Porter, and the Virtue of Solidarity*. Eugene, OR: Pickwick Publications, 2019.

Fois, Mario. "La Risposta confraternale alle Emergenze sanitarie e sociali della prima metà del Cinquecento Romano: Le Confraternite del Divino Amore e di S. Girolamo della Carità." *Archivum Historiae Pontificiae* 41, (2003): 83–107. https://www.jstor.org/stable/23564738.

Foner, Eric. "What Is American Exceptionalism?" *Ethics and International Affairs*, August 8, 2013. https://www.ethicsandinternationalaffairs.org/2013/what-is-american-exceptionalism/.

Forbes, Gregory. "Repentance and Conflict in the Parable of the Lost Son (Luke 15:11–32)." *Journal of the Evangelical Theological Society* 42, no. 2 (June 1999): 211–29.

Forrest, Jim. *The Ladder of the Beatitudes*. Maryknoll, NY: Orbis Books, 1999.

Francis. *Amoris Laetitia*. Last modified March 19, 2016. Accessed August 7, 2022. https://www.vatican.va/content/dam/francesco/pdf/apost_exhortations/documents/papa-francesco_esortazione-ap_20160319_amoris-laetitia_en.pdf.

Fraser, Nancy, and Axel Honneth. *Redistribution or Recognition?: A Political-Philosophical Exchange*. Brooklyn: Verso Books, 2003.
Fullam, Lisa. *The Virtue of Humility*. Lewiston, NY: Edwin Mellen Press, 2009.
Gallagher, David M. "Desire for Beatitude and Love of Friendship in Thomas Aquinas." *Mediaeval Studies* 58 (1996): 1–47.
Gilleman, Gérard. *The Primacy of Charity in Moral Theology*. Translated by William F. Ryan and André Vachon. Westminster, MD: Newman Press, 1959.
———. *Le Primat de la charité en théologie morale*. Louvain, Belgium: Nauwelaerts, 1952.
———. *Le rôle de la charité en théologie morale: Essai méthodologique*. Paris: Institut Catholique de Paris, 1947.
Gilligan, Carol. *In a Different Voice: Psychological Theory and Women's Development*. Cambridge, MA: Harvard University Press, 1982.
Gilson, Erinn C. *The Ethics of Vulnerability: A Feminist Analysis of Social Life and Practice*. New York: Routledge, 2014.
Giubilini, Alberto. "Conscience." *Stanford Encyclopedia of Philosophy*. Last modified February 11, 2021. Accessed August 6, 2022. https://plato.stanford.edu/entries/conscience/#ConsMotiActMora.
Goertz, Stephan, Rudolf B. Hein, and Katharina Klöcker, eds. *Fluchtpunkt Fundamentalismus?: Gegenwartsdiagnosen katholischer Moral*. Freiburg im Breisgau, Germany: Herder, 2013.
Goldstein, Valerie Saiving. "Human Situation: A Feminine View." *Journal of Religion* 40, no. 2 (April 1960): 100–112.
Gowler, David. "Venerable Bede and the Parables." Parables Reception. August 12, 2015. https://parablesreception.blogspot.com/2015/08/the-venerable-bede-and-parables-part-2.html.
Griener, George E., and James F. Keenan, eds. *A Lúcás Chan Reader: Pioneering Essays on Biblical and Asian Theological Ethics*. Bangalore: Dharmaram, 2017.
Grimes, Katie Walker. *Christ Divided: Antiblackness as Corporate Vice*. Minneapolis: Fortress Press, 2017.
Guido, Pettinati. "Confraternita dei Bianchi sede presso Ospedale Incurabili." Accessed August 8, 2022. https://ospedaleincurabili.jimdofree.com/religiose-santi-beati-e-laici/confraternita-dei-bianchi/.
Gula, Richard. *Reason Informed by Faith: Foundations of Catholic Moral Theology*. Mahwah. NJ: Paulist Press, 1989.
Gustafson, James. "The Communion of Saints; A Dogmatic Inquiry into the Sociology of the Church, by Dietrich Bonhoeffer." *Theology Today* 21, no. 4 (1965): 527–29. https://doi.org/10.1177/004057366502100423.
Gutierrez, Gustavo. "Sermon: Gutierrez on the Liberating of Man Born Blind." *New Blackfriars* 70, no. 826 (1989): 158–60. http://www.jstor.org/stable/43248370.
Haker, Hille. "The Fragility of the Moral Self." *Harvard Theological Review* 97, no. 4 (October 2004): 359–81. https://doi.org/10.1017/S0017816004000756.
———. "Recognition and Responsibility." *Religions* 12, no. 7 (2021): 467. https://doi.org/10.3390/rel12070467.
———. *Towards a Critical Political Ethics: Catholic Ethics and Social Challenges*. Würzburg, Germany: Echter Verlag, 2020.
Hamilton, Brian. "It's in You: Structural Sin and Personal Responsibility Revisited." *Studies in Christian Ethics* 34, no. 3 (2021): 360–80. https://doi.org/10.1177/09539468211009764.

Häring, Bernhard. *Das Gesetz Christi*. Freiburg, Germany: Verlag Wewel, 1954.
———. *The Law of Christ: Moral Theology for Priests and Laity*. Translated by Edwin G. Kaiser. Westminster, MD.: Newman Press, 1961.
———. *My Witness for the Church*. Mahwah, NJ: Paulist Press, 1992.
———. *Teologia morale verso il terzo millennio*. Class notes. Rome: Alfonsianum University, 1987.
Harrington, Daniel, and James Keenan. *Jesus e a ética da virtude*. São Paolo: Edições Loyola, 2013.
———. *Jesus and Virtue Ethics: Building Bridges between New Testament Studies and Moral Theology*. Lanham, MD: Sheed and Ward, 2002.
———. *Paul and Virtue Ethics*. New York: Rowman and Littlefield, 2010.
Haskins, Susan. *Mary Magdalen: Myth and Metaphor*. New York: Harcourt Press, 1994.
Hauerwas, Stanley. "Jesus: The Story of the Kingdom." In *A Community of Character: Toward a Constructive Christian Social Ethic*, 36–52. Notre Dame, IN: University of Notre Dame Press, 2005.
Hellwig, Monika K. "The Blessedness of the Meek, the Merciful, and the Peacemakers." In *New Perspectives on the Beatitudes*, edited by Francis A. Eigo, 193. Villanova, PA: Villanova University Press, 1995.
Heschel, Abraham Joshua. *The Prophets*. New York: Harper, 1969.
Heyer, Kristin, and Linda Hogan. "Beyond the Northern Paradigm: Catholic Theological Ethics in Global Perspective." *Journal of the Society of Christian Ethics* 39, no. 1 (Spring/Summer 2019): 21–38.
———. "Social Sin and Immigration: Good Fences Make Bad Neighbors." *Theological Studies* 71, no. 2 (2010): 410–36. https://doi.org/10.1177/004056391007100207.
———. "Walls in the Heart: Social Sin in Fratelli Tutti." *Journal of Catholic Social Thought* 19, no. 1 (2022): 25–40.
Heyer, Kristin, Andrea Vicini, and James F. Keenan, eds. *Building Bridges in Sarajevo: The Plenary Papers of Sarajevo 2018*. Maryknoll, NY: Orbis books, 2019.
Himes, Kenneth R. "Hiroshima and Nagasaki: 75th Anniversary Reflections." *Asian Horizons* 14, no. 2 (June 2020): 507–24.
Hirschman, Charles, Samuel Preston, and Vu Manh Loi. "Vietnamese Casualties during the American War: A New Estimate," *Population and Development Review* 21, no. 4 (1995): 783–812. https://doi.org/10.2307/2137774.
Hogan, Linda. *Keeping Faith with Human Rights*. Washington, DC: Georgetown University Press, 2015.
———. "Moral Leadership: A Challenge and a Celebration." *Theological Studies* 82, no. 1 (2021): 138–54. https://doi.org/10.1177/0040563921993456.
———. "Vulnerability: An Ethic for a Divided World." In *Building Bridges in Sarajevo: The Plenary Papers of Sarajevo 2018*, edited by James F. Keenan, Kristin Heyer, and Andrea Vicini, 216. Maryknoll, NY: Orbis Books, 2019.
Honneth, Axel. *The Struggle for Recognition: The Moral Grammar of Social Conflicts*. Cambridge, MA: MIT Press, 1995.
Hooton, Peter. *Bonhoeffer's Religionless Christianity in Its Christological Context*. Minneapolis: Fortress Press, 2020.
Human, Dirk J. "God Accepts a Broken Spirit and a Contrite Heart—Thoughts on Penitence, Forgiveness and Reconciliation in Psalm 51." *Verbum et ecclesia* 26, no. 1 (2005): 114–32. https://doi.org/10.4102/ve.v26i1.215.

Insidecom. "Hospital for the Incurable in Venice Zattere Pavement." Accessed August 8, 2022. https://www.venetoinside.com/hidden-treasures/post/incurable-hospital-in-venice-zattere-pavement/.
Iozzio, Mary Jo. "Radical Dependence and the *Imago Dei*: Bioethical Implications of Access to Healthcare for People with Disabilities." *Christian Bioethics* 23, no. 3 (2017): 234–60.
———. *Self-Determination and the Moral Act: A Study of the Contributions of Odon Lottin, O.S.B.* Leuven, Belgium: Peeters, 1995.
Jackson, Helen Hunt. *A Century of Dishonor: The Classic Exposé of the Plight of the Native Americans*. Garden City, NY: Dover Publications, 2003. First published as *A Century of Dishonor: A Sketch of the United States Government's Dealings with Some of the Indian Tribes*. New York: Harper & Brothers, 1881.
James, William. *The Varieties of Religious Experience*. London: Routledge, 2002.
Jennings, Willie James. *The Christian Imagination: Theology and the Origins of Race*. New Haven, CT: Yale University Press, 2010.
Jesuits. "The Ignatian Examen." Accessed August 5, 2022. https://www.jesuits.org/spirituality/the-ignatian-examen/.
Jocano, Landa. "Rethinking 'Smooth Interpersonal Relations.'" *Philippine Sociological Review* 14, no. 4 (1966): 282–91.
Johnson, Elizabeth A. *Friends of God and Prophets: A Feminist Theological Reading of the Communion of Saints*. New York: Continuum Press, 1998.
———. "The Incomprehensibility of God and the Image of God Male and Female." *Theological Studies* 45, no. 3 (1984): 441–65. https://doi.org/10.1177/004056398404500302.
———. *She Who Is: The Mystery of God in Feminist Theological Discourse*. New York: Herder and Herder, 2017.
———. *Truly Our Sister: A Theology of Mary in the Communion of Saints*. New York: Continuum, 2006.
Johnston, Douglas, and Cynthia Sampson, eds. *The Missing Dimension of Statecraft*. New York: Oxford University Press, 1994.
Jones, Frederick M., ed. "Advice for Priests Who Minister to Those Condemned to Death." In *Alphonsus de Liguori: Selected Writings*, 330–36. New York: Paulist Press, 1999.
Kaag, John. *Sick Souls, Healthy Minds: How William James Can Save Your Life*. Princeton, NJ: Princeton University Press, 2020.
Katsanis, Bobbi Dykema. "Meeting in the Garden: Intertextuality with the Song of Songs in Holbein's *Noli Me Tangere*." *Interpretation* 61, no. 4 (October 2007): 402–16.
Kaveny, M. Cathleen. "Anger, Lamentation, and Common Ground." *Theological Studies* 82, no. 4 (November 2021): 663–85. https://doi.org/10.1177/00405639211053648.
———. *A Culture of Engagement: Law, Religion, and Morality*. Washington, DC: Georgetown University Press, 2016.
———. *Prophecy without Contempt: Religious Discourse in the Public Square*. Cambridge, MA: Harvard University Press, 2016.
Keen, Sam. "Foreword." In *The Denial of Death*, by Ernest Becker. New York: Free Press, 1997.
Keenan, James F. "The Bible and Ethics." In *The Jerome Biblical Commentary for the Twenty-First Century*. 3rd fully rev. ed., edited by John Collins and Gina Hens-Piazza, 2120–37. New York: T & T Clark, 2022.
———. "Blessed Are the Poor in Spirit: A Response to Homelessness by a Reading of Matthew's Beatitudes." In *Street Homelessness and Catholic Theological Ethics*, edited by James Keenan and Mark McGreevy, 176–86. Maryknoll, NY: Orbis Books, 2019.

———. "Building Blocks for Moral Education: Vulnerability, Recognition and Conscience." In *Conscience and Catholic Education*, edited by Kevin Baxter and David DeCosse, 17–30. Maryknoll, NY: Orbis Books, 2022.

———. "Can a Wrong Action Be Good? The Development of Theological Opinion on Erroneous Conscience." *Église et Théologie* 24 (1993): 205–19.

———. "Catholic Conscience Awakening: The Evolution of Our Contemporary Dependence on Conscience." In *Conscience and Catholicism*, edited by David DeCosse and Kristin Heyer, 1–15. Maryknoll, NY: Orbis Books, 2015.

———. "Collective Conscience and Collective Guilt." In *VATICANUM 21 Erschließung und bleibende Aufgaben des Zweiten Vatikanischen Konzils für Theologie und Kirche im 21. Jahrhundert*, edited by Christoph Böttigheimer and René Dausner, 78–86. Freiburg, Germany: Herder, 2016.

———. "The Color Line, Race and Caste: Structures of Domination and the Ethics of Recognition." *Theological Studies* 82, no. 1 (2021): 69–94. https://doi.org/10.1177/0040563921992550.

———. "The Community Colleges: Giving Them the Ethical Recognition They Deserve." *Journal of Moral Theology* 9, no. 2 (November 2020): 143–64. https://jmt.scholasticahq.com/article/18040-the-community-colleges-giving-them-the-ethical-recognition-they-deserve.

———. "Costruire ponti a Sarajevo: Un incontro internazionale di etica teologica." *La Civiltà Cattolica* 4038 (2018): 513–20.

———. "Distinguishing Charity as Goodness and Prudence as Rightness: A Key to Thomas' Pars Secunda." *Thomist* 56, no. 3 (1992): 407–26. https://doi.org/10.1353/tho.1992.0017.

———. "Examining Conscience: Ancient Wisdom on Judgment, Justice, and the Heart." *America* 214, no. 11 (April 4–11, 2016): 15–17.

———. "Exploring Vulnerability: Theological Ethics Today." Lecture delivered as the Campion Lecture at Campion Hall, Oxford University, Oxford, England, November 2019.

———. "Faith, A Journey to Dachau." In *Virtues for Ordinary Christians*, 37–41. Kansas City, MO: Sheed and Ward, 1996.

———. "To Follow and to Form over Time: A Phenomenology of Conscience." In *Conscience and Catholicism: Rights, Responsibilities, and Institutional Policies*, edited by David DeCosse and Kristin Heyer, 1–15. Maryknoll, NY: Orbis Books, 2015.

———. "Grieving in the Upper Room: Vulnerability, Recognition, Conscience and the Holy Spirit." Lecture delivered as the Holy Spirit Lecture at Duquesne University, Pittsburgh, PA, October 2021.

———. *A History of Catholic Moral Theology in the Twentieth Century: From Confessing Sins to Liberating Consciences*. New York: Continuum, 2010.

———. *A History of Catholic Theological Ethics*. Mahwah, NJ: Paulist Press, 2022.

———. "Impasse and Solidarity in Theological Ethics." *Catholic Theological Society of America Proceedings* 64 (2009): 47–60.

———. "John Mahoney's *The Making of Moral Theology*." In *The Oxford Handbook of Theological Ethics*, edited by Gilbert Meilaender and William Werpehowski, 503–19. Oxford: Oxford University Press, 2005.

———. "Linking Human Dignity, Vulnerability and Virtue Ethics," *Interdisciplinary Journal for Religion and Transformation in Contemporary Society* 6 (July 2020): 56–73. https://doi.org/10.30965/23642807-00601004.

———. *Moral Wisdom: Lessons and Texts from the Catholic Tradition*. Lanham, MD: Sheed and Ward, 2004.

———. On Public Expressions of Guilt, of Conscience, and of Confession." *Confessio: Schuld bekennen in Kirche und Öffentlichkeit*, edited by Julia Enxing and Jutta Koslowski, 165–77. Leipzig, Germany: Evangelische Verlagsanstalt, 2018.

———. "Pathways To Modernity II: Confraternities and the School of Salamanca." In *A History of Catholic Theological Ethics*, 208–36. Mahwah, NJ: Paulist Press, 2022.

———. "Proposing Cardinal Virtues." *Theological Studies* 56, no. 4 (1995): 709–29. https://doi.org/10.1177/004056399505600405.

———. "Pursuing Ethics by Building Bridges beyond the Northern Paradigm." *Religions* 10, no. 8 (2019): 490.

———. *Readings in Moral Theology*. Vol. 11, *The Historical Development of Fundamental Moral Theology in the United States*, edited by Curran and McCormick, 281–306. Reprint. Mahwah, NJ: Paulist Press, 1999.

———. "Rethinking Humanity's Progress in Light of COVID-19." *Asian Horizons* 14, no. 3 (September 2020): 713–35.

———. "Sin." In *Moral Wisdom: Lessons and Texts from the Moral Tradition*, 45–67. Lanham, MD: Rowman and Littlefield, 2010.

———. "Vatican II and Theological Ethics." *Theological Studies* 74, no. 1 (2013): 162–90. https://doi.org/10.1177/004056391307400109.

———. "Vicious Structures of Social Formation: Acquired Vices, Embodied Anthropology, Social Practices, and Human Freedom." In *Zlo nasilja u etničkim sukobima. Poraz moralno-povijesnog imperativa: Nikad više*, edited by Zorica Maros and Darko Tomašević, 17–28. Sarajevo: Catholic University of Sarajevo, 2016.

———. "Virtue Ethics." In *Basic Christian Ethics: An Introduction*, edited by Bernard Hoose, 84–94. London: Chapman, 1997.

———. "Virtue, Grace and the Early Revisionists of the Twentieth Century." *Studies in Christian Ethics* 23, no. 4 (2010): 365–80.

———. *Virtues for Ordinary Christians*. Kansas City, MO: Sheed and Ward, 1996.

———. "The Virtue of Prudence (IIa IIae 47–56)." In *The Ethics of Aquinas*, edited by Stephen Pope, 259–71. Washington, DC: Georgetown University Press, 2002.

———. "Vulnerability and the Father of the Prodigal Son." *Alfonsiana*, September 27, 2019. https://www.alfonsiana.org/blog/2019/09/27/vulnerability-and-the-father-of-the-prodigal-son/.

———. "Vulnerability and Hierarchicalism." *Melita Teologica* 68, no. 2 (2018): 129–42. https://core.ac.uk/download/pdf/333554648.pdf.

———. "Vulnerable to Contingency," *Journal of the Society of Christian Ethics* 40, no. 2 (2021): 221–36. https://muse.jhu.edu/article/787428/pdf.

———. *The Works of Mercy: The Heart of Catholicism*. Lanham, MD: Sheed and Ward, 2005.

———. "The World at Risk: Vulnerability, Precarity and Connectedness." *Theological Studies* 81, no. 1 (April 2020): 132–49. doi.org/10.1177/0040563920907633.

Keenan, James F., and Mark McGreevy. *Street Homelessness and Catholic Theological Ethics*. Maryknoll, NY: Orbis Books, July 2019.

Keenan, James, and Connor Murphy. "When the Public Remembrance of an Injustice is an Ethical Necessity." In *Pravda u BH društvu. Izazov temeljne ljudskosti*, edited by Zorica Maros and Darko Tomašević, 41–54. Zagreb: Glas Koncila, 2017.

Kekes, John. *The Examined Life*. Lewisburg, PA: Bucknell University Press, 1988.

Kelley, Melissa. *Grief: Contemporary Theory and the Practice of Ministry*. Minneapolis: Fortress Press, 2010.

Kelly, Conor M. "Everyday Solidarity: A Framework for Integrating Theological Ethics and Ordinary Life." *Theological Studies* 81, no. 2 (2020): 414–37. https://doi.org/10.1177/0040563920928333.

Kierkegaard, Søren. *Purity of Heart Is to Will One Thing*. New York: Harper, 2014.

King, Martin Luther, Jr. *Letter from a Birmingham Jail*. New York: Penguin, 2018.

Kleber, Karl-Heinz. *Historia Docet: Zur Geschichte der Moraltheologie*. Münster, Germany: LIT Verlag, 2005.

Kopfensteiner, Thomas R. "The Metaphorical Structure of Normativity." *Theological Studies* 58, no. 2 (1997): 331–46. https://doi.org/10.1177/004056399705800206.

Kotva, Joseph, Jr. *The Christian Case for Virtue Ethics*. Washington, DC: Georgetown University Press, 1996.

LaCocque, André. *Onslaught against Innocence: Cain, Abel and the Yahwist*. Cambridge, UK: James Clarke and Co, 2015.

LaCouter, Travis. *Balthasar and Prayer*. New York: T & T Clark, 2021.

Lactantius. "Of the Kinds of Beneficence, and Works of Mercy." In *The Divine Institutes*. Vol. 6 of *True Worship*. https://www.newadvent.org/fathers/07016.htm.

Lampe, G. W. H. "Some Notes on the Significance of *basileia tou theou, basileia christou*, in the Greek Fathers." *Journal of Theological Studies* 49 (1948): 58–73.

Lamson-Scribner, Jennifer. "Disorder and Distortion: A Theological Approach to Addiction." PhD diss., Boston College, 2022.

Langan, John. "Sins of Malice in the Moral Psychology of Thomas Aquinas." *Annual of the Society of Christian Ethics* 12 (1987): 179–98.

Lapide, Cornelius. "Who Is My Neighbor?" In *The Great Commentary of Cornelius À Lapide*. Vol. 4, *St. Luke's Gospel*, translated by Thomas Mossman. Edinburgh: John Grant, 1908.

Lazare, Aaron. *On Apology*. Oxford: Oxford University Press, 2004.

Levinas, Emmanuel. *Difficult Freedom: Essays on Judaism*. London: Athlone Press, 1990.

Levine, Amy-Jill. *Short Stories by Jesus: The Enigmatic Parables of a Controversial Rabbi*. New York: HarperOne, 2014.

Lewis, C. S. *A Grief Observed*. New York: Harper Collins Publishers, 2001.

Lewis, Karoline M. *John*. Minneapolis: Fortress Press, 2014.

Lindsay, Rebecca. "Overthrowing Nineveh: Revisiting the City with Postcolonial Imagination." *Bible and Critical Theory* 12, no. 1 (2016): 49–61. https://doi.org/10.2104/BCT.V12I1.638.

Lohfink, Gerhard. *Jesus of Nazareth: What He Wanted, Who He Was*. Collegeville, MN: Liturgical Press, 2012.

Long, Stephen D. "The Way of Aquinas: Its Importance for Moral Theology." *Studies in Christian Ethics* 19, no. 3 (2006): 339–56. https://doi.org/10.1177/0953946806071557.

Lorrimar, Victoria. "Church and Christ in the Work of Stanley Hauerwas." *Ecclesiology* 11, no. 3 (2015): 306–26. https://doi.org/10.1163/17455316-01103004.

Lottin, Odon. *Au cœur de la morale chrétienne*. Tournai, Belgium: Declée, 1957.

———. *Morale fondamentale*. Tournai, Belgium: 1954.

———. *Principes de morale*. Louvain, Belgium: Abbaye du Mont César, 1946.

———. *Psychologie et morale aux XIIe et XIIIe siècles*. 4 vols. Gembloux, Belgium: J. Duculot, 1942–1960.

MacIntyre, Alasdair. *After Virtue: A Study in Moral Theory*. Notre Dame, IN: University of Notre Dame Press, 1981.

Mackenzie, Catriona, Wendy Rogers, and Susan Dodds, eds. *Vulnerability: New Essays in Ethics and Feminist Philosophy*. New York: Oxford University Press, 2013.

Mahoney, Jack. *The Holy Spirit and Moral Action in Thomas Aquinas.* Lanham, MD: Rowman and Littlefield, 2021.
Mahoney, John. *The Making of Moral Theology: A Study of Roman Catholic Tradition.* Oxford: Clarendon Press, 1987.
Malley, Edward. "The Gospel According to Mark." In *The Jerome Biblical Commentary,* edited by Raymond Brown, Joseph Fitzmyer, and Roland Murphy, 20–61. Englewood Cliffs, NJ: Prentice-Hall, 1968.
Markell, Patchen. *Bound by Recognition.* Princeton, NJ: Princeton University Press, 2003.
Massingale, Bryan N. *Racial Justice and the Catholic Church.* Maryknoll, NY: Orbis Books, 2010.
Mathewes, Charles. "Vulnerability and Political Theology." In *Exploring Vulnerability,* edited by Heike Springhart and Günther Thomas, 165–84. Bristol, CT: Vandenhoeck and Ruprecht, 2017.
Mattison, William C., III. *The Sermon on the Mount and Moral Theology: A Virtue Perspective.* New York: Cambridge University Press, 2017.
Mawson, Michael, and Philip Ziegler, eds. *The Oxford Handbook of Dietrich Bonhoeffer.* Oxford: Oxford University Press, 2019.
McCosker, Phillip, Luigi Gioia, and Travis LaCouter, eds. *Clericalism and Sexuality.* Cambridge: Cambridge University Press, 2022.
McCoy, Marina Berzins. *Wounded Heroes: Vulnerability as a Virtue in Ancient Greek Literature and Philosophy.* New York: Oxford, 2013.
McDonagh, Enda. *Vulnerable to the Holy: In Faith, Morality and Art.* Dublin: Columbia Press, 2005.
McKenna, Joseph H. "Evil and the Possibility of Social Sin: A Theological Anthropodicy." PhD diss., Fordham University, 1993. Ann Arbor, MI: ProQuest.
———. "The Possibility of Social Sin." *Irish Theological Quarterly* 60, no. 2 (1994): 125–40.
McKenzie, John L. "The Gospel According to Matthew." In *The Jerome Biblical Commentary,* edited by Raymond Brown, Joseph Fitzmyer, and Roland Murphy, 62–114. Englewood Cliffs, NJ: Prentice-Hall, 1968.
McLaughlin, Eliott. "Three Videos Piece Together the Final Moments of George Floyd's Life." *CNN,* June 23, 2020. https://www.cnn.com/2020/06/01/us/george-floyd-three-videos-minneapolis/index.html.
McQueen, Paddy. "Social and Political Recognition." *The Internet Encyclopedia of Philosophy.* https://www.iep.utm.edu/recog_sp/#SH3a.
Meilaender, Gilbert. *The Theory and Practice of Virtue.* Notre Dame, IN: University of Notre Dame Press, 1984.
Menninger, Karl. *What Became of Sin?* New York: Hawthorn, 1973.
Merriell, Juvenal D. *To the Image of the Trinity. A Study in the Development of Aquinas' Teaching.* Toronto: Pontifical Institute of Medieval Studies, 1990.
Metz, Johann Baptist. *Mystik der offenen Augen: Wenn Spiritualität aufbricht.* Freiburg, Germany: Herder, 2011.
Mikulich, Alex, Laurie Cassidy, and Margaret Pfeil. *The Scandal of White Complicity in U.S. Hyper-incarceration: A Nonviolent Spirituality of White Resistance.* New York: Palgrave-Macmillan, 2013.
Miller, Jerome A. "The Way of Suffering: A Reasoning of the Heart." *Second Opinion* 17, no. 4 (April 1992): 21–33.
Miller, Joshua H. "Christian Communal Parrhesia and the Case of the 1965 Bloody Sunday March." In *New Directions in Rhetoric and Religion: Exploring Emerging Intersections of Religion,*

Public Discourse, and Rhetorical Scholarship, edited by James W. Vining, 9–28. Lanham, MD: Rowman and Littlefield, 2021.

Milton, John. *Paradise Lost*. 2nd ed. London: Samuel Simmons, 1674.

Moltmann, Jürgen. "The Justification of Life." In *The Spirit of Life: A Universal Affirmation*, 123–43. Minneapolis: Fortress Press, 1992.

Müncker, Theodor. *Die psychologische Grundlegung*. Düsseldorf, Germany: Patmos, 1947.

Nelson, Daniel Mark. *The Priority of Prudence*. University Park: Pennsylvania State University, 1992.

Niebuhr, Reinhold. *Moral Man and Immoral Society: A Study in Ethics and Politics*. Louisville, KY: Westminster John Knox Press, 2001.

Nieuwenhove, Rik Van. "In the Image of God: The Trinitarian Anthropology of St Bonaventure, St Thomas Aquinas and the Blessed Jan Van Ruusbroec." *Irish Theological Quarterly* 66, no. 3 (2001): 227–37. https://doi.org/10.1177/002114000106600303.

Nussbaum, Martha. "Non-relative Virtues: An Aristotelian Approach." *Midwest Studies in Philosophy*. Vol. 13, *Ethical Theory: Character and Virtue*, edited by Peter A. French, Theodore E. Uehling, and Howard K. Wettstein, 32–53. Notre Dame, IN: University of Notre Dame Press, 1988.

Obama, Barack. "Barack Obama's Speech on Race." Transcript of speech delivered at the Constitution Center, Philadelphia, March 18, 2008. http://www.nytimes.com/2008/03/18/us/politics/18text-obama.html.

———. "Remarks by President Obama and Prime Minister Abe of Japan at Hiroshima Peace Memorial." Transcript of speech delivered at Hiroshima Peace Memorial, Hiroshima, Japan, May 27, 2016. https://www.nytimes.com/2016/05/28/world/asia/text-of-president-obamas-speech-in-hiroshima-japan.html.

Odozor, Paulinus. *Moral Theology in an Age of Renewal*. Notre Dame, IN: University of Notre Dame, 2003.

Okano, Haruko. "Theological Ethics in Relation to Japanese Religions regarding Moral Responsibility." In *Doing Catholic Theological Ethics in a Cross Cultural and Interreligious Asian Context*, edited by Yiu Sing Lúcás Chan, James F. Keenan, and Shaji George Kochuthara, 194–204. Bangalore: Dharmaram Press, 2016.

O'Malley, John. *The First Jesuits*. Cambridge, MA: Harvard University Press, 1993.

Orphanopoulos, Carolina Montero. *Vulnerabilidad: Hacia una ética más humana*. Madrid: Dykinson, 2022.

———. "Narrative and the Social Dynamics of Virtue." In *Changing Values and Virtues*, edited by Dietmar Mieth and Jacques Pohier, 69–80. Edinburgh: T & T Clark, 1987.

Paul II. *Veritatis splendor*. Written August 6, 1993. Accessed August 6, 2022. https://www.vatican.va/content/john-paul-ii/en/encyclicals/documents/hf_jp-ii_enc_06081993_veritatis-splendor.html. Quoted in Yiu Sing Lúcás Chan, *The Ten Commandments and the Beatitudes: Biblical Studies and Ethics for Real Life*. Lanham, MD: Rowman and Littlefield, 2012.

Paul VI. *Gaudium et spes*. Promulgated December 7, 1965. Accessed August 6, 2022. https://www.vatican.va/archive/hist_councils/ii_vatican_council/documents/vat-ii_const_19651207_gaudium-et-spes_en.html.

Pearman, Sara Jane. "The Iconographic Development of the Cruciform in the Throne of Grace from the Twelfth-Century to the Sixteenth-Century." Fine Arts Department, PhD diss., Case Western Reserve, Cleveland, OH, 1974. https://www.proquest.com/docview/302709048/fulltextPDF/6E56D11FC72F4B84PQ/1?accountid=9673.

Pellauer, David, and Paul Ricœur. *The Course of Recognition.* Cambridge, MA: Harvard University Press, 2007.
Pincoffs, Edmund L. *Quandary Ethics: Against Reductivism in Ethics.* Lawrence: University of Kansas, 1986.
Pontifical Justice and Peace Commission. *What Have You Done to Your Homeless Brother?: The Church and the Housing Problem.* London: Catholic Truth Society, 1988.
Pope, Stephen. "Expressive Individualism and True Self-Love: A Thomistic Perspective." *Journal of Religion* 71, no. 3 (1991): 384–99. https://www.jstor.org/stable/1204562.
Porter, Jean. *Natural and Divine Law: Reclaiming the Tradition for Christian Ethics.* Grand Rapids, MI: Eerdmans, 1999.
———. *Nature as Reason: A Thomistic Theory of the Natural Law.* Grand Rapids, MI: Eerdmans, 2005.
———. *The Recovery of Virtue: The Relevance of Aquinas for Christian Ethics.* Louisville, KY: Westminster Press, 1990.
Prejean, Helen. *Dead Man Walking.* New York: Vintage Press, 1994.
Prosperi, Adriano. *Crime and Forgiveness: Christianizing Execution in Medieval Europe.* Cambridge, MA: Harvard University Press, 2020.
Pugh, Jeffrey. *Religionless Christianity: Dietrich Bonhoeffer in Troubled Times.* New York: T & T Clark, 2009.
Puhl, Louis J. *The Spiritual Exercises of St. Ignatius.* Chicago: Loyola University Press, 1951.
Ratzinger, Joseph. *Relationship between Magisterium and Exegetes.* Last modified May 10, 2003. Accessed August 11, 2022. https://www.vatican.va/roman_curia/congregations/cfaith/pcb_documents/rc_con_cfaith_doc_20030510_ratzinger-comm-bible_en.html.
Regan, Ethna. "The Criteria of 'Authentically' Catholic Theology: Reading *Theology Today* a Decade Later." *Religions* 12, no. 12 (2021): 1071. https://doi.org/10.3390/rel12121071.
Reiter, Johannes. "Die Katholische Moraltheologie Zwischen den Beiden Vatikanischen Konzils." In *Die Katholischtheologische Disziplinen in Deutschland 1870–1962. Ihre Geschichte, ihre Zeitbezug,* edited by Hubert Wolf, 231–42. Paderborn, Germany: Schöningh, 1999.
Ricœur, Paul. "Love and Justice." In *Radical Pluralism and Truth: David Tracy and the Hermeneutics of Religion,* edited by Werner G. Jeanrond and Jennifer L. Rike, 187–202. New York: Crossroad, 1991.
Riordan, Patrick. "Common Good: Theological, Philosophical, Political Aspects." Lecture delivered at Campion Hall, March 24, 2021. https://www.campion.ox.ac.uk/news/darcy-lectures-2021.
Robinson, David. "Confessing Race: Towards a Global Ecclesiology after Bonhoeffer and Du Bois." *Journal of the Society of Christian Ethics* 36, no. 2 (2016): 121–39.
Rogers-Vaughn, Bruce. "Recovering Grief in the Age of Grief Recovery." *Journal of Pastoral Theology* 13, no. 1 (2003): 36–45. https://doi.org/10.1179/jpt.2003.13.1.005.
Romeo, Giovanni. *Aspettando il boia: Condannati a morte, confortatori e inquisitori nella Napoli della Controriforma.* Firenze, Italy: Sansoni, 1993.
Rothschild, Bruce M. "History of Syphilis." *Clinical Infectious Diseases* 40, no. 10 (2005): 1454–63. https://doi.org/10.1086/429626.
Roukema, Riemer. "The Good Samaritan in Ancient Christianity." *Vigiliae Christiana* 58, no. 1 (February 2004): 56–74. https://www.jstor.org/stable/1584537.
Ryan, Gerard. *Mutual Accompaniment as Faith-Filled Living: Recognition of the Vulnerable Other.* New York: Palgrave Macmillan, 2022.

Ryan, Thomas. "Jesus—'Our Wisest and Dearest Friend': Aquinas and Moral Transformation." *New Blackfriars* 97, no. 1071 (2016): 575–90. https://doi.org/10.1111/nbfr.12223.
Sanchis, Dominique. "Samaritanus ille. L'exegese augustinienne de la parabole du Bon Samaritain." *Recherches de Science Relgieuse* 49 (1961): 406–25. http://www.worldcat.org/oclc/800637268.
Sarot, Marcel. "Patripassianism and the Impassibility of God." *Svensk Teologisk Kvartalskrift* 72 (1996): 73–81.
———. "Patripassianism, Theopaschitism and the Suffering of God. Some Historical and Systematic Considerations." *Religious Studies* 26, no. 3 (1990): 363–75. https://www.jstor.org/stable/20019419.
Schimmel, Solomon. "Joseph and His Brothers: A Paradigm for Repentance." *Judaism* 37, no. 1 (Winter 1988): 60–66.
Shriver, Donald W., Jr. *An Ethic for Enemies: Forgiveness in Politics*. New York: Oxford University Press, 1995.
Slater, Thomas. *A Manual of Moral Theology for English-Speaking Countries*. London: Benziger Brothers, 1906.
Smith, Adam. *The Theory of Moral Sentiments*. New York: Penguin Classics, 2010.
Sorabji, Richard. *Moral Conscience through the Ages: Fifth Century BCE to the Present*. Chicago: University of Chicago Press, 2014.
Spicq, Ceslaus. *Agape in The New Testament*. St. Louis, MO: Herder, 1963.
———. *Charity and Liberty in the New Testament*. New York: Alba Press, 1965.
Spohn, William. *Go and Do Likewise: Jesus and Ethics*. New York: Continuum, 1999.
———. "The Return of the Virtues." *Theological Studies* 33, no. 1 (1992): 60–75. https://doi.org/10.1177/004056399205300104.
Stein, Robert. *An Introduction to the Parables of Jesus*. Philadelphia: Westminster, 1981.
Steinbüchel, Theodor. *Die philosophische Grundlegung*. Düsseldorf, Germany: Patmos, 1947.
Strom, Paul. *Conscience: A Very Short Introduction*. New York: Oxford University Press, 2011.
Stuhlmueller, Carroll. "The Gospel According to Luke." In *The Jerome Biblical Commentary*, edited by Raymond Brown, Joseph Fitzmyer, and Roland Murphy, 115–64. Englewood Cliffs, NJ: Prentice-Hall, 1968.
Taylor, Charles. "The Politics of Recognition." In *Multiculturalism: Examining the Politics of Recognition*, edited by Amy Gutmann, 25–74. Princeton, NJ: Princeton University Press, 1994.
Terpstra, Nicholas. "The Bologna Comforter's Manual: Comforting by the Books: Editorial Notes on *the Bologna Comforters' Manual* Book 1." In *The Art of Executing Well: Rituals of Execution in Renaissance Italy*, edited by Nicholas Terpstra, 183–292. Kirksville, MO: Truman State University Press, 2008.
———. *Cultures of Charity: Women, Politics, and the Reform of Poor Relief in Renaissance Italy*. Cambridge, MA: Harvard University Press, 2013.
———. *Lay Confraternities and Civic Religion in Renaissance Bologna*. Cambridge: Cambridge University Press, 1995.
———. *Lost Girls: Sex and Death in Renaissance Florence*. Baltimore: Johns Hopkins University Press, 2012.
———. "Piety and Punishment: The Lay Conforteria and Civic Justice in Sixteenth-Century Bologna." *Sixteenth Century Journal* 22, no. 4 (1991): 679–94. https://doi.org/10.2307/2542371.

Terpstra, Nicholas, Adriano Prosperi, and Stefania Pastore, eds. *Faith's Boundaries: Laity and Clergy in Early Modern Confraternities*. Turnhout, Belgium: Brepols, 2013.
Tessman, Lisa. *Burdened Virtues: Virtue Ethics for Liberatory Struggles*. New York: Oxford University Press, 2005.
Thalhammer, D. "Der Meister ruft." *Zeitschrift für Katholische Theologie* 62 (1938): 451.
Thurman, Howard. "Good News for the Underprivileged." In *The Papers of Howard Washington Thurman*, vol. 1 (June 1918–March 1936), edited by Walter Earl Fluker, 263–70. Columbia, SC: University of South Caroline Press, 2009.
———. *Jesus and the Disinherited*. Boston: Beacon Press, 1976.
Tierney, Brian. *The Idea of Natural Rights: Studies on Natural Rights, Natural Law and Church Law 1150–1625*. Atlanta: Scholars Press, 1997.
Tilley, Terrence. *The Disciples' Jesus: Christology as a Reconciling Practice*. Maryknoll, NY: Orbis Books, 2008.
Tillmann, Fritz. *Die Idee der Nachfolge Christi*. Düsseldorf, Germany: Verlag, 1939.
———. *The Master Calls: A Handbook of Morals for the Layman*. Translated by Gregory J. Roettger. Baltimore: Helicon Press, 1960.
———. *Der Menschensohn: Jesu Selbstzeugnis für seine messianische Würde*. Bonn, Germany: University of Bonn, 1905.
———. *Der Meister ruft: Eine Laienmoral für gläubige Christen*. Düsseldorf, Germany: L. Schwann Verlag, 1937.
———. *Persönlichkeit und Gemeinschaft in der Predigt Jesu*. Cologne: Schwann, 1919.
———. *Das Selbstbewusstsein des Gottessohnes: auf Grund der synoptischen Evangelien*. Münster, Germany: Aschendorff, 1911.
———. *Die Wiederkunft Christi: Nach den Paulinischen Briefen*. Freiburg: Herder, 1909.
Timmer, Daniel. "Jonah's Theology of the Nations: The Interface of Religious and Ethnic Identity." *Revue Biblique* 120, no. 1 (2013): 13–23. http://www.jstor.org/stable/44092183.
Torrell, Jean-Pierre. "Nature et grâce chez Thomas d'Aquin." *Revue Thomiste* 101 (2001): 167–202.
Townes, Emilie M., ed. "'Wading through Many Sorrows': Towards a Theology of Suffering in Womanist Perspective." In *A Troubling in My Soul: Womanist Perspectives on Evil and Suffering*, 109–29. Maryknoll, NY: Orbis, 1993.
Vacek, Edward. *Love, Human and Divine*. Washington, DC: Georgetown University Press, 1995.
Van Leeuwen, Bart. "A Formal Recognition of Social Attachments: Expanding Axel Honneth's Theory of Recognition, Inquiry." *An Interdisciplinary Journal of Philosophy* 50, no. 2 (March 2007): 180–205. https://doi.org/10.1080/00201740701239897.
Vann, Gerald. *The Divine Pity: A Study in the Social Implications of the Beatitudes*. New York: Sheed and Ward, 1946.
Vasko, Elisabeth. *Beyond Apathy: A Theology for Bystanders*. Minneapolis: Fortress, 2015.
Vawter, Bruce. "The Gospel According to John." In *The Jerome Biblical Commentary*, edited by Raymond Brown, Joseph Fitzmyer, and Roland Murphy, 414–66. Englewood Cliffs, NJ: Prentice-Hall, 1968.
Verhey, Allen. *The Christian Art of Dying: Learning from Jesus*. Grand Rapids, MI: Wm. B. Eerdmans, 2011.
Vermeulen, Karolien. "Mind the Gap: Ambiguity in the Story of Cain and Abel." *Journal of Biblical Literature* 133, no. 1 (Spring 2014): 29–42. https://doi.org/10.15699/jbibllite.133.1.29.

Viviano, Benedict T. "The Kingdom of God in Albert the Great and Thomas Aquinas." *Thomist: A Speculative Quarterly Review* 44, no. 4 (October 1980): 502–22. https://doi.org/10.1353/tho.1980.0001.

Vogt, Christopher P. *Patience, Compassion, Hope and the Christian Art of Dying Well*. Oxford: Rowan and Littlefield, 2004.

Volf, Miroslav. *Exclusion and Embrace: A Theological Exploration of Identity, Otherness, and Reconciliation*. Nashville: Abingdon, 1996.

———. *After Our Likeness: The Church as the Image of the Trinity*. Grand Rapids, MI: Wm. Eerdmans, 1997.

Walzer, Michael. *Thick and Thin: Moral Argument at Home and Abroad*. Notre Dame, IN: University of Notre Dame Press, 1996.

Ward, Kate. "'Mere Poverty Excites Little Compassion': Adam Smith, Moral Judgment and the Poor." *Heythrop Journal* 61, no. 1 (March 2015): 97–114. https://doi.org/10.1111/heyj.12260.

Weaver, Darlene Fozard. *The Acting Person and Christian Moral Life*. Washington, DC: Georgetown, 2011.

———. "Intimacy with God and Self-Relation in the World: The Fundamental Option and Categorical Activity." In *New Wine, New Wineskins: A Next Generation Reflects on Key Issues in Catholic Moral Theology*, edited by William C. Mattison, 143–63. Lanham, MD: Sheed and Ward, 2005.

———. "Taking Sin Seriously." *Journal of Religious Ethics* 31 (2003): 45–74.

White, T. H. *The Once and Future King*. New York: Ace Books, 1987.

Wilkerson, Isabel. *Caste: The Origins of Our Discontent*. New York: Random House, 2020.

Williams, Reggie L. *Bonhoeffer's Black Jesus: Harlem Renaissance Theology and an Ethic of Resistance*. Waco, TX: Baylor University Press, 2014.

Wink, Walter. *When the Powers Fall: Reconciliation in the Healing of Nations*. Minneapolis: Fortress Press, 1998.

Yearley, Lee H. *Mencius and Aquinas: Theories of Virtue and Conceptions of Courage*. Albany: State University of New York Press, 1990.

INDEX

Abel, 42–43, 48
Adam, 28, 39
Advice for Priests Who Minister to Those Condemned to Death (Liguori), 139–40
Affordable Care Act, 68
Allison, Dale, Jr., 7
Ambrose, 39
anamchara, 105, 133
Aquinas, Thomas, 22–23, 56, 83–84, 99–101, 102, 103, 104, 106, 108, 113–14, 116, 117, 119, 120–21, 124–25, 126–27, 131, 134
Arbery, Ahmaud, 45, 47
Aristotle, 119
ars moriendi (the art of dying): tradition of, 1, 11
Art of Dying Well (Bellarmine), 10
Au Coeur de la moral chrétienne (Lottin), 100
Augustine, 39, 114, 137; on humility, 35, 37n48; on virtues, 124–25
Austin, Nicholas, 93, 134–36
Autiero, Antonio, 55, 133–34

baptism, 37, 48, 78, 82, 96
Beatitudes, the, 140–42; eighth Beatitude, 146–47; fifth Beatitude, 144–45; first Beatitude, 142; fourth Beatitude, 144; second Beatitude, 142–43; seventh Beatitude, 145–46; third Beatitude, 143–44
Becker, Ernest, 10–11, 12
Bellarmine, Robert, 10
Bethge, Eberhard, 6
Bethge, Renate, 6
Betz, Hans Dieter, 7

Beyond Apathy: A Theology for Bystanders (Vasko), 58
Biblical Ethics in the 21st Century: Developments, Emerging Consensus, and Future Directions (Chan), 78–79
Black Lives Matter (BLM), 45, 47, 52, 60
Block, Elizabeth Sweeny, 57–58, 142
Böckle, Franz, 70, 106
Boff, Leonardo, 114
Bonhoeffer, Dietrich, 5–6, 9, 12, 94–97, 107, 133
Boopalan, Sunder John, 13
Bourdieu, Pierre, 59
Burdened Virtues (Tessman), 31
Burridge, Richard A., 75–76, 83–85
Butler, Judith, 14–15, 25, 26, 30, 32, 51; on grievability, 45–48
Bynum, Caroline Walker, 134

Cahill, Lisa Sowle, 98–99
Cain, 42–43, 48
Cajetan, Thomas, 135
"Call to Action, A: Global Moral Crises and the Inadequacy of Inherited Approaches to Conscience," 57–58
Campin, Robert, 119
Caritas forma omnium virtutum (charity is the form of all the virtues), 103
Carpentier, René, 77, 101, 110n39
caste, 49–51, 54n49
Caste: The Origins of Our Discontent (Wilkerson), 49–50
Catholics, call of conscience of, 66, 67
Catholic Theological Ethics in the World Church (CTEWC), 33, 55
Cavanaugh, William, 106

Chan, Yiu Sing Lúcás, 7–8, 16, 78, 141; on the Beatitudes, 142–47
charity, 101–2, 123, 126; Divine charity, 104; union with God through charity, 102–3
Cholbi, Michael, 12–13
Christian Art of Dying, The: Learning from Jesus (Verhey), 11
Christian community, 137
Christian funeral, 5, 6
Christianity, 86; growth of, 137; "religionless Christianity," 94, 95, 96
Christian piety, 10
Christian spiritual life, 10
Christians, 11, 13, 82, 84, 137; Black Christians, 95–96; self-governing Christians, 100; self-understanding of before God, 82; vocation of to follow Christ in holiness, 99–100
Church of St. James, 138
Cicero, 65
Clement of Alexandria, 39
Cochran, Clarke, 63–64, 73n36
Columbus, Christopher, 137
Commentary on Romans (Aquinas), 117
Communion of Saints, 133–36
Compagnia del Divino Amore (Confraternity of Divine Love), 138
Cone, James, 69, 85
confraternities, 138–40
Confraternity of the Imprisoned, 139
Confraternity of Mercy, 139
Confraternity of Pietá, 139
Connelly, Hugh, 104–5
conscience, 22–23, 55, 70–72; Christian conscience, 67, 100; and the collective guilty consciences of Nineveh and the brothers of Joseph, 61–63, 64, 66, 70, 107; differences between continental Europe and the United States on the phenomenology of conscience, 66–69; "engaged" conscience, 57; the guilty conscience and the birth of conscience itself, 64–66; movement toward a socially responsible conscience, 55–56; recent critical works on conscience, 57–60; "reflexive" conscience, 57; searching for a meditation on collective guilty conscience, 57–58
Conscience: A Very Short Introduction (Strom), 65
consciousness, divine, 27
Copeland, M. Shawn, 68, 85
Cost of Discipleship (Bonhoeffer), 96
creation narratives, 29
Cross and the Lynching Tree, The (Cone), 69
cultures, Catholic, 128
Curran, Charles, 98
Cyprian, 136

Daly, Daniel J., 51–52
Das Gesetz Christi (Häring), 97
David, 64, 66; Nathan's accusation against, 57
Davies, William, 7
De Anda, Neomi, 31
Democritus, 65
Denial of Death, The (Becker), 10–11
Die Idee der Nachfolge Christi (Tillman et al.), 77, 79
Die Meister ruft (Tillman), 77
Dionysius, 136
discipleship, 75–87, 93, 99; grace of, 86–87
Disciples' Jesus, The: Christology as a Reconciling Practice (Tilley), 115
disciples (of Christ), 34, 35, 90; fidelity to Christ of, 85
"Disorder and Distortion: Theological Approach to Addiction" (Lamson-Scribner), 26–27
Dworkin, Andrea, 58

Elephant Man (1980), 47
Emmaus, Jesus's meeting with the two disciples on, 4, 6, 85
Equal Justice Initiative (EJI), 47
Erasmus, 10
Ermecke, Gustav, 77
Ethics of Vulnerability, The: A Feminist Analysis of Social Life and Practice (Gilson), 25
evil, 9, 23, 66, 67, 68, 69, 102, 108, 125
exceptionalism, American, 69

Farley, Margaret, 123–24
fasting, 144
fidelity, 85, 126
Finn, Daniel, 59
Fleming, Daniel J., 30
Floyd, George, 45, 47, 52; public murder of, 46
Forbes, Greg, 48
"Fragility of the Moral Self, The" (Haker), 31
Frames of War: When Life is Grievable (Butler), 15
Friends of God and Prophets: A Feminist Theological Reading of the Communion of Saints (Johnson), 132–33
Fuchs, Josef, 98
Fundamental Moral Theology (Böckle), 70

Gaudium et spes, 66–67, 71, 124
Gilleman, Gérard, 77, 98, 101–4, 106; ordering of love by, 103
Gilligan, Carol, 126
Gilson, Erinn C., 25
Giubilini, Alberto, 56
Giving an Account of Oneself (Butler), 30
God, 5–6, 28, 82–83, 106; grace of, 83; judgment of, 64–65; love of, 103; as relational, 114; revelation of, 27; union with God through charity, 102–3; workmanship of, 137. *See also* humans, as made in God's image
Goldstein, Valerie Saiving, 31
Golgotha, 20–21, 24, 28
"Good News for the Underprivileged" (Thurman), 85
Good Samaritan, the, parable of, 22, 25, 29–30; as allegory, 39–40
Gospel according to St. Matthew, 83
grace, 97–98; cheap grace, 96; of discipleship, 99; gift of, 98, 107; of self-doubt, 123–24; and sin, 93–94, 105
grief, 14, 118; Christian grief, 11, 13; as existential, 11; as a form of love, 4; as meant to be shared, 2; moving forward with, 12; "preconditions" of, 1; and the revelation of human vulnerability, 6
Grief: A Philosophical Guide (Cholbi), 12–13

Grief Observed, A (Lewis), 12
guilt, admission of, 70–71
Gula, Richard, 55–56
Gutiérrez, Gustavo, 85, 88

"habitus," 59
Haker, Hille, 31–33, 42–43, 127
Hamilton, Brian, 58–60, 73n26
Häring, Bernhard, 66, 77, 97–98
Harrington, Daniel, 80
Harvey, James, 40
Hauerwas, Stanley, 114
Hellwig, Monika, 143
Heschel, Abraham, 27–28, 30
Heyer, Kristin, 55, 60
History of Catholic Theological Ethics, A (Keenan), 98–99, 137
HIV/AIDS, ethics concerning, 21
Hogan, Linda, 33–34, 55, 120
Holy Spirit, the, 1, 116–17; life-giving work of, 6, 133; vulnerability of, 117
Holy Spirit and Moral Action in Thomas Aquinas, The (Mahoney), 116
Holy Trinity (El Greco [1577]), 119
homelessness, 140–41
Honneth, Axel, 43–44
hope, 7, 9, 11, 13, 16, 86, 95, 119, 135–36; Christian hope, 19–21
Humanae vitae, 68
human behavior, motivation for, 10–11
humans: as made in God's image, 27, 38, 114; primary identity of, 125; relational identity of, 126
humility, 34, 135, 142; "epistemic humility," 34, 124; foundational stance of, 35

Iconographic Development of the Cruciform in the Throne of Grace from the Twelfth-Century to the Sixteenth-Century (Pearman), 117
Ignatian Contemplation, 115
Imitating Jesus: An Inclusive Approach to New Testament Ethics (Burridge), 75–76, 83
inclination, 102–3
In a Different Voice (Gilligan), 126

Irish Penitentials, The (Connelly), 104–5
"It's in You: Structural Sin and Personal Responsibility Revisited" (Hamilton), 58–59

James, William, 8, 17n13, 87
Jennings, Willie James, 85
Jeremiah, 8
Jesuits, 139; community liturgy of, 16
Jesus Christ, 79, 84, 86, 88, 96, 104, 106; ascension of, 3; as the *autobasileia*, 114; crucifixion of, 5; default assumption that Jesus is white, 95; ministry of, 136; moral theology of, 97; Passion of, 116; as rabbi, 82–83; relation to the Father and the Spirit, 112; religion of, 87; resurrection of, 85; teachings of, 114–15; vulnerability of, 116; vulnerability of to Lazarus, 7
Jesus and the Disinherited (Thurman), 76
Jesus and Virtue Ethics: Building Bridges between New Testament Studies and Moral Theology (Keenan and Harrington), 82
Jesus of Nazareth: What He Wanted, Who He Was (Lohfink), 75, 80
"Jesus—'Our Wisest and Dearest Friend': Aquinas and Moral Transformation" (Ryan), 116
Jim Crow laws, 69
Joanna, 3
John, 6, 9
John, Gospel of: focus of on love, 83–84
John Paul II (pope), 141
Johnson, Elizabeth, 118, 132, 133, 135
Joseph, 61–63; brothers of, 61–63, 64, 66, 70, 107; contemporary relevance of the Joseph story, 63–64
Joseph of Arimathea, 81
"Joseph and the Politics of Memory" (Cochran), 63–64
Julius Caesar, 65
justice, 126, 127; insufficiency of, 125; and peace, 146; without charity, 125. *See also* Philippines, the, justice in

Kant, Immanuel, 126
Kaveny, M. Cathleen, 17n21
Keen, Sam, 10, 11
Keenan, Bobby, 5, 8
Kelley, Melissa, 12
King, Martin Luther, Jr., 87, 120
Kingdom of God, 83, 87, 114, 115, 141
Kleber, Karl-Heinz, 77
Kubler-Ross, Elizabeth, 11

Lamson-Scribner, Jennifer, 26–27
Lazarus (as raised from the dead by Jesus), 7, 84
Lazarus (of the Good Samaritan story), 22, 24
Letter 118 (Augustine), 35
Letter from a Birmingham Jail (King), 120
Letters and Papers from Prison (Bonhoeffer), 94
Levinas, Emmanuel, 30
Lewis, C. S., 12
Lewis, Joy, 12
Liguori, Alphonsus, 139–40
Lohfink, Gerhard, 75, 80–83, 87
Lottin, Dom Odon, 66, 98–101, 106; writing style of, 101
lynching museum, 69

magnanimity, 135–36; Christian magnanimity, 135
Mahoney, Jack, 116
man born blind, the, 88–90
Manual of Moral Theology for English-Speaking Countries, A (Slater), 102
Mark, Gospel of: canonical ending of, 2–3
Maros, Zorica, 55
Marquette University, 2, 16
Marrow, Stanley, 5
Marsh, Rob, 94
Martha, 7, 84
Mary, 3, 7, 9, 24
Mary Magdalen, 2–3, 4, 6, 9, 19–21, 24
Mary (mother of Jesus), 3, 5, 31, 34
Mary of Bethany, 84
Massingale, Bryan N., 8, 85
Master Calls, The (Tillman), 78
Mathewes, Charles, 26
McDonagh, Edna, 27, 30
McGreevy, 140–41

McQueen, Paddy, 41
meekness, 143–44
Memory, Grief and Agency (Boopalan), 13
Menninger, Karl, 105
mercy, 145; corporal works of, 136–40; agenda of mercy, 136
"'Mere Poverty Excites Little Compassion': Adam Smith, Moral Judgment and the Poor" (Ward), 49
Merrick, Joseph, 47
Military Order of Our Lady of mercy and the Redemption of the Captives, 139
Milton, John, 29
Moltmann, Jürgen, 70
Montero, Carolina, 34
moral agency, 135
Moral Conscience through the Ages (Sorabji), 65
Morale fundamentale (Lottin), 99, 100
moral formation, stages of, 21–24
moral law, 57
"Moral Leadership: A Challenge and a Celebration" (Hogan), 120
Moral Man and Immoral Society: A Study in Ethics and Politics (Niebuhr), 48
Mount of Olives, 4
mourning: object of, 7–8; and a responsive God, 8
Mourning Trinity (Campin), 119
Müncker, Theodor, 76, 77

Nathan, accusation of against David, 57
Nathaniel, 84
National Memorial for Peace and Justice, 47
Nicomachean Ethics (Aristotle), 119
Niebuhr, Reinhold, 48, 123, 134
Nineveh, guilt of, 60–63
Nolasco, Peter, 139

Obama, Barack, 70
O'Malley, John, 139
Once and Future King, The (White), 28
Origen, 39, 114
Ospedali degli incurabili, 138
Outline of a Theory of Practice (Bourdieu), 59

Paradise Lost (Milton), 29
Pasolini, Pier Paolo, 83
Patience, Compassion, Hope and the Christian Art of Dying Well (Vogt), 10
"Patripassianism," 118
Paul, 71, 79, 106; on suffering, 9
Pearman, Jane, 117
Pegoraro, Renzo, 55
Pentecost, 1, 19, 136; grieving at Pentecost, 2–3, 4
Perkins, William, 10
Personality and Community in the Preaching of Jesus (Tillman), 77
Peter, 4, 5, 6, 9, 84
Pharisees, 90
Philippines, the, justice in, 127–28
Powell, Clayton, 96
Praxeas, 118
Precarious Life: The Powers of Mourning and Violence (Butler), 14
precarity, 9, 14, 25, 29, 35, 40, 61, 99
Prejean, Helen, 148n28
Preparing for Death (Erasmus), 10
prodigal son, parable of, 47–48
"Protestantism without Reformation" (Bonhoeffer), 95
prudence, 100, 120–21, 127
Puri, Sunita, 12

Quintilian, 65

race, 50
racism, 49, 68, 69, 94, 96
recognition, 38, 51; and the call to recognition, 48–51; importance of, 52; mutual recognition, 40–41; of the other, 39; as a precondition for a moral life, 21; refusal of, 42; social impact of, 51–52; three stages of, 41–42; threshold of, 42–44
"Recognition and Responsibility" (Haker), 42–43
Reiter, Johannes, 77
responsibility: emergence of, 27; and vulnerability, 27
Rhetorica ad Herennium, 65
Ricoeur, Paul, 32, 34, 125

Robinson, David, 95
Rogers-Vaughan, Bruce, 14
Rublev, Andrei, 115
Rule and exercises of Holy Dying (Taylor), 10
Ryan, Thomas, 116

Saint Joseph of Matha, 139
salvation history, 122–23
Salve for a Sicke Man (Perkins), 10
Schimmel Solomon, 63
scholasticism, 99
Sermon on the Mount, 141
sin/sinfulness, 9, 85, 104–9; confession of, 105–6; as a desire to do harm, 106; structural sin, 58–59, 70. *See also* grace, and sin
Sisters of the Dominican Third Order, 139
Slater, Thomas, 102
slavery, 54n49; history of in the United States, 68–69
Smith, Adam, 48–49
Sorabji, Richard, 65
soul, distinction between the healthy and the sick soul, 9
Spiritual Exercises, The (Ignatius), 106
Steinberger, Johannes, 77
Steinbüchel, Theodor, 76, 77
Stelzenberger, Johannes, 77
Street Homelessness and Catholic Theological Ethics (Keenan and McGreevy), 141
Strom, Paul, 65
Struggle for Recognition, The: The Moral Grammar of Social Conflicts (Honneth), 43–44
Summa Theologiae (Aquinas), 119, 134
sympathy: "divine sympathy," 27; prophetic sympathy, 28; sympathy with the divine pathos, 27–28
synderesis, 23
Synoptic Gospels, 4, 75, 80, 82, 84
syphilis, 137–38

Taylor, Breonna, 45, 47
Taylor, Jeremy, 10
Ten Commandments and the Beatitudes: Biblical Studies and Ethics for Real Life (Chan), 7, 141

Tertullian, 118
Tessman, Lisa, 31
Thiene, Gaetano da, 138
theology: achievement of moral theology, 102; biblical theology, 78; Black theology, 85; canon law's influence on, 99–100; Catholic moral theology, 77–78; charity-centered moral theology, 103–4; liberation theology, 85; manuals of moral theology, 102; moral theology, 79, 82; moral theology of Jesus, 97; revisionist moral theology, 98; theological anthropology, 1, 120, 142
Theory of Moral Sentiments, The (Smith), 48–49
Thomas, 84, 85 *See also* Aquinas, Thomas
Throne of Grace, 20, 114, 115, 117–18, 119
Thurman, Howard, 76, 85–87, 94, 107
Tilley, Terrence, 115
Tillman, Fritz, 75, 76–80, 87, 97, 98; publications of, 76–77
Tomašević, Darko, 55
Torah, the, 81
Towards a Critical Political Ethics: Catholic Ethics and Social Challenges (Haker), 32–33
Trinitarians, 138–39
Trinity, the, 20, 38, 112, 125; how vulnerable are the persons of the Trinity, 114–19; is the Trinity vulnerable?, 113–14
Trinity, The (Veronese [1582]), 119

Upper Room: disciples' experience of after the death of Christ, 1, 2, 15, 19, 85; grieving in, 2–5

van Leeuwen, Bart, 44
Vann, Gerald, 7
Vasko, Elizabeth, 58
Verhey, Allen, 11
Vernazza, Ettore, 138
Vietnam Veterans Memorial, 70
Vietnam War, 68
virtues, 112, 124, 134; cardinal virtues, 124–25, 126; skeletal virtues, 127–28; virtue ethics, 119–23; virtues for those

made in the image of the vulnerable Triune God, 123–28
Vogt, Christopher P., 10
Volf, Miroslav, 114
Vulnerable to the Holy: In Faith, Morality and Art (McDonagh), 27
Vulnerabiliad (Montero), 34
vulnerability, 6, 19, 35–36, 83–84, 101; critique of, 31–33; divine vulnerability, 27–30; at the foot of the cross, 19–21; as foundational, 24–27; and human dignity, 33–34; meaning of, 25; and moving forward philosophically, 30–31; as a precondition for a moral life, 21; priority of, 26; and responsibility, 27; retrieving of as capacious and responsive, 25; virtue of, 34–35; vulnerability going social, 33–34. *See also* moral formation, stages of

Walsh, Thomas F., 9–10
Ward, Kate, 48–49
Weaver, Darlene Fozard, 106–7
What Became of Sin? (Menninger), 105
White, T. H., 28
whiteness, 95–96
Wilkerson, Isabel, 49–50, 54n49, 123, 134

ABOUT THE AUTHOR

JAMES F. KEENAN, SJ, is the Canisius Chair, Director of the Jesuit Institute, and Vice Provost of Global Engagement at Boston College. A Jesuit priest since 1982, he received a licentiate and a doctorate from the Pontifical Gregorian University in Rome. He has edited or written over twenty-five books and published over 400 essays, articles, and reviews worldwide. In 2003 he founded Catholic Theological Ethics in the World Church (CTEWC), an international network of ethicists, and subsequently hosted three international and six regional conferences. Today CTEWC has its own book series and is a live network of over 1,000 Catholic ethicists (www.catholicethics.com). In 2015 Keenan wrote *University Ethics: How Colleges Can Build and Benefit from a Culture of Ethics* (Rowman and Littlefield), and in 2022 *A History of Catholic Theological Ethics* (Paulist Press). From 1993 to 2013 he was the founding editor of Georgetown University Press's Moral Traditions Series. In 2019 he received the John Courtney Murray Lifetime Achievement Award from the Catholic Theological Society of America, and from 2020 to 2021 he was President of the Society of Christian Ethics.

www.ingramcontent.com/pod-product-compliance
Lightning Source LLC
Chambersburg PA
CBHW031441160426
43195CB00010BB/814